Fossilization in Adult Second Language Acquisition

SECOND LANGUAGE ACQUISITION 5
Series Editor: David Singleton, *Trinity College, Dublin, Ireland*

Fossilization in Adult Second Language Acquisition

ZhaoHong Han

Viva Books
New Delhi | Mumbai | Chennai | Kolkata
Bangalore | Hyderabad | Kochi | Guwahati

First Indian Edition 2010

VIVA BOOKS PRIVATE LIMITED

- 4737/23 Ansari Road, Daryaganj, New Delhi 110 002
  E-mail: vivadelhi@vivagroupindia.net, Tel. 42242200
- Plot No. 76, Service Industries, Shirvane, Sector 1, Nerul, Navi Mumbai 400 706
  E-mail: vivamumbai@vivagroupindia.net, Tel. 27721273, 27721274
- Jamals Fazal Chambers, 26 Greams Road, Chennai 600 006
  E-mail: vivachennai@vivagroupindia.net, Tel. 28290304, 28294241
- B-103, Jindal Towers, 21/1A/3 Darga Road, Kolkata 700 017
  E-mail: vivakolkata@vivagroupindia.net, Tel. 22836381, 22816713
- 7, Sovereign Park Apartments, 56-58, K. R. Road, Basavanagudi, Bangalore 560 004
  E-mail: vivabangalore@vivagroupindia.net, Tel. 26607409, 26607410
- 101-102 Mughal Marc Aptt., 3-4-637 to 641, Narayanguda, Hyderabad 500 029
  E-mail: vivahyderabad@vivagroupindia.net, Tel. 27564481, 27564482
- First Floor, Beevi Towers, SRM Road, Kaloor, Kochi 682 018, Kerala
  E-mail: vivakochi@vivagroupindia.net, Tel: 0484-2403055, 2403056
- 232, GNB Road, Beside UCO Bank, Silpukhuri, Guwahati 781 003
  E-mail: vivaguwahati@vivagroupindia.net, Tel: 0361-2666386

Published by arrangement with

Multilingual Matters Ltd.
Frankfurt Lodge, Clevedon Hall
Victoria Road, Clevedon BS21 7HH
England

ISBN 978-81-309-0516-7

Published by Vinod Vasishtha for Viva Books Private Limited, 4737/23, Ansari Road, New Delhi - 110 002. Printed and bound by Jaina Offset Printers, Delhi.

Contents

Preface

As a multilingual speaker, a second language educator and a researcher, I have always been fascinated by the notion of fossilization (Selinker, 1972), that is, cessation of learning in spite of rich exposure to input, adequate motivation to learn, and abundant opportunity for communicative practice. Yet it was not until after I became a student of Larry Selinker at the University of London that I began research in this area. The longitudinal study (Han, 1998) I performed then not only convinced me of the reality of fossilization, but kindled in me an even greater interest in seeking an understanding of its etiology. Why is it that learners suffer fossilization differentially? Why do L2 learners wind up with differential success in learning the L2 under seemingly identical learning conditions? What does the existing constellation of explanations tell us about lack of learning, and about the general understanding of adult second language acquisition (SLA)? Can instruction salvage learners from fossilization? These are some of the issues that have appealed to my attention and that I have tried to address in this book.

With no pretense of offering an exhaustive account of fossilization, the book synthesizes the major research on the topic, provides a conceptual framework for interpreting various manifestations of lack of learning, and explores the relationship between instruction and fossilization, an issue of extensive interest to second language researchers and educators.

In the preparation for this book, I have benefited, in no small measure, from discussions on various issues with the following individuals (in alphabetical order): David Birdsong, William Davies, Robert DeKeyser, Lynn Eubank, Susan Foster-Cohen, Gillies Houghton, Jan Hulstijn, Scott Jarvis, Eric Kellerman, Donna Lardiere, Diane Larsen-Freeman, Mike Long, Brian MacWhinney, Terry Odlin, Bonnie Schwartz, Tom Scovel, Larry Selinker, Mike Sharwood Smith, Rex Sprouse, and Paul Wiita, though I should point out that none of them is responsible for any of the ideas presented in this book.

Many other individuals have also provided valuable support in various forms, and I am grateful to them all. In particular, I am indebted to Joowon Suh, Paula Korsko, Jung-Eun Year, and Amy BaoHan for their bibliographic assistance. I, too, want to thank Marjukka Grover, Ken Hall and their colleagues at Multilingual Matters for their support and efficiency.

A special thanks goes to the Dean of Teachers College, Columbia University for having provided a research grant (2000–2001) in support of my writing.

Last but not least, I wish to thank my students at Teachers College for sharing their second language learning experiences and for never failing to feed me with stimulating questions about the various conundrums of SLA, including fossilization.

It is my hope that this book, albeit limited in breadth and depth and possibly biased in many ways, will stir an interest among SLA researchers, second language teachers, and graduate students in the issue of fossilization and will serve as a springboard onto more substantive research than has been hitherto attempted.

ZhaoHong Han
New York

Chapter 1

Introduction

People marvel at the ease and rapidity with which children acquire their first language. It is generally observed that by the age of five every normal child obtains a full knowledge of the grammar of the language of the community in which they live. This amazing feat is often contrasted with the hopeless failure encountered by adults acquiring a second language (L2):

> The outcome of first language acquisition is success: normal children acquire the grammar of the ambient language. Adult second language acquisition, on the other hand, results in varying degrees of success. Failure to acquire the target language is typical. (Birdsong, 1992: 706)

> It is true that many adults learn to communicate effectively using an L2, and some few appear to have extensive if not perfect knowledge of the grammar of the L2. Nevertheless, the overwhelming majority are not able to achieve anything like the same level of mastery as that achieved by every normal child. (Schachter, 1996a: 160)

> It is much more difficult to learn a second language in adulthood than a first language in childhood. Most adults never master a foreign language, especially the phonology – hence the ubiquitous foreign accent. Their development often 'fossilizes' into permanent error patterns that no teaching or correction can undo. (Schwartz, 1997)

> It has been widely observed that children from immigrant families eventually speak the language of their new community with native-like fluency, but their parents rarely achieve such high levels of mastery of the spoken language . . . Many adult second language learners become capable of communicating very successfully in the language but, for most, differences of accent, word choice, or grammatical features distinguish them from native speakers and from second language speakers who began learning the language while they were very young. (Lightbown & Spada, 1999: 60)

The difference in outcome between the child first language (L1) and adult L2 cases, as Schachter (1996a) puts it, is strong and unambiguous.

As early as 1972, Selinker conjectured that the absolute success in a second language affects a mere 5% of learners.[1] Similarly, Eubank and Gregg (1999: 77) claim that 'with few exceptions adult learners fail, often miserably, to become indistinguishable from members of the ambient L2 speech community'.

If the 5% success rate in L2 acquisition[2] is compared to the success rate in L1 development, the figures appear to be reversed, since in the latter case it is the failure rate that seems to stand at a mere 5%, and this is accounted for exclusively by those with specific language impairments (Eubank, 1997, SLART-L on-line communication; see also Bley-Vroman, 1989; Selinker, 1972; Selinker & Lamendella, 1978).

The overwhelming success surrounding first language acquisition (FLA) begs an important question: *How is acquisition possible*? This question was originally formulated as a logical problem in language acquisition (Hornstein & Lightfoot, 1981) to address the fact that learners' linguistic knowledge or competence transcends the input to which they have been exposed. Child first language acquirers have been noted to be capable of developing a robust and highly generative grammar despite exposure to input that is degenerate, under-determinate and finite. The general explanation given for the logical problem has been that child first language acquisition is driven by an innate language-specific mechanism known as Universal Grammar (UG). As Chomsky (1965: 58) states:

> A consideration of the character of the grammar that is acquired, the degenerate quality and narrowly limited extent of the available data, the striking uniformity of the resulting grammars, and their independence of intelligence, motivation and emotional state, over wide ranges of variation, leave little hope that much of the structure of language can be learned by an organism initially uninformed as to its general character.

Some researchers (e.g., Gregg, 1996; L. White, 1989) maintain that the same logical problem also obtains in second language acquisition (SLA). That is, in SLA there exists a similar gap between input on the one hand and the acquired competence on the other (L. White, 1996). Gregg (1996) argues that insofar as second language grammar (i.e., interlanguage) – however imperfect – is underdetermined by input data, the logical problem obtains.

Other researchers (e.g., Bley-Vroman, 1989; Schachter, 1988, 1996a), however, challenge the straightforward application of the logical problem to SLA, pointing out that SLA is characterized more by failure than by success:

> Few adults are completely successful; many fail miserably, and many achieve very high level of proficiency, given enough time, input, effort and given the right attitude, motivation and learning environment. (Bley-Vroman, 1989: 49)

By presenting a different view on the ultimate attainment of SLA, these researchers suggest an alternative version of the logical problem, namely, *why is complete acquisition impossible*? The explanation sought subsequently is that unlike first language acquirers whose acquisition is guided by UG, adult second language acquirers rely on their general problem-solving capacity for L2 development.

In postulating his Fundamental Difference Hypothesis, Bley-Vroman (1989) underscores nine major characteristics of second language acquisition: (1) lack of success; (2) general failure; (3) variation in success, course and strategy; (4) variation in goals; (5) fossilization; (6) indeterminate intuitions; (7) the importance of instruction; (8) the need for negative evidence; and (9) the role of affective factors. These features set SLA distinctively apart from FLA. In a similar vein, Schachter (1996a: 160–161; see also Schachter, 1988) points out four major dimensions along which SLA differs from FLA: (1) ultimate attainment (i.e., 'the ultimate attainment of most, if not all, of adult L2 learners is a state of incompleteness with regard to the grammar of the L2'); (2) fossilized variation (i.e., 'long after cessation of change in the development of their L2 grammar, adults will variably produce errors and non-errors in the same linguistic environments'); (3) lack of equipotentiality (i.e., 'the adult's knowledge of a prior language either facilitates or inhibits acquisition of the L2, depending on the underlying similarities or dissimilarities of the languages in question'); and (4) the role of prior knowledge (i.e., 'the adult learner's prior knowledge of one language has a strong effect, detectable in the adult's production of the L2').

The debate on the logical problem of SLA continues. Nonetheless, it becomes increasingly clear that unlike in FLA, a monolingual context, where success dominates, in SLA, a multilingual interactive context, success and failure co-exist, with both warranting explication. The logical problem in SLA, therefore, has dual facets, and given so, it is imperative that any theories of SLA that purport to be explanatorily adequate account for both. In other words, an adequate theory of SLA should be capable both of explaining how and why learning occurs and *how and why it fails to occur* (cf. Gass, 1988; Towell & Hawkins, 1994). Such theories, as yet, remain sparse. This theoretical gap is, in my view, attributable to the fact that we still lack a coherent understanding of failure.

Hence, for the ultimate purpose of facilitating the development of adequate theories, this book offers a preliminary attempt at constructing a systematic account of failure in adult SLA. Failure is here defined as permanent lack of mastery of a target language (TL) despite continuous exposure to the TL input, adequate motivation to improve, and sufficient opportunity for practice.[3] In SLA research, such kind of failure has largely been dealt with under the construct of 'fossilization' (Selinker, 1972).

Over the past 30 years, the SLA literature appears to have documented a considerable bulk of evidence of fossilization across and within adult L2 learners, as well as a rich spectrum of explanations thereof from a myriad of perspectives. Due, however, to the lack of uniformity in the interpretation and application of the construct of 'fossilization', the empirical phenomena that have been designated as fossilization seem widely disparate, and the explanatory accounts rather fragmented, thereby creating more confusion than clarity in the literature. For example, by one researcher, fossilization is associated with slow learning, but by another, it is connected to habitual errors. Then, in one case, fossilization is an empirical phenomenon, but in another, it serves as explanation for other learning phenomena. And so on. Such idiosyncratic application of the construct, among other things, obstructs a systematic understanding of failure, which, as can be speculated, could only be of little help to SLA theory construction.

My goal in this book is therefore three-fold: (1) to take stock of the major theoretical and empirical findings that have accumulated in this area, (2) to introduce a framework for interpreting them, and (3) to offer a principled perspective on adult L2 learners' lack of ability to fully acquire the target language. What I attempt to show also is that research on fossilization offers heuristics that can yield insights into resources for, processes of, and most importantly, constraints on, adult L2 learning. The understanding thereby derived can be central not only to SLA theory but also to second language instruction. In terms of the latter, for instance, a sound understanding of the constraints would enable second language educators to set more realistic goals for adult L2 learning. Moreover, an understanding of what renders linguistic features fossilizable might help educators to better sequence and present the instructional materials. Furthermore, knowledge of factors underlying fossilization may guide educators in search of compensatory strategies to maximize learning opportunities and, in MacWhinney's (2001: 90) words, to 'promote the functioning of neuronal loops for rehearsal, memory and learning' in the classroom, thus reducing the scope of fossilization and simultaneously expanding that of learning.

Prior to proceeding further, I have two caveats. First, in examining failure in L2 learning, I am not oblivious of Cook's (1992, 1995) notion of *multicompentence*, namely that the competence attained by a multilingual speaker is categorically different from that attained by a monolingual speaker.[4] It is not my intent in this book to suggest that L2 learning should be measured against the competence of a monolingual native speaker (NS), but rather to reveal a reality of adult SLA which, in the general perception, warrants explanation. In fact, as will be seen, the views expressed in this book, to a considerable extent, corroborate with Cook's view that it is unrealistic to expect adult L2 learners to be native-like in all language domains (for recent discussions of the notion of 'native speaker', see Cook, 1999; Davies, 2003; Han, in press).

My second caveat is that while devoting the entire book to a discussion of failure in adult SLA, I am mindful of Larsen-Freeman's (1997: 159) caution that 'an IL must be conceived as the evolving grammar of the learner adapting to an evolving target grammar'. However, I also recognize that despite the natural language dynamism, an interlanguage (IL) can simultaneously exhibit systematicity and fragmentation; permeability and resistance; and variability and premature stability (cf. Selinker & Han, 2001), and thus that studies of its non-dynamic nature make a paramount contribution to an authentic picture of L2 acquisition.

As a point of departure for our discussion, let us briefly review an important concept in SLA: ultimate attainment, in relation to fossilization.

Fossilization and Ultimate Attainment

As has been revealed in the quotes cited towards the beginning of this chapter, L2 ultimate attainment – which, after Birdsong (1999: 10), is understood as 'synonymous with the end state or asymptote of L2A, however close to or far from nativelike that state may be' – has served as a major lens through which researchers observe failure in adult SLA.[5] One contentious issue has been whether L2 ultimate attainment is isomorphic with fossilization.

A cross-learner view of the L2 ultimate attainment indicates that complete success is rare (if not impossible) in post-adolescent L2 acquisition; there are few nativelike attainers (see, e.g., Bongaerts, 1999; Ioup *et al.*, 1994; Nikolov, 2000). It is in this sense that L2 ultimate attainment has been seen as characterized by *general failure*. However, in tandem with the latter, as researchers have noted, is *differential success*. Below we will look at each in turn.

General failure

Despite the lack of large-scale and comprehensive studies able to demonstrate the phenomenon scientifically, an impressionistic look at learners in different acquisition contexts produces *prima facie* evidence that the 'majority of adult learners wind up far from the target,' and that 'their interlanguage remains distinct from the mature L2 in a good number of ways' (Eubank, 1997, SLART-L on-line communication).

Success in this context, in the view of some researchers, means complete mastery of a second language, namely, the attaining of 'all levels of linguistic structure and in all discourse domains' (Selinker & Lamendella, 1978: 373; see also Sharwood Smith, 1997, SLART-L on-line communication). The general lack of such success is characteristically seen to reside in the imbalance between the rate of success and the rate of failure. Over the years, the 5% success rate proposed by Selinker (1972) has been widely quoted. Some argue that this figure is too conservative (Seliger *et al.*, 1975), while others claim that even 5% is a gross overestimate (Gregg, 1996; Long, 1990).[6] If we follow Gregg's (1996: 52) speculative argument that 'truly native-like competence in an L2 is never attained', there can be no question of any imbalance since no learner would ever achieve perfect mastery of an L2 (cf. Sorace, 1993). Still other researchers (e.g. Kellerman, 1995a) who quote the 5% figure do so merely as a general recognition of the fact that there is overwhelmingly more failure than success in adult L2 acquisition.

In the SLA literature, it is also worth noting, there exist different views on what success should entail. As mentioned, for some, success means complete mastery of every facet of the L2; for others (e.g., Schachter 1996b), however, it means achieving only native-like competence in the core grammar of an L2 without taking account of linguistic peripherals. Despite the lack of consensus, the point nevertheless remains that in whichever sense, complete success is not achievable in post-adolescent L2 acquisition, and it has gained considerable support from studies of ultimate attainment in so-called 'near-natives' (e.g., Coppieters 1987; Sorace, 1993).[7] Although they each focused only on a small number of linguistic subsystems, Coppieters (1987) and Sorace (1993) both presented convincing evidence of the existence of a significant gap, assumed to be permanent, between the interlanguage grammar and the mature native grammar.

Counterevidence, to a lesser extent, is also available (Birdsong, 1992; Bongaerts, 1999; Ioup *et al.*, 1994; White & Genesee, 1996). White and Genesee (1996), for instance, come to the conclusion that it is possible for adult L2 learners to acquire native-like competence. Birdsong (1992), on the other hand, offers mixed evidence from his informants showing that with some subsystems complete mastery is possible, whereas with other subsystems it is not. Findings such as this speaks to the necessity of a non-monolithic view on ultimate attainment. And this takes us to the second facet of the L2 ultimate attainment: differential success and failure.

Differential success/failure

In addition to general failure, L2 ultimate attainment features differential success and failure (Bley-Vroman, 1989).

In writing on the longitudinal studies of the European Science Foundation (ESF) project, Perdue (1993: 8) particularly mentions the following as a salient feature of the untutored L2 learners:

> They achieve very different degrees of language mastery. Few, it seems, achieve native-like proficiency. Some stop (or, to use Selinker's [1972] term, 'fossilize') at a very elementary level. Others come between the two extremes.

Similarly, Hyltenstam and Abrahamsson (2001: 164) note:

> The ultimate attainment of individual L2 learners varies enormously in its approximation to nativelike proficiency, although some individuals may reach very high levels of proficiency and in some cases even pass as native speakers.

All these researchers, adopting a cross-learner view, stress qualitative individual variations in attaining competence in an L2, and that learners, instead of arriving at an identical terminal state of interlanguage competence that is short of the target, may end up with differential terminal interlanguage states in which they have successfully covered varying distances towards that target.[8]

The issue of differential success is not limited to a cross-learner view, however. If we look at the interlanguage of a particular learner, we can also see differential success. Bialystok (1978: 69) notes, for instance, that 'for a particular individual, some aspects of language learning are mastered more easily than are others'. In fossilization terms, Selinker and Lamendella (1978) claim that for a given learner, part of his interlanguage system fossilizes, and part of it does not. The existence of such kind of intra-learner variation is suggestive of differential ultimate attainments within an individual learner's system (cf. Sorace, 1993), with some subsystems successfully reaching the target and others falling short of it (Lardiere, 1998a).

Thus viewed, the L2 ultimate attainment has at least three facets: (1) cross-learner general failure; (2) inter-learner differential success/failure; and (3) intra-learner differential success / failure. Moreover, the three facets are interrelated such that the general failure is a conglomeration of inter-learner and, further, of intra-learner failure. To return to the question we posed at the beginning of this section, namely whether or not L2 ultimate attainment is isomorphic with fossilization, the answer is definitely no, for clearly, within the ultimate attainment, *success and failure co-exist*. Nevertheless, the three facets of ultimate attainment do exhibit fossilization in that they all involve permanently arrested development of some sort (cf. Selinker & Lamendella, 1978; Towell & Hawkins, 1994).

A Conceptual Framework

Guided by the above-elaborated conception of L2 ultimate attainment and of fossilization, in this book I attempt to offer a systematic analysis of fossilization that incorporates a macroscopic and a microscopic perspective, as schematized in Figure 1.1.

As illustrated, the macroscopic analysis involves examining general failure, while the microscopic analysis investigates inter- and intra-learner failure. The two-way arrow between general failure and inter-/intra-learner differential failure, on the other hand, signifies the interdependence between the two. A brief foreshadowing of each of the two levels of analysis follows.

On the macroscopic level, SLA research to date has advanced a number of explanations for the overall lack of success in L2 learning, two of which appear to be the most convincing: L1 transfer and the Critical Period Hypothesis (CPH). Language transfer, herein defined as a unidirectional influence of the native language (NL) on L2 learning, has been a perennial issue of SLA. Research over the past 30 years has taken us afar from an all-or-none view, which prevailed in the early days of SLA research, to a much more qualitative understanding of how native language may influence L2 learning. For example, transfer is now generally recognized to be a cognitive, an idiosyncratic, and a selective process that to a significant extent determines the quantity and quality of success in an L2. Even

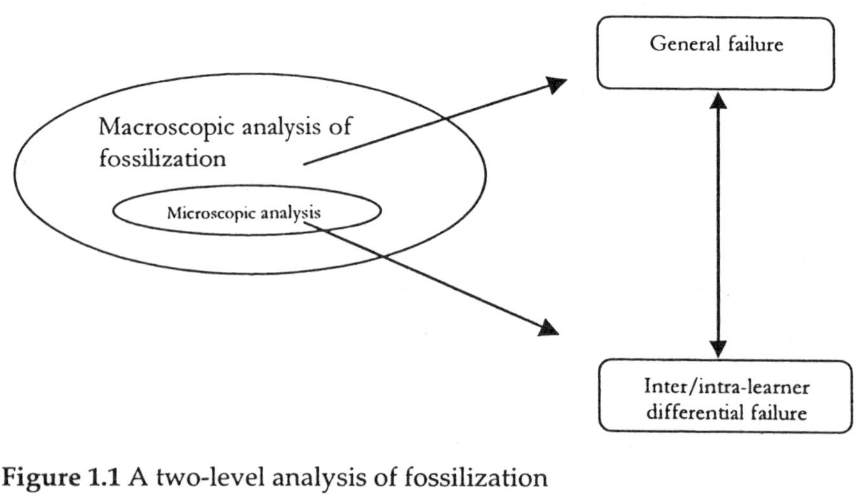

Figure 1.1 A two-level analysis of fossilization

though it may consciously be acted upon (Andersen, 1983), L1 influence is largely an implicit force that drives language acquisition (Kellerman, 1995a). Moreover, SLA research by now has produced a wealth of evidence showing that L1 influence, as a cognitive factor, can interact with a host of other factors, external (e.g., input) and internal (e.g., maturational constraints), leading to long-term stabilization (see, e.g., Han, 2000; Han & Selinker, 1999; Kellerman, 1989; Schachter, 1996a; Schumann, 1978a; Selinker & Lakshmanan, 1992)

Contributing equally, if not more, to the observed general failure in L2 acquisition are maturational constraints. Selinker and Lamendella (1978: 167) have asserted that 'it is an inescapable conclusion that there is indeed a biologically based upper bound on fossilization, an age related point in ontogeny after which successful IL learning becomes impossible'.[9] Research on the biological influence has largely centered around testing out the Critical Period Hypothesis (CPH) (Lenneberg, 1967), which stipulates that 'there is a limited developmental period during which it is possible to acquire a language, be it L1 or L2, to normal, nativelike levels' and that 'once the window of opportunity is passed, the ability to learn language declines' (Birdsong, 1999: 1). What is implied in this proposition is that children are biologically predisposed to be better language learners than adults are. Long's (1990) review, examining both the findings and the methodological designs of the past studies on the CPH, points to the certainty of maturational constraints and their potential consequences. Of particular relevance to understanding fossilization is his insight that there exists a cause-and-effect relationship between the timing of the first exposure and the ultimate attainment. Following from this understanding, adult second language learners begin with some degree of 'biological handicap' (Slobin, 1993), and because of this, their learning is doomed to incompleteness.

Thus, it will be argued that under the cognitive and biological constraints, adult learners are *preconditioned* to fossilize, with asymptotic performance as the characteristic behavioral reflex. The bio-cognitive constraints, however, are inadequate to serve as an explanation for the other two facets of ultimate attainment, namely, the inter-learner and intra-learner differential failure (and success). With respect to the latter, a microscopic analysis of fossilization is warranted to address such questions as 'why do some adults fossilize at a greater distance from TL norms than others?' (Selinker & Lamendella, 1978: 151), and why does a given individual fossilize in some aspects of the TL while successfully meeting the target in others? Two pieces of evidence garnered from the literature, in particular, will be brought to bear on these issues. The first is that the two general constraints may interact with one another to engender differential failure

(Bialystok & Miller, 1999; Birdsong & Molis, 2001; DeKeyser, 2000; Kellerman, 1995b). The second piece of evidence is that language transfer may interact with a host of other factors (social, psychological, linguistic, etc.) to further halt progress in individual learners.

An Outline of the Book

Unifying the macroscopic and microscopic perspectives on failure (i.e., fossilization) constitutes a major goal of this book. To that end, the ensuing chapters are organized as follows. In Chapter 2, a brief survey of definitions of fossilization is provided to enable the reader a quick overview of the evolution of the conceptual scope of fossilization since its inception (Selinker, 1972). Chapter 3 presents, first in a cursory manner, a range of behavioral reflexes with which the term 'fossilization' has come to be associated, and then in a more detailed way, a spectrum of putative causal variables culled from the SLA literature. The question is, then, raised as to whether fossilization arises from lack of ability to learn or from the influence of individual-oriented variables such as the socio-psychological ones? It is argued that fossilization is internally determined, due to the functioning of bio-cognitive constraints, yet it can be modulated (i.e., aggravated or alleviated) by environmental, social, and psychological forces. In further pursuit of this line of argumentation, in Chapter 4, a macroscopic analysis is conducted of the critical period research, the major thrust of which is to reveal a genetic cause for the observed general lack of success among adult L2 learners. Chapter 5 shifts the focus of the macroscopic analysis to the cognitive factor of native language transfer. A microscopic analysis, then, follows in Chapter 6 with a focus on examining specific behavioral reflexes of fossilization and exploring inter-learner and intra-learner differential failure. For that purpose, several major empirical studies are brought under scrutiny for a close analysis of their findings and methodological designs. Next, in the spirit of relating theory to practice, Chapter 7 delves into the relationship between second language instruction and fossilization. Finally, by way of conclusion, Chapter 8 sums up the thesis of each chapter, explores the implications of the foregoing discussion for research and practice, and outlines future research directions.

Notes

1. Over the past three decades, there has been limited yet continued interest in researching the 5% population who seem to have been exempted from maturationally imposed limitations on language acquisition ability. Studies along this line typically target a small number of exceptional learners, and subsequently make inferences, based on the observed traits, about what underlies their successful acquisition. Schneiderman and Desmarais (1988), for example,

studied two talented informants by administering to them a number of contrived tasks, from which they inferred that their informants possessed a unique neuropsychological substrate, i.e., 'a non-left lateralized substrate' (1988: 102), that features neurocognitive flexibility.

2. Throughout this book, the terms *learning* and *acquisition* are used more or less with no differentiation.
3. This therefore eliminates consideration of those instances of failure, due, for example, to lack of exposure to input and lack of motivation. As Oyama (1976: 262) has aptly pointed out, 'failure to learn a language well under unnatural and restricted circumstances may say less about their general ability to acquire languages than it does about our difficulty in providing the proper conditions for learning'.
4. Jarvis and Pavlenko (2000) invoke the notion of 'multicompetence' (Cook, 1991) to argue that the end state of interlanguage development is not merely a fossilized state short of the target, but of the native language as well. In their words, 'an interlanguage might be characterized more accurately as a continuum from monolingual competence to multicompetence, where the end state of second language acquisition is not comparable to two independent monolingual states'.
5. Patkowski (1980) notes that studies which have not focused on eventual achievement have generally shown child–adult differences favoring adults.
6. Long and Robinson (1998: 20) have gone further to claim that 'very few, if any, older learners achieve even *near-native* abilities' (emphasis added).
7. Selinker and Han (2001) cast doubts on the validity of using 'near-natives' for studying ultimate attainment. In their view, fallibility is likely to result if the assumed 'near-natives' are not true 'near-natives' and/or if the putative 'near-natives' have not indeed reached ultimate attainment. White and Genesee (1996) have expressed a similar concern, though the question they pose relates primarily to the procedures adopted in previous studies for selecting near-natives as informants.
8. Marinova-Todd *et al.* (2000: 18) remind us that 'adults are not a homogeneous group of linguistically incompetent creatures', and they highlight the fact that despite the seemingly vast amount of failure, successful adult L2 learners do exist whose linguistic performance even surpasses that of native speakers.
9. Selinker and Lamendella (1978) argue that satisfaction of the interactive needs of the individual learners provides the lower bound on fossilization. By 'upper bound', they refer to the point at which fossilization will *necessarily* develop, whereas the 'lower bound' provides the point at which fossilization will *possibly* occur.

Chapter 2

What is Fossilization?

In *The Guardian*, May 13, 1997, we read the following obituary of the renowned physicist, Chien-Shiung Wu (1912–1997):

> Professor Chien-Shiung Wu, who has died aged 83, was a physicist whose brilliance carried her from obscurity in China during the early thirties to fame in the United States during and after the second world war. As a postdoctoral physicist, **speaking idiosyncratic English** but with a unique knowledge of gaseous fission products, she was called in by the great Enrico Fermi when, **in 1942**, an experimental reactor began to run down within weeks of going critical. She quickly and correctly diagnosed poisoning by the rare gas xenon, produced in the fission process.
>
> . . .
>
> In 1992, Wu came to Europe for an 80th birthday symposium held in her honor at the international Cern laboratory at Geneva. She was delighted and, **with her early difficulties with English still evident**, talked about her beta decay work and the importance of choosing critical experiments. It is said that few left the meeting uninspired by her amazing clarity of thought, or unmoved by the power of her quiet yet very special genius. (emphasis added)

Professor Chien-Shiung Wu, who arrived in the U.S. in 1936 at the age of 24 and had since lived and worked there until her death at 83, had 56 years of exposure to English, her second language. She was nevertheless unable to overcome all of her early difficulties with English, despite her undoubted intelligence and her enormous scientific achievements over the intervening decades. Why were some of her early language difficulties insurmountable? Professor Wu's case is typical of millions of adult L2 learners who, despite long exposure and concerted efforts, become caught up somewhere in the learning process and find themselves unable to progress.

This phenomenon of non-progression of learning despite continuous exposure to input, adequate motivation to learn, and sufficient opportunity for practice – generally referred to in the literature as 'fossilization' – became a central concern for SLA researchers almost as soon as the research field itself came into existence, and may even have propelled the field into existence (Selinker, personal communication, 1996). More profoundly, it has been seen as part of a larger background issue:

> One of the most enduring and fascinating problems confronting researchers of second language acquisition (SLA) is whether adults can ever acquire native-like competence in a second language (L2), or whether this is an accomplishment reserved for children who start learning at a relatively early age. As a secondary issue, there is the question of whether those rare cases of native-like success reported amongst adult learners are indeed what they seem, and if they are, how it is that such people can be successful when the vast majority are palpably not. (Kellerman, 1995b: 219)

While Kellerman pinpointed the difference in ultimate attainment between child FLA and adult SLA, Towell and Hawkins (1994: 2) further noted:

> For most of us the acquisition of second language is less spectacular. If we are past the age of around 7–10 years the acquisition of an L2, in marked contrast to the way we acquired our first language (L1), can turn out to be rather slow, laborious and, even in talented L2 learners, tends to stop short of native-like proficiency. This 'stopping short' has been referred to as fossilization (Selinker, 1972) or incompleteness (Schachter, 1990). It is one of the noticeable characteristics of second language acquisition. Even after many years of exposure to an L2, in a situation where the speaker might use that L2 every day for normal communicative purposes, even to the extent of 'losing' the native language, it is not uncommon to find that the speaker still has a strong 'foreign' accent, uses non-native grammatical constructions, and has non-native intuitions about the interpretation of certain types of sentence.

Thus, Towell and Hawkins explicitly tie L2 ultimate attainment to fossilization.

For more than three decades now, the construct of fossilization has been subjected to theoretical and empirical queries under a range of different terms, not only under its by now traditional name of 'fossilization' (Selinker, 1972; *passim* the SLA literature), but also as 'virtual halt' (e.g., Lowther, 1983; Perdue, 1984), 'linguistic monstrosities' (Hammerly, 1983), 'plateau' (e.g. Flynn & O'Neil, 1988), 'rigor mortis' (Long, 1988, 1997), 'stopping short' (Towell &

Hawkins, 1994), 'fossilized variation' (Schachter, 1996a), 'permanent optionality' (Sorace, 1996), 'siesta' (Sharwood Smith, 1997, SLART-L on-line communication), 'endstate' (Lardiere, 1998a), and so forth.

In this chapter, we examine and discuss a selection of definitions, starting from the earliest to the more recent, with a view to revealing the evolution of the concept and the existence of conceptual differences, and further, to identifying key conceptual issues surrounding fossilization.

Selinker's Definitions

The notion of 'fossilization' dates back to scholars such as Weinreich (1953) and Nemser (1971). Weinreich, for example, talked about 'permanent grammatical influence' (cited in Selinker, 1992: 41) and Nemser about 'permanent intermediate systems and subsystems' (p. 174). Both researchers not only recognized the phenomenon but also integrated it into their theoretical perspectives (For an accessible discussion of the earliest thoughts on fossilization, see Selinker, 1992).

The term 'fossilization' was introduced to the field of SLA by Selinker in 1972 on the basis of his observation that the vast majority of second language learners fail to achieve native-speaker competence. Fossilization, as then conceptualized, implicated both a cognitive mechanism known as the *fossilization mechanism* (Selinker, 1972: 221) and a performance-related structural phenomenon. As a cognitive mechanism, it was thought to be a constituent of a *latent psychological structure* that dictates a learner's acquisition of a second language. As a performance-related structural notion, it denoted specifically 'the regular reappearance in second-language performance of linguistic phenomena which were thought to be eradicated in the performance of the learner' (p. 211). The two functions were conceived to be interrelated:

> *Fossilization*, a mechanism . . . underlies surface linguistic material which speakers will tend to keep in their IL productive performance, no matter what the age of the learner or the amount of instruction he receives in the TL. (Selinker, 1972: 229)

Further, as a performance-based structural notion, fossilization was indirectly, rather than directly, defined in terms of putative fossilizable structures:

> Fossilizable linguistic phenomena are linguistic items, rules, and subsystems which speakers of a particular L1 tend to keep in their IL relative to a particular TL, no matter what the age of the learner or amount of explanation and instruction he receives in the TL . . . (Selinker, 1972: 215)

This earliest conception suggests, *inter alia*, several properties of fossilization. First, fossilizable structures are persistent; second, they are resistant to external influences; and third, fossilization affects both child and adult L2 learners alike. Behind these, it is important to note, is the implication that L2 learners lack the ability to attain native-like competence. And precisely it is this view that accords the construct of fossilization its intrinsic interest; it is what has drawn the attention of many second language researchers and practitioners.

Since 1972, the notion of fossilization has seen a gradual abstraction and an expansion in scope. In 1978, Selinker and Lamendella explicitly defined it in terms of:

> . . . a permanent cessation of IL learning before the learner has attained TL norms at all levels of linguistic structure and in all discourse domains in spite of the learner's positive ability, opportunity, and motivation to learn and acculturate into target society. (1978: 187)

Fossilization, in the view expressed above, is coterminous with permanent cessation of learning, thereby going beyond the 'backsliding' of linguistic structures that were thought to be eradicated. The scope of 'fossilizable structures' was also extended from 'linguistic items, rules and subsystems' to 'all levels of linguistic structure and in all discourse domains'. The role played by the 'learner's positive ability, opportunity, and motivation' was minimized, thereby suggesting the inevitability of fossilization and thus its innateness.

In Selinker and Lakshmanan (1992), fossilization is defined structurally in terms of persistent non-target-like structures, thus incorporating long-term persistence as a defining feature of empirical discovering of fossilization.

Fossilization in the sense of a general cessation of learning would, in Selinker's view, culminate in ultimate *fossilized competence* (Selinker, 1996a, b):

> Fossilization is the process whereby the learner creates a cessation of interlanguage learning, thus stopping the interlanguage from developing, it is hypothesized, in a permanent way . . . The argument is that no adult can hope to ever speak a second language in such a way that s/he is indistinguishable from native speakers of that language. (Selinker, 1996b)

On this view, then, the ultimate attainment of adult L2 acquisition is a fossilized interlanguage; fossilization is inevitable; and no adult L2 learner would ever be able to pass for native in all contexts.

In sum, since 1972, Selinker has broadened the referential scope of fossilization: from 'backsliding' to 'cessation of learning' and to 'ultimate attainment', gradually moving away from the 5% estimate that he made initially concerning the hypothesized successful population of SLA to the claim that no adult L2 learner can hope to achieve native-like competence in all discourse domains (Selinker, 1996b). Accompanying this change in conception.is also an expansion of the linguistic scope of fossilization, from fossilizable structures (i.e., local fossilization) to a fossilized interlanguage (i.e., global fossilization).

Meanwhile, the dual functions of fossilization, namely, its being both a cognitive mechanism and a structural-behavioral phenomenon, which were explicit in the earliest postulation, tend to be less clear-cut in his later definitions (Selinker & Douglas, 1985).

Others' View

Beyond Selinker's definitions, the SLA literature over the past three decades has seen numerous interpretations of fossilization. In this section, a selection of these, which are largely representative of the general views, are presented. As can be seen, many are in essence extended interpretations of the notion as originally proposed by Selinker in 1972. Lowther (1983: 127), for example, has the following interpretation of fossilization:

> Fossilization, as presented in much of the literature, is understood to be the *inability* of a person to attain nativelike ability in the target language. (emphasis added)

This is reminiscent of Selinker's view of fossilization as fundamentally a cognitive mechanism. Most SLA researchers, however, have followed and built on the performance dimension of Selinker's (1972) dual definition. R. Ellis (1985: 48), for instance, offers the following view:

> Fossilized structures can be realized as errors or as correct target language forms. If, when fossilization occurs, the learner has reached a stage of development in which feature *x* in his interlanguage has assumed the same form as in the target language, then fossilization of the correct form will occur. If, however, the learner has reached a stage in which feature *y* still does not have the same form as the target language, the fossilization will manifest itself as error.

Thus, R. Ellis has suggested, among other things, that as part of the interlanguage process, fossilization happens at a certain point in interlanguage development, and as a result, there are fossilized errors as well as fossilized target-like forms.

The origin of this view, namely that fossilization applies to both incorrect and correct forms, can be traced back to Vigil and Oller (1976: 282):

> We will extend the notion of fossilization to any case where grammatical rules, construed in the broadest sense, become relatively permanently incorporated into a psychologically real grammar.
>
> . . .
>
> An adequate explanation must account for the incorporation of rules into developing grammars in relatively permanent form regardless of whether those rules conform or do not conform to the norms of the language which is being learned. It is not only the fossilization of so-called 'errors' that must be explained, but also the fossilization of correct forms that conform to the target language norms.

Here, viewing fossilization as the relatively permanent incorporation of grammatical rules in the interlanguage grammar, Vigil and Oller argue that the presence of fossilization should be felt not only in incorrect forms but in correct ones also.

This opinion, however, is not widely endorsed. Most researchers are, instead, of the view that fossilization should be reserved exclusively for non-target-like forms. Hyltenstam (1988: 68), for example, gives the following definition of fossilization:

> Fossilization – according to observations – is a process that may occur in the second language acquisition context as opposed to first language acquisition. It covers features of the second language learner's inter- language that deviate from the native speaker norm and are not developing any further, or deviant features which – although seemingly left behind – re-emerge in the learner's speech under certain conditions. Thus, the learner has stopped learning or has reverted to earlier stages of acquisition.

Here, fossilization – in line with Selinker's (1972) view– is associated with deviant forms, and 'backsliding' identified as the prime phenomenological manifestation of fossilization. A similar conception has been entertained by many others, including Preston (1989: 245) who identifies fossilization with the 'persistence of an incorrect form in the emerging interlanguage'.

While fossilization has so far been largely construed as an IL product, some researchers see it as a process – 'a process whereby repeated practice and exposure to the language does not lead to any further development' (Sharwood Smith, 1994a: 37).

Further, there is also the conception that fossilization is a stage in the interlanguage process. Bley-Vroman (1989: 47–49), for example, asserts:

> It has long been noted that foreign language learners reach a certain stage of learning – a stage short of success – and that learners then permanently stabilize at this stage. Development ceases, and even serious conscious efforts to change are often fruitless. Brief changes are sometimes observed, but they do not 'take'. The learner backslides to the stable state.

Fossilization is thus taken to be 'permanent stabilization', and as such, an ultimate stage in the interlanguage process. Corroborating this view, Tarone (1994: 1715) notes:

> A central characteristic of any interlanguage is that it fossilizes – that is, it ceases to develop at some point short of full identity with the target language.

Tarone's claim is worth noting for its strong implication that fossilization is inevitable, and that it is what characterizes the ultimate attainment of every learner.

In summary, within the SLA literature there exist a wide range of differing conceptions *vis-à-vis* the nature and scope of fossilization. What about outside this realm? With this question, we now turn to the dictionary definitions.

Dictionary Definitions

A by now widely recognized, significant feature of SLA, fossilization has figured in a number of popular dictionaries, from which three definitions are extracted below for discussion.

First, in the *Unabridged Random House Dictionary* (Flexner, 1993: 755), 'fossilize' is defined in the following way:

> Ling. (of a linguistic form, feature, rule, etc) to become permanently established in the interlanguage of a second-language learner in a form that is deviant from the target-language norm and that continues to appear in performance regardless of further exposure to the target language.

This definition identifies deviant forms as the target of fossilization. Persistence and resistance are seen to be the primary characteristics of fossilization. It is worth noting that persistence here takes the form of continuous appearance rather than backsliding.

Second, in the Longman Dictionary of Language Teaching and Applied Linguistics (Richards *et al.*, 1992: 145), 'fossilization' is defined as:

> ... a process (in second and foreign language learning) which *sometimes* occurs in which incorrect linguistic features become a permanent part of the way a person speaks or writes a language. Aspects of pronunciation, vocabulary usage, and grammar may become fixed or fossilized in second or foreign language learning. Fossilized features of pronunciation contribute to a person's foreign accent. (emphasis added)

As in the preceding definition, here the target of fossilization is the deviant (as opposed to target-like) forms, and the fossilized forms are assumed to be permanent. Moreover, fossilization is thought to be a process which occurs only sometimes, thus hinting at the possibility of some interlanguages or part of one interlanguage being free of the process. In addition, the definition suggests that fossilization happens only to interlanguage subsystems rather than the entire system.

Third, in the *Routledge Dictionary of Language and Linguistics* (Bussman, 1996), 'fossilization' is defined as:

> Permanent retention of his habits which when taken together, constitute a learner's interlanguage (e.g. French uvular /r/ in the English interlanguage of native speakers of French, American English retroflex /r/ in the French of native speakers of American English, German time-place word order in the English interlanguage of native speakers of German, etc.). Fossilization may occur despite optimal teaching factors and corrective feedback; it may result, in particular, when a language learner perceives that his communication strategies are effective and adequate.

Here, an interlanguage is considered a collection of habits, and fossilization the retention of particular habits. The examples given illustrate what the habits are meant to be, namely, incorrect forms. These habits, resulting largely from the adequacy of a learner's use of communication strategies, are impervious to pedagogic attempts.

Hence, taken together, the dictionaries have offered various (though not entirely dissimilar) perceptions on what fossilization is – quite akin to what we see in the SLA literature.

An Alternative Definition

A major criticism of the definitions of fossilization developed thus far is that they lack sophistication, thereby making the phenomenon non-measurable (K. Gregg, 1997, SLART-L discussion). In response, Han (1998) suggests a two-tier definition, taking into account both the innateness and the external manifestation of the phenomenon:

> COGNITIVE LEVEL: Fossilization involves those cognitive processes,[1] or underlying mechanisms that produce permanently stabilized IL forms.
>
> EMPIRICAL LEVEL: Fossilization involves those stabilized interlanguage forms that remain in learner speech or writing over time, no matter what the input or what the learner does.

This two-tier definition defines fossilization at two interrelated levels. At the cognitive level, it specifies that fossilization is a cognitive mechanism made up of more than one process; at the empirical level, it ties fossilization with stabilization over time that has manifestations in interlanguage output. The two levels are also tied respectively to fossilization as a process and as a product; that is, the cognitive level pertains to fossilization as a process whereas the empirical level speaks to its product dimension. The two imply a cause–effect relationship in that it is the cognitive level of fossilization (i.e., fossilization as a process) that gives rise to the empirical level (i.e., fossilization as a product). Moreover, fossilization on the whole is predicated on the condition of 'no matter what the input or what the learner does,' hence suggesting that as a cognitive mechanism, fossilization would function regardless of learning conditions, and that when showing up in interlanguage output, it would be out of a learner's control.[2]

Whether or not this is a better definition than its predecessors is as yet to be judged by the field. Nevertheless, what does seem clear at this point is that the definition still leaves considerable room for interpretation. For example, at the cognitive level, it is still not clear what processes make up the mechanism(s), and presuming we do know what they are, the questions that ensue are how and when they are activated. At the empirical level, though fossilization is associated with stabilization over time, both the length of the stabilization and its manner remain to be determined.[3]

Another already discernible flaw in this definition lies in its use of 'cognitive processes' in the upper tier as a lump term for learner-internal processes. This may imply, to some, a by-now classic view on the scope of cognition. After all, the intellectual world surrounding 'fossilization' is different now than it was in the 1970s. What used to come under 'cognition' are, in fact, internal processes, some of which (e.g., neural and socio-affective processes) are not really cognitive.

Last but not least, the two-tier definition is reminiscent of Selinker's dual functions of fossilization (i.e., it being a cognitive mechanism and at the same time a performance-related phenomenon). Long (2003) has pointed out that Selinker's view is essentially ambiguous in that it suggests fossilization both as *explanandum* (i.e., the thing to be explained) and as *explanans* (i.e., an explanation). From this criticism, it will follow, then, that the two-tier definition, in that it invokes the same term for two (albeit related) properties, may as well create ambiguity.

Key Issues

As is clear from the preceding review, the various attempts made over the years at defining fossilization have resulted more in conceptual diversity than uniformity, notwithstanding the fact that they all recognize fossilization as a central characteristic of SLA (Towell & Hawkins, 1994). The major differences seem to have stemmed from a number of issues (Han, 2002a), of which we will now briefly discuss two: (1) whether fossilization is global or local; and (2) whether fossilization is a product or a process.

Is fossilization global or local?

Some researchers have viewed fossilization as occurring *globally* to the entire interlanguage system, yet others have maintained that fossilization could only happen *locally* in parts of the interlanguage system. It may be recalled that Selinker himself has shifted his perception from local to global. Mirroring this difference, the SLA literature sees the use of 'fossilized error', on the one hand, suggesting local fossilization, but 'fossilized competence' and 'fossilized learner', on the other hand, suggesting global fossilization. By way of illustration, Tarone *et al.* (1976; see also Selinker, 1992) argue that two types of learners can be distinguished: fossilized learners (referred to as 'Type 1 learners') and non-fossilized learners (referred to as 'Type 2 learners'). According to the researchers, a Type 1 learner's interlanguage is characterized by cessation of learning or stability due to his or her inability to change the IL system. In contrast, a Type 2 learner's interlanguage is dynamic in that it changes over time, thereby suggesting continuation of learning. Apparently, such a bifurcation of L2 learners is conceptually flawed. For one thing, it essentially relies only on learners' output (i.e., the observable behavior) to determine whether learning is occurring or not, and inasmuch as it ignores the underlying cognitive processes, it reflects a simplistic and behavioristic view of learning.

As of yet, it is crucial to note, evidence of global fossilization remains entirely impressionistic (cf. VanPatten, 1988).[4] More precisely, global fossilization is assumed as opposed to established. Rather, the preponderance of the available empirical evidence has been pointing to local fossilization;

that is, fossilization only hits certain linguistic features in certain subsystems of the interlanguages of individual learners while other linguistic features in the *same* subsystems are successfully acquired or continue to evolve. It is worth mentioning that the empirical results are largely in line with the general conceptual framework established in Chapter 1, namely that L2 ultimate attainment is made up of cross-learner as well as within-learner differential success, which features local fossilization, but which denies the existence of global fossilization. In light of that conceptualization, it would be a misconception that some learners are fossilized. The issue of global vs. local fossilization will be further discussed in Chapter 6 as we examine empirical studies of fossilization.

Is fossilization a product or a process?

L2 researchers differ also in their view on whether fossilization is a process or a product. Apparently, some think it is one, not the other; others think just the opposite, and still others think it is both. Importantly, underlying the three positions are three different perspectives. That is, the first has adopted a cognitive perspective on fossilization, the second a phenomenological perspective, and the third both a cognitive and a phenomenological perspective.

Viewed from a phenomenological perspective, fossilization is a product, and as such, it should, according to some of the definitions, manifest itself as permanently stabilized linguistic deviance. The word 'permanent' is elusive, though: should we take it inferentially or literally? A literal interpretation would necessarily predict that fossilization will never be proven, because we will never be able to find any evidence of it. Interestingly, some have indeed taken the literal meaning, and in so doing, they are going down such a garden path:

> To make any decisive claims [on fossilization] . . . it would be necessary to demonstrate that the fossilized item in question has completely ceased developing towards the L2 norm. However, this would require the researcher analyzing the learner's performance over a sufficient length of time, ideally from the moment of observation of a fossilized item until the learner's death, to be sure that no destabilization had occurred. (Jung, 2002: 16)

This kind of suggestion, though oversimplistic at best, hints at the difficulty in documenting fossilization. Indeed, under a phenomenological approach, as apparently is the case above, it would be empirically impossible to establish fossilization as a product. However, the absence of such evidence should not be taken as evidence of absence of fossilization. The question is: How should we approach it? Given the methodological difficulty, it would seem necessary (and plausible) to conceptualize fossilization as a process, a process whereby learning manifests a strong tendency toward cessation in spite of 'repeated practice and exposure to the [target] language' (Sharwood Smith, 1994a: 37).

Summary

In this chapter, we have looked at a broad spectrum of views on fossilization. According to the earliest formulation (Selinker, 1972), *fossilization* is a mechanism existing in the latent psychological structure underlying a learner's L2 acquisition; it is overtly a process that affects every learner's interlanguage; and is manifested in the form of 'backsliding'. It is important to note that in this earliest conceptualization, fossilization is largely monolithic, linked primarily with 'backsliding'. For other researchers, *fossilization* is a product as well as a process; it affects the entire IL system as well as its subsystems; it is literally permanent as well as relatively permanent; it is persistent and resistant; and for some it happens to every learner but to only some learners for others. It is a stage of interlanguage learning, therefore, incorporating the fossilization of correct as well as of incorrect forms. It is externally manifested as well as internally determined. Furthermore, it is suggested that fossilization may represent the ultimate outcome of L2 learning. The definitions offered by the three dictionaries, in contrast, are relatively uniform and are representative of the general prevailing view. *Fossilization* is regarded as pertaining only to interlanguage forms that are deviant from the target-language norms. *Fossilization* in this sense becomes synonymous with 'error fossilization' (Lennon, 1991: 130). It is a process which affects interlanguage subsystems rather than the entire interlanguage system. It is persistent and resistant.

What is fossilization, then? To date, there is no uniform answer. However, from the miscellaneous conceptions, two broad and (by now) uncontroversial features are deducible, namely: (1) that fossilization involves premature cessation of development in defiance of optimal learning conditions; and (2) that fossilizable structures are persistent over time, against any environmental influences, including consistent natural exposure to the target language and pedagogic interventions. In addition, several issues are identifiable as lying at the heart of the conceptual differences, and we discussed two: (1) whether fossilization should be seen as global or local, and (2) whether it should be viewed as a product or a process. I have argued that fossilization occurs locally rather than globally, and that it is an observable process, with the product only being inferable.

Notes

1. In this context, 'cognitive' assumes a broader meaning than is traditionally accorded it, encompassing not only aspects of knowledge development and use but also the dimension of emotion (see, e.g., Mandler, 1999; Schumann, 1998).
2. The reader may question this point, given that 'backsliding' shows that the L2 learner is able, through special effort, to control the interlanguage form by 'suppressing'. it. It is therefore important to point out that 'out of control' is here intended to mean that the fossilized form, including 'backsliding', would remain permanently in the interlanguage, and that the L2 learner is not able to shed it in all situations.
3. Long (2003) suggests that an arbitrary minimum period be stipulated for fossilization to be inferred.
4. David Birdsong, in many of his publications, has referred to the L2 ultimate attainment as asymptotic (see, e.g., Birdsong, 1999). It is important to point out that his notion of 'asymptote' is not identical to 'fossilized competence'. According to Birdsong (personal communication, 2002), '[asymptote] is an idealization of an end state (L1 or L2) that doesn't commit one to a literal "steady state", allowing for Johnson *et al.* 1996 "indeterminacy", accumulation of lexis, that kind of thing'. This view makes no presumption about whether L2 ultimate attainment is target-like or non-target-like, but it does suggest that 'any further development would be scarcely measurable'.

Chapter 3

Behavioral Reflexes and Causal Variables

In the previous chapter we have seen that *fossilization* as a theoretical construct has been interpreted in a variety of different ways. The lack of uniformity in the general understanding of the notion, as a consequence, has led researchers, over the years, to apply the term to a wide array of learner behaviors. In this chapter, I will first provide a quick sketch of the putative behavioral reflexes and causal variables of fossilization, and then offer a more in-depth view on a selection of sample explanations. After that, I will highlight and discuss two what I believe are primary determinants of lack of ability to learn a second language.

An Overview

Below is a list of what researchers have recognized as behavioral reflexes of fossilization (cf. Selinker & Han, 2001; Han, 2003):

- Backsliding (e.g., R. Ellis, 1985; Schachter, 1988; Selinker; 1972).
- Stabilized errors (e.g., Schumann, 1978a).
- Persistent non-target-like performance (e.g., Mukattash, 1986).
- Learning plateau (e.g., Flynn & O'Neil, 1988).
- Typical error (Kellerman, 1989).
- Low proficiency (e.g. Thep-Ackrapong, 1990).
- De-acceleration of the learning process (e.g., Washburn, 1991).
- Ingrained errors (Valette, 1991).
- Systematic use of erroneous forms (Allwight & Bailey, 1991).
- Variable outcomes (Perdue, 1993).
- Cessation of learning (e.g., Odlin, 1993).
- Structural persistence (e.g., Schouten, 1996).
- Errors that are impervious to negative evidence (Lin & Hedgcock, 1996).

- Random use of grammatical and ungrammatical structures (Schachter, 1996).
- Habitual errors (SLART-L, 1997).
- Errors made by advanced learners (e.g., Selinker & Mascia, 1999).
- Long-lasting free variation (R. Ellis, 1999).
- Persistent difficulty (Hawkins, 2000).
- Ultimate attainment (*passim* the SLA literature).
- Inability to fully master target language features (*passim* the SLA literature).

As the above list indicates, over the years the term 'fossilization' has come to be associated with a wide array of learner behaviors. The lack of uniformity in the application of the notion, while creating confusion, nevertheless points to the fact that fossilization is no longer a monolithic concept as it was in its initial postulation, but rather a complex construct intricately tied up with a myriad of manifestations of failure, some of which are local, and some of which are global. Examples in the global category include 'low-proficiency', 'de-acceleration of the learning process', and 'ultimate attainment', whereas in the local category there are such variables as 'typical error', 'habitual errors', and 'persistent difficulty', and so on.

The proliferation of uses of the term 'fossilization' is matched in excess by explanatory accounts exhibiting a rich spectrum with almost every existent perspective on SLA represented. Just as each idiosyncratic application of the term adds a new empirical property to the discovery of fossilization, each explanatory account reveals a new underlying factor, and together they weave a large and delicate picture of fossilization.

In the SLA literature, explicit and implicit explanations of fossilization abound. Some of them are based on empirical studies ostensibly devoted to the subject matter of fossilization, and some are sheer speculations without any empirical basis. Fossilization, in association with the above list of behavioral reflexes, has been found to be explained in terms of the following variables, among others (see also Selinker & Han, 2001; Han, 2003):

- Multiple factors acting in tandem (e.g., Han & Selinker, 1999; Jain, 1974; Kasper, 1982; Kellerman,1989; Selinker, 1992; Selinker & Lakshmanan, 1992; Sharwood Smith, 1994a).
- Absence of instruction (Krashen & Seliger, 1975, 1976; Schmidt, 1983; Seliger, 1975).
- Absence of corrective feedback (Higgs & Clifford, 1982; Lightbown & Spada, 1999; Tomasello & Herron, 1988; Valette, 1991; Vigil & Oller, 1976).

- Satisfaction of communicative needs (Corder, 1978, 1983; R. Ellis, 1985; Klein, 1986; Klein & Perdue, 1993; Kowal & Swain, 1997; Selinker & Lamendella, 1978).
- Lack of acculturation (e.g., Preston, 1989; Schumann, 1978a,b; Stauble 1978).
- Lack of input (Schumann, 1978a,b).
- Changes in the neural structure of the human brain (e.g., Pulvermüller & Schumann, 1994; Scovel, 2000; Selinker & Lamendella, 1978).
- Maturational constraints (e.g., DeKeyser, 2000; Seliger, 1978).
- Reinforcement from linguistic environment (Harley & Swain, 1978; Larsen-Freeman & Long, 1991; Lightbown, 1985, 1991, 2000).
- L1 influence (e.g., Andersen, 1983; Han, 2000; Kellerman, 1989; Schouten, 1996; Selinker & Lakshmanan, 1992; Zobl, 1980).
- Age (e.g., Schmidt, 1983).
- Lack of attention (e.g., Schmidt, 1983).
- Inappropriate learning strategy (R. Ellis, 1999; Schmidt, 1983).
- Lack of written input (Schmidt, 1983; VanPatten, 1988).
- Language complexity (Lightbown, 1985, 2000).
- Lack of opportunity to use the target language (Swain, 1985, 1995).
- Lack of communicative relevance (Færch & Kasper, 1986).
- Inability to notice input-output discrepancies (e.g., Klein, 1986).
- Lack of access to universal grammar (e.g., Hale, 1988; Schachter, 1996a).
- Will to maintain identity (e.g., Preston, 1989, Zuengler, 1989a, 1989b, 1989c).
- Change in the emotional state (e.g., Preston, 1989; Selinker, 1972).
- False automatization (Hulstijn, 1989; 2002a).
- Quality of input (e.g., Flege & Liu, 2001; Gass & Lakshmanan, 1991; Schwartz & Sprouse, 1996; Valette, 1991).
- Failure of parameter resetting (e.g., Eubank, 1995; L. White, 1991).
- Automatization of the first language system (MacWhinney, 1992).
- Using top-down processes in comprehension (MacWhinney, 1992).
- Lack of understanding (Perdue, 1993).
- Reluctance to take the risk of restructuring (Klein & Perdue, 1993).
- Simplification (Selinker, 1993).
- End of sensitivity to language data (Schnitzer, 1993).
- Lack of talent (Ioup *et al.*, 1994).
- Decrease of cerebral plasticity for implicit acquisition (Paradis, 1994).
- Possession of a mature cognitive system (Birdsong, 1994).

- Use of domain-general problem-solving strategies (Birdsong, 1994).
- The speed with which, and extent to which, automatization has taken place (K. Johnson, 1996).
- Processing constraints (Schachter, 1989, 1996a).
- Lack of access to learning principles (L. White, 1996).
- Learning inhibiting learning (Elman *et al.*, 1996).
- Natural tendency to focus on content, not on form (Skehan, 1998).
- Avoidance (Nakuma, 1998).
- Failure to detect errors (Carroll, 2001).
- Failure to resolve the inherent variation in the interlanguage (R. Ellis, 1999).
- Transfer of training (Han & Selinker, 1999).
- Reduction in the computational capacity of the language faculty (Lardiere, 1998a,b, 2000).
- Representational deficits of the language faculty (Hawkins, 2000).
- Instruction (Han, 2001a; Han & Selinker, 2001; Kasper, 1982; Stenson, 1975; Takahashi, 1996),
- Lack of verbal analytical skills (DeKeyser, 2000).
- Neural entrenchment (N. Ellis, 2002a).
- Lack of sensitivity to input (Long, 2003).
- Socio-psychological barriers (Tarone, 2003).

Clearly, these explanations originated from miscellaneous perspectives at different points in time. Broadly conceived, they fall into the following categories: environmental, cognitive, neurobiological, and socio-affective (see Table 3.1).

As Table 3.1 suggests, both external and internal factors contribute to fossilization. Within the internal factors we can differentiate between cognitive, neuro-biological and social-affective ones. The cognitive factors – in line with current thinking – include those that pertain to knowledge representation, knowledge processing and psychological processes such as attention, avoidance, and emotion (Mandler, 1999; Schumann, 1998). In the following section, a more detailed description is provided of some of the putative causal variables.

Sample Explanations

Absence of corrective feedback

Some researchers claim that fossilization occurs because of absence of corrective feedback. Representative of this view are Vigil and Oller (1976) who distinguish between two dimensions of feedback: the cognitive and

Table 3.1 A taxonomy of putative causal factors of fossilization

EXTERNAL	Environmental		Absence of corrective feedback Lack of input Reinforcement from linguistic environment Lack of instruction Lack of communicative relevance Lack of written input Language complexity Quality of input Instruction
INTERNAL	Cognitive	Knowledge representation	L1 influence conspiring with other factors L1 influence Lack of access to UG Failure of parameter-resetting Possession of a mature cognitive system Non-operation of UG learning principles Learning inhibiting learning Representational deficits of the language faculty
		Knowledge processing (receptive/productive)	Lack of attention Inability to notice input-output discrepancies False automatization Automatization of the first language system Using top-down processes in comprehension Lack of understanding Use of domain general problem-solving strategies End of sensitivity to language data Lack of opportunity to use the target language The speed with which, and extent to which, automatization has taken place Processing constraints Failure to detect errors Failure to resolve the inherent variation in the interlanguage Reduction in the computational capacity of the language faculty Lack of verbal analytical skills Lack of sensitivity to input
		Psychological	Inappropriate learning strategy Change in the emotional state Reluctance to take the risk of restructuring Simplification Natural tendency to focus on content, not on form Avoidance Transfer of training
	Neuro-biological		Changes in the neural structure of the brain Maturational constraints Age Decrease of cerebral plasticity for implicit acquisition Neural entrenchment Lack of talent
	Socio-affective		Satisfaction of communicative needs Lack of acculturation Will to maintain identity Socio-psychological barriers

the affective. Cognitive feedback transmits messages about facts, suppositions, beliefs, etc. that are usually coded by linguistic devices such as words, phrases and sentences. Affective feedback, on the other hand, transmits messages realized by kinestic and paralinguistic devices such as facial expression, tone of voice, and gesture. Each of the two dimensions, in their view, could be either positive or negative. However, it is largely the nature of the cognitive dimension (i.e., positive or negative) that determines change or fossilization (for a rebuttal of this view, see Selinker & Lamendella, 1979). We will refer again to Vigil and Oller (1976) in Chapter 7 when discussing the relationship between instruction and fossilization.

Quality of input

Gass and Lakshmanan (1991) advocate the necessity of understanding L2 learning from the perspective of linguistic environment. For them, there exists an essential difference between child first language acquisition and second language acquisition in terms of the quality of input. In the former case, the input is simple yet accurate, but in SLA, particularly naturalistic as opposed to instructed learning, ungrammatical input abounds. Focusing on null subjects in the 'fossilized interlanguage' of Alberto, Schumann's (1978a) informant, Gass and Lakshmanan revealed that the existence of incorrect positive evidence in the input to Alberto correlated with the persistent occurrence of null subjects in his English interlanguage. The study therefore suggests quality of input as a contributing factor to fossilization.

Lack of access to universal grammar

Adult learners' lack of access to a full range of UG, in Schachter's (1996b: 163) view, directly contributes to their incomplete L2 ultimate attainment:

> What a mature speaker of an L1 has as a result of L1 learning is a grammar stripped of those aspects of UG not incorporated into the L1 grammar, and further, that the adult learner of an L2 does not have independent access to UG – hence that adult-formed L2 grammars are necessarily incomplete.

Following this argument, fossilization is inevitable in adult SLA.

Failure of parameter resetting

For researchers who believe in continued full access to UG in adult SLA, the fact that many L2 learners fossilize with divergent interlanguage grammars is not an indication that UG is not available in SLA, but rather of failure to reset certain parameters. Eubank (1995: 96), for example, claims:

> Those who argue that parameter resetting cannot take place face the difficult task of explaining away the apparent counterexamples to this view from other studies . . . *There is, on the other hand, a clear appeal to claiming that parameters cannot be reset*: One is in a much better position, without appealing to complete pathology (i.e. no 'access'' to Universal Grammar), to explain the general failure of adult L2 learners to attain a state of competence identical to that of the native speaker. (Emphasis added)

Learning inhibiting learning

Some researchers, assuming a connectionist perspective, attribute the lack of second language learning ability to what they describe as 'neural entrenchment', i.e., a consequence of the neural system having committed itself to first language learning. Under this view, learning is a matter of creating neural associations in response to environmental stimuli (i.e., input). Once formed and fixed, as a result of first language acquisition, the connections are hard to sever. L2 development, subsequently, builds on such an existent network of mental representations, and thus involves, among other things, supplanting it to accommodate new input data. However, due to the resistance of the prior system (i.e., NL), restructuring in second language learning is not always possible, hence learners' failure to acquire certain TL features. It is in this sense that learning (i.e., L1 learning) inhibits learning (L2 learning).

Automatization of faulty knowledge

Fossilization, for researchers who assume an information-processing perspective on SLA, is equivalent to automatized non-target forms. Viewing SLA as consisting primarily of two phases, controlled processing and automatic processing, Hulstijn (1989) posits three possibilities for the production of any form in an L2, namely that the required information could be: (1) present and automatized; (2) present, but not yet automatized; and (3) absent. He then goes on to claim that fossilization is most likely to come into existence when the third possibility is real. In his view, lack of information for even controlled processing might lead the L2 learner to seek various kinds of heuristics or strategies, the application of which could result in the production of non-target forms. 'Some of these nontarget forms can become automatized in their turn (resulting in so-called fossilizations)' (Hulstijn, 1989: 17). Assuming that the fossilized non-target forms are automatized and would thus require the least attention in their production, Hulstijn (1989: 20) asserts:

> Automatized nontarget forms (fossilization) . . . are more likely to

occur in casual than in careful style. If the learner knows what the corresponding target forms are, he or she is more likely to use the correct target form in careful style (due to heightened attention to correctness), while still using the fossilization in the vernacular style.

Lack of understanding

Lack of understanding is a potential cause of fossilization. This has been the view of Perdue (1993: 57) who sees it as capable of having a positive or negative impact on learners' motivation to learn. It may make them linguistically more aware, thus motivating them to learn, but it may also lead them to 'avoid all but inevitable linguistic contact with TL native speakers, thus provoking fossilization at an elementary stage'.

Processing constraints

L2 learners are typically found to produce grammatical and ungrammatical sentences on a random basis. When associated with this kind of behavior, fossilization is considered to arise from processing constraints rather than from lack of grammatical competence. As Schachter (1996b: 161) notes:

> A perfectly fluent adult non-native speaker (NNS) of English will produce 'I see him yesterday' and shortly thereafter 'I saw him yesterday', apparently on a random basis. This phenomenon, more properly labeled *fossilized variation*, is typically associated with morphemes that do not carry a heavy semantic load, yet it makes the adult L2 speech as distinctly non-native and is a phenomenon not found in the speech of NSs. Fossilized variations . . . may well be a processing phenomenon not directly attributable to differences in grammatical competence between NS and NNSs of a language.

Lack of sensitivity to input

Long (2003: 516) argues that L2 learners' reduced sensitivity to input is a strong predictor of failure, stating that 'while several factors predict stabilization, including L1-L2 and typological markedness relationships, and various combinations of social-psychological factors, just one factor, sensitivity to input, is the most likely explanation for fossilization . . . '. For him, the reduced sensitivity is a corollary of 'incremental losses of plasticity with increasing brain maturation, possibly associated with myelination' (Long, 1990: 280).

According to developmental psycholinguists (e.g., Gleason & Ratner, 1998), humans begin to lose their perceptual ability as early as by the end of their first year. During the first few weeks of life, infants are said to be able to make fine phonological distinctions that adults cannot, but this phonetic sensitivity begins to vanish as soon as they have begun to learn the sounds of the language around them. That is, 'perceptual loss is a consequence of the infant's continued interaction with her language' (1998: 357). From this it clearly follows that adult L2 learners are, by default, devoid of the ability to fully acquire an additional sound system of any additional language, due to having already acquired the sound system of their native language.

Change in emotional state

Fossilization in the form of *backsliding* (Selinker, 1972) could, according to Preston (1989; see also Selinker, 1972), be caused by one's emotional state:

> Apparently, the degree to which emotional involvement distracts a speaker from attention to form is reflected in backsliding for language learners . . . (1989: 180)

In support of his argument, Preston cites several studies:

> Lantolf and Ahmed [1989] show decreasing L2 accuracy in an Arabic learner from interview style to conversational style, indicating that the respondent was emotionally engaged in the conversation topic, which he nominated himself at the end of a data gathering session. Eisenstein and Starbuk [1989] also found greater L2 inaccuracy in respondents' emotionally invested conversations. (1989: 180)

Natural inclination to focus on content, not on form

Skehan (1998: 3) highlights L2 learners' natural inclination to focus on meaning, not on form. He claims that in the processes of comprehension and production, 'meaning takes priority for older learners, and that the form of language has secondary importance'. Such a natural inclination is largely psychological. As they grow older, learners are more and more capable of availing themselves of strategies of communication, exploiting schematic knowledge, exploiting the collaborative construction of meaning, and saying less but meaning more. Besides, the social context in which communication takes place presents a variety of cues (e.g., role relationship, power status, setting, topic) which adult learners can readily capitalize on to extract the meaning of communication without exhaustive analyses of the structural aspects of language. As a consequence, in interaction with the target language input, the language acquisition device (LAD) is seldom engaged, thus rendering large amounts of otherwise crucial properties of input obsolete.

Skehan further notes that as a result of the meaning priority, learners tend to employ a 'dual-coding' approach to L2 learning: rule-based and instance-based, both of which together enable economical, parsimonious and effective performance. In his view, fossilization, i.e., the erroneous exemplar, is the premature product of the rule-based approach, which is then adopted under the instance-based approach in language use, and 'if the underlying system does not so evolve, and if communicative effectiveness is achieved, the erroneous exemplar may survive and stabilize, and becomes a syntactic fossil' (1998: 61).

Avoidance

Nakuma (1998: 251) suggests that fossilization is not the product of acquisition but of avoidance, namely, 'the deliberate choice of an L2 learner not to acquire a given L2 form, probably because the given target L2 form is believed to be available already in the L2 learner's acquired cognitive baggage'. He posits 'interlingual identifications' (Weinreich, 1953) as the underlying mechanism:

> Interlingual identification between specific L1 and L2 elements by the L2 learner will induce the latter to avoid duplicating his or her L1 knowledge (Weinreich, 1953). To successfully avoid duplication of L1 knowledge, the L2 learner will have to choose not to learn the L2 counterparts of the identified L1 forms. If such is the case, then it must be true that the only way that the avoided L2 elements may be produced subsequently by the L2 learner will have to be through 'transfer' of the L1 element to cover for the avoided L2 element. Therefore, one can expect the L2 user to continue producing the same deviant form for as long as the interlingual identification is maintained, granted that the L1 and L2 elements which have been (mis)perceived to be 'identical' are actually not identical. (Nakuma, 1998: 251)

Thus, for Nakuma, fossilization arises from L2 learners' individual perception of L1-L2 equivalents, the result of which may be positive or negative, depending on whether the form transferred from the L1 overlaps with the target L2 form. In this sense, fossilization is highly idiosyncratic. In the researcher's own words, 'the exact cause of fossilization in individual learners is beyond generalization, since individuals perceive reality idiosyncratically' (1998: 253).

Satisfaction of communicative needs

Many researchers have considered 'satisfaction of communicative needs' a major causal factor of fossilization. As K. Johnson (1996) notes, the concept of stopping when needs are met persists in fossilization studies. Corder (1978, 1983) was among the earliest exponents of this view, which regards communicative needs as the immediate motivation for interlanguage development, suggesting that the interlanguage grammar would fossilize when these needs are satisfied. Klein (1986) sheds some interesting new light on the link between fossilization and communicative needs by speculating that some L2 learners might be aware of the fossilized deviances in their interlanguage, yet they would not make any attempt to restructure them because their fossilized varieties, despite lacking expressive power, are easy to handle and can satisfy their basic communicative needs.

Other researchers have also expressed similar views based on their observations made in different learning contexts. In reviewing research on the French immersion program, Kowal and Swain (1997: 284) conclude that 'although immersion students can reach native-speaker levels on receptive tasks such as listening and reading comprehension, their productive skills, spoken and written, remain below these levels', and they trace the lag in the development of productive skills to the fact that 'once [the students] are able to communicate their intended meaning to one another, there is little impetus for them to be more accurate in the form of the language they are using to convey their message'. Schmidt (1983), Long (1985), Skehan (1994) and K. Johnson (1996) all concur that the development of strategic competence (Canale & Swain, 1980), when preceding the development of linguistic competence, may become the threshold of fossilization.

Lack of acculturation

Some researchers (e.g., Schumann, 1978a,c, 1986) argue that there exists an isomorphism between the cessation of acculturation into the target society and the onset of fossilization. In his longitudinal study of an adult Costa Rican immigrant (named Alberto) in the U.S., Schumann (1978a,c) noticed, among other things, the persistence of what he called pidginized forms such as the 'uniform negative "no" for most of his negative utterances' (Schumann, 1978c: 367). These forms were considered fossilized, and thought to be best explained in terms of Alberto's social and psychological distance:

> Alberto was . . . socially and psychologically distant from native speakers of English in that he was a member of a subordinate socioeconomic minority group; he had little contact with Americans either socially or at work and he had little desire to integrate with American society. Thus he needed English to handle only basic denotative referential communication with shopkeepers, work supervisors, co-workers

> and occasionally with a doctor, dentist or postal clerk. (Schumann, 1978c: 368)

The fossilized forms in Alberto's interlanguage were thus attributed to his lack of acculturation into the TL community. 'Acculturation' is, as Schumann (1978b: 165) explains, an integration strategy for adapting to the life style and values of the TL group while maintaining one's own life style and values for intragroup use, and it 'yields varying degrees of contact between the two groups and thus varying degrees of acquisition of the target language'.

Schumann (1986) further elaborates on the construct as a cluster of social factors (e.g., social dominance patterns, assimilation, preservation, adaptation) and affective factors (e.g., language shock, motivation, cultural shock, ego-permeability). He thereby suggests that there can be two types of acculturation: the social and the psychological, and that different configurations thereof (e.g., +social, -psychological) may lead to different degrees of success in L2 learning. Yet, he also concedes that acculturation, though a major causal variable, functions only as a remote cause of SLA:

> Acculturation as a remote cause brings the learner into contact with TL-speakers. Verbal interaction with those speakers as a proximate cause brings about the negotiation of appropriate input which then operates as the immediate cause of language acquisition. Acculturation then is of particular importance because it initiates the chain of causality. (1986: 384)

Schumann's argument, by extension, can be understood to mean that lack of acculturation would lead to lack of exposure to the L2 input data, which, in turn, would result in fossilization.

Will to maintain identity

Schumann's socio-psychological perspective on fossilization is shared and enhanced by Preston (1989: 254) who differentiates between social fossilization and sociolinguistic fossilization. Social fossilization has to do with 'the social and psychological make-up of the learners, their relationship to other, especially shared L1, learners, and their feelings to other, especially shared L1, learners, and their feelings toward the reception in the new speech community'. In Preston's view, what occurred in Schumann's informant, Alberto, was social fossilization. Sociolinguistic fossilization, on the other hand, occurs as a result of the learner's will to maintain his/her identity, hence the 'fossilized forms represent a more subtle construction of the variability which characterizes his or her identity in the speech community' (Preston, 1989: 255). This variability, unlike in social fossilization where it is genuine, is symbolic (i.e., a deliberate attempt) in sociolinguistic fossilization.

In summary, over the past 30 years various competing explanations of fossilization have been advanced, with some appearing to be directed at global fossilization (i.e., pertaining to the entire interlanguage system) but others at local fossilization (i.e., pertaining to interlanguage subsystems). Despite the divergence of their perceptions, researchers, collectively, have nevertheless raised a fundamental question: Does fossilization arise from lack of ability to learn or does it occur due to the influence of individual-oriented variables such as the socio-psychological ones? If we take fossilization to mean, as we do in this book, cessation of learning in spite of continuous exposure to input, adequate motivation to learn, and sufficient opportunity for practice, fossilization should, in the first place, be considered ability-related. Yet, given what we know about individual differences in adult L2 learning, it is highly conceivable that the lack of ability to learn can be modulated through internal and external influences for individual learners. In other words, it is highly likely that while L2 learners generically suffer from a reduced ability to learn, which leads to fossilization, individual learners differ in their capacity to exploit the limited learning ability, and importantly, that such a capacity is susceptible to environmental, cognitive, social and psychological influences – hence the possibility of differential fossilization across and within individual learners. This conception is, in fact, in accord with the three facets of fossilization we identified in Chapter 1, namely (1) cross-learner general failure, (2) cross-learner differential failure and (3) within-learner differential failure.

From the same conception, it also follows that any effort to explain fossilization through one unitary account would prove to be less than adequate. For example, while the biological line of argument appears to be capable of accounting for the lack of ability on the part of the overwhelming majority of adult L2 learners to reach native speaker (NS) competence in an L2, it is clearly incapable of explaining differential success in the L2 ultimate attainment, either at an inter-learner or an intra-learner level. By the same token, satisfaction of communicative needs, which many have contended is a major causal factor of fossilization, is not likely to constitute a universal ontological account of what brings fossilization into existence. The reason is quite straightforward: comparing L2 classroom learners with the so-called 'street learners' (Willems, 1987), the classroom learners are generally known to have no genuine communicative needs while the 'street learners' normally do, yet the classroom learners are generally more successful than the 'street learners' (Corder, 1981). What is the relationship, then, between the putative causal variables and the various facets of fossilization? What determines the lack of ability and what leads to differential fossilization? These two questions constitute the subject matter of discussion in much of the remainder of the book. To begin, let us briefly explore factors that can independently circumscribe L2 learner's ability to learn.

Two Primary Determinants of Lack of Ability

Several major theoretical models have identified maturational constraints and native language interference as key factors influencing the degree of success in adult L2 learning. Two such models are discussed in this section: the Competition Model (Bates & MacWhinney, 1981) and the UG approach.

Drawing on facts about brain development, the Competition Model (Bates & MacWhinney, 1981; MacWhinney, 2001) predicts two fundamental, interrelated constraints on adult L2 learning: (1) neuronal commitment and (2) the parasitic nature of learning. As the human brain matures, its plasticity declines, and so does its capacity for new forms of learning. Crucially, such decline intersects with what appears to be an epiphenomenal consequence of first language learning, namely that certain neural areas of the brain have become committed. Learning a second language, then, becomes imposing another system upon the existing neural template, hence parasitic in nature. In this context, transfer – primarily from the old system to the new system– is set to occur, not only due to the interconnected nature of the brain but importantly as a compensatory strategy for the loss of plasticity. Thus, processing the stimuli of a second language in comprehension and production – the core concern of the Competition Model – would involve the competition between L1-based processing cues and those required for processing the L2; learning a second language amounts to adjusting one's internal speech processing mechanisms from those appropriate for the native language to those appropriate for the other language. Failure to do so would result in (sometimes permanent) L2 interpretation and production errors. MacWhinney (2001: 86–87) points out that 'this declining plasticity of the brain is at the root of the difficulties that older adults have in acquiring full competence in L2. . . . it is important to recognize that the plasticity of the brain places important limits on what the adult has to do to achieve successful L2 acquisition . . . a full control over L2 requires the learner to reduce this parasitism and to automatize L2 processes apart from L1 processes'.

While the Competition Model has sought to explicate SLA from a processing, functional perspective, the UG approach to SLA focuses on the nature of L2 grammatical competence. A major task confronting the UG approach to SLA is to explain, as L. White (1998: 321) has summarized it,

Table 3.2 Summary of claims on UG availability and transfer

	FT/PA	*NT/FA*	*FT/FA*	*PT/FA*	*PT/PA*
Initial state	L1	UG	L1	UG and parts of L1	Parts of UG and L1
Grammar development	UG principles (via L1)	UG principles	UG principles	UG principles	(Some) UG principles
	L1 parameter settings + local adjustments	L2 parameter settings	Parameter resetting from L1 → L2/Ln	Parameter resetting from L1 → L2	Parameters associated with functional features remain unspecified
	Possibility of 'wild' grammars[1]	No wild grammars	No wild grammars	No wild grammars	Locally wild grammars
Final state	L1 (+local adjustments) L2 not attainable	L2	Ln (L2 possible but not inevitable)	L2 (Ln)	L2 not attainable

Note: FT = full transfer; PA = partial access; NT = no transfer; FA = full access; PT = partial transfer

'the extent to which second language (L2) competence or L2 performance diverges from native speakers, from first language (L1) acquirers, or from other L2 speakers, and the implications of such divergence for theories of mental representation of interlanguage competence'. Over the past several decades, research centering around this task has given rise to an array of theoretical positions, divided primarily over the extent to which adult L2 learners have access to UG and the extent to which the L1 functions in SLA. Table 3.2, reproduced from L. White (2000), provides a succinct summary of these positions and of the claims they each make on UG and transfer *vis-à-vis* the initial state, the developmental stage, and the final state of L2 learning.

As Table 3.2 shows, each of these positions makes a different set of assertions about the various phases of L2 learning. Starting from the second column, the Full Transfer/Partial Access (FT/PA; Schachter, 1989) position asserts:

(1) The L1 grammar constitutes the initial stage of L2 learning, hence 'full transfer';

(2) UG functions, via the L1, to guide L2 parameter setting, hence 'partial or indirect access', with some local adjustments to accommodate new features in the L2;
(3) wild grammars possibly exists as a result of partial access to UG, and
(4) the ultimate outcome of learning is a grammar characterized largely by L1 features, hence an incomplete L2 grammar.

Moving on, the No Transfer/Full Access (NT/FA; Epstein *et al.*, 1996) position takes UG as the starting point of L2 learning. UG principles are assumed to function in toto during L2 learning. There will be no wild grammars and learners ultimately develop a target-like L2 grammar. Next is the Full Transfer/Full Access (FT/FA; Schwartz & Sprouse, 1996) position which holds that the L1 grammar is the point of departure for L2 learning, but UG, in toto, guides through the L2 developmental stages to such effect that learners will switch from L1 parameter settings to L2 required settings. As a consequence, there will be no wild grammars, and the end state of L2 learning will possibly be a target-like L2 grammar, but it is not inevitable. Following on, the Partial Transfer/Full Access (PT/FA; Vainikka & Young-Scholten, 1994) position assumes that UG and parts of the L1 grammar form the initial state of L2 learning. UG principles are thought to guide the L2 learning process. As a consequence, learners will be able to reset parameters from the L1 to the L2. No wild grammars are to be expected, and the final state of L2 learning shall feature full attainment of the target grammar. The last position displayed in Table 3.2 is called 'Partial Transfer/ Partial Access' (PT/PA; Eubank *et al.*, 1997). By now the reader may be able to decipher its meaning: parts of UG and the L1 provide the grammatical knowledge that L2 learners start with; some UG principles will operate to guide the learning process; only some parameters will be successfully reset; locally there will be wild grammars; and full attainment of the L2 grammar is not possible.

Now what do we surmise from this array of disparate positions? One interesting categorical observation we can make is that whenever language transfer is recognized to be a (main) part of the initial process, learners'

Table 3.3 Predictions on ultimate attainment

Theoretical positions		*Ultimate attainment*
Full Transfer/Partial Access	→	Divergent
No Transfer/Full Access	→	Convergent
Full Transfer/Full Access	→	Divergent (possibly convergent)
Partial Transfer/Full Access	→	Convergent
Partial Transfer/Partial Access	→	Divergent

ultimate attainment is predicted to diverge from the L2 grammar, and that ultimate convergence with the L2 grammar is predicted to result only from UG functioning in its entirety throughout the learning process (i.e., initial state and grammar development). Table 3.3 displays the predictions each of the five positions makes on L2 ultimate attainment.

Clearly, even within the UG-SLA paradigm, there is recognition of transfer as a major factor affecting L2 learning and effecting its ultimate attainment. Transfer, however, is not the only source of constraint on L2 learning in the UG perspective.

A compounding force, which appears to be capable of affecting the UG capacity as well, is neuro-biological maturation. On this issue, Eubank and Gregg's (1999) discussion is particularly illuminating. Citing evidence from both neuro-biological research and from generative linguistics studies, Eubank and Gregg argue for a modular view of the mind and brain and of linguistic competence:

> There are various, relatively autonomous, mental faculties – memory, face recognition, visual perception, and so forth – and that these may also be broken down further into (perhaps less mutually autonomous) subfaculties – short-term memory, episodic memory, and so forth. Similarly ... linguistic competence (i.e., knowledge) is relatively autonomous from other forms of competence on the one hand and includes various relatively autonomous competences on the other. (1999: 65)

On this view, first of all, the human brain is compartmentalized into different domain-specific faculties, one of which is responsible for linguistic competence. Second, each faculty is subdivided into subfaculties, and so when applied to linguistic competence, this would imply the existence of linguistic subcompetences such as phonology, syntax, and morphology. Third, each of the faculties (and subfaculties) may have a different biological timetable for its maturation; that is, linguistic subcompetences may be differentially subject to age effects, hence possibly the existence of multiple critical periods.

Importantly, Eubank and Gregg argue that the CPH-L1A (L1 acquisition) should be differentiated from the CPH-L2A (L2 acquisition). In their view, the CPH-L2A is not on a par with CPH-L1A. For one thing, in the latter case, missing a CP entails that 'the relevant neural architecture is presumably unorganized and unspecific, and the relevant dendritic pathways for neural intercommunication remain significantly redundant or simply unavailable; but in the case of exposure to secondary stimuli after the CP has been successfully traversed – the case, for instance, of adult L2 acquisition – the neural architecture is already developed' (1999: 78). In other words, change in the neural architecture of an adult L2 learner (i.e., from one mature state to another) occurs on a much more limited scale than that occurring in a child L1 acquirer (i.e., a metamorphosis from preexposure state to the mature state). The gross physiological difference, in turn, predicts differential behavioral reflexes: whereas late L1 acquisition (i.e., past the critical period) would result in near-total incompetence, late L2 acquisition would still lead to variational success across different linguistic domains.

With these understandings as a foundation, Eubank and Gregg challenge a conception held by many participants in the UG-L2 Access debate, namely that UG and CPs are mutually exclusive. This conception – 'if there is a CP for L1, then L2 grammars should fall outside of the range of grammars permitted by UG, whereas if there is no CP, then these grammars should be UG constrained' (1999: 79) – clearly defies the modular nature of mind-brain and of linguistic competence mentioned above, since it views UG as monolithic that is either accessible to L2 learners or otherwise. Drawing on recent developments in generative theories as well as evidence from L2 empirical studies, Eubank and Gregg contradict the popular conception by noting that some aspects of UG, e.g., structure dependence, may be easily fixed on the provision of some minimal amount of linguistic stimuli, while others, e.g., morphophonological and morphosyntactic parameters, may be contingent on the provision of relevant linguistic stimuli during a critical period (see also Schachter [1996a] discussed in the next chapter). The suggestion, then, is that even within UG, some properties are susceptible to CP effects and some are not, and that those that are will unlikely be fully acquired by adult L2 learners.

Given the centrality of maturational constrains and language transfer to understanding fossilization, in the next two chapters we will carry out a much more detailed and systematic discussion of each, the aim being to provide the reader with some understanding of how each can operate to affect the ability of L2 learners to learn.

Summary

Over the years, the term 'fossilization' has come to be associated with a wide range of learner behaviors. The lack of uniformity exhibited in the conceptualization and application of the term, though creating confusion in the literature, is nevertheless an indication of advances in the general understanding of the notion; it points to the fact, among other things, that fossilization is no longer a monolithic concept as it was in its initial postulation, but rather an increasingly complex construct intricately tied up with a myriad of manifestations of failure and a wide spectrum of underlying acquisition processes and factors.

With the conceptual developments, the question has also come to the fore: does fossilization arise from lack of ability to learn or does it occur due to the influence of individual-oriented variables such as the socio-psychological ones? I have argued that fossilization is internally determined, due to the constant functioning of maturational and NL constraints, yet it can be modulated (aggravated or alleviated) by environmental, social, and psychological forces.

Note

1. The term 'wild grammar' refers to interlanguage features that do not conform to UG constraints.

Chapter 4

A Macroscopic Analysis: Critical Period Effects

In this and the next chapter, I attempt to provide a macroscopic analysis of general failure (see also Fig. 1.1). A central argument to be advanced is that adult L2 learners are *universally preconditioned* to fossilization. Two lines of research – the critical period effects and the NL influence – are brought to bear on the argument. Both lines of inquiry, one being biologically oriented and the other cognitively oriented, have been subject to long-term, substantial investigation over the past 30 years and both by now have mature implications for understanding lack of success in adult SLA.

The focus of this chapter is on examining the critical period effects. I will begin by reviewing the Critical Period Hypothesis (Lenneberg, 1967), and then discuss it in relation to first and second language acquisition. In the section that then follows, I will discuss the modular nature of the critical period, and in the final section, highlight the critical period effects.

The Critical Period Hypothesis

In 1967, Lenneberg, a psycho-biologist, who was inspired by findings from ethological studies and insights from the work of his contemporaries (e.g., Penfield & Roberts, 1959), proposed for human language learning a Critical Period Hypothesis (CPH), suggesting there is a period during the human life span from infancy to puberty (age 2 to 13) that is critical to language learning, during which learning is successful and after which it is marginal. Such a period is thought to be neurobiologically determined in that it is coinceptive and conterminous with a series of neurological processes – lateralization of cognitive, linguistic, and perceptual functions, myelination, the proliferation of neurons in the cerebral cortex, the increase in neurotransmitters, and the variation of amplitudes of certain brain waves, to name a few – that take place during the first years of life and that taper off and plateau by puberty (Scovel, 1988).

On the relevance of the CPH for second language acquisition, Lenneberg made, albeit in passing, the following claim:

> Most individuals of average intelligence are able to learn a second language after the beginning of their second decade, although the incidence of 'language – learning – blocks' rapidly increases after puberty. Also automatic acquisition from mere exposure to a given language seems to disappear after this age, and foreign languages have to be taught and learned through a labored effort. Foreign accents cannot be overcome easily after puberty. However, a person can learn to communicate in a foreign language at the age of forty. (Lenneberg, 1967: 176)

In simple terms, Lenneberg's hypothesis predicts a rectangular function in the relationship between age of acquisition and ultimate performance. It is worth noting that the proposal evinces considerable vagueness. It, for example, gives no specification of whether language ability declines only at the end of the critical period (CP), whether changes at the critical turning point should be abrupt or gradual, whether the CP affects every aspect of language development or selectively a few, whether the CP arises from biology alone or from lack of exercise of the learning capacity, and so forth. These are some of the issues that subsequent research has sought to clarify, as will be shown in the remaining sections of this chapter.

Before taking a snapshot of empirical studies that attempt to refine the notion, however, it is instructive to look at a theoretical suggestion made by Colombo (1982). Following a critical review of a large number of ethological and human pathological studies, Colombo suggests that the term 'critical period' should be used only when it satisfies the following five criteria: (1) the onset; (2) the terminus; (3) organizational plasticity; (4) the critical stimulus; and (5) the critical system. First, the onset of the critical period is gradual and 'may not be entirely maturationally determined but may be influenced in some way by exogenous input as well' (1982: 262). Second, the terminus, the upper bound of the period, is set primarily by biology, and is gradual, though less so than the onset. Third, the critical period is essentially 'the time between the emergence anatomically or functionally of a given biobehavioral system and its maturation' (1982: 263), during which neurobiological changes affect the sensitivity to stimuli and plasticity in development. Fourth, even though the CP phenomenon is mainly biologically driven, external stimuli may play a critical role; their effects can be permanent once the system reaches maturity. The idea is that only certain stimuli (or input) are critical to learning. We will return to this issue later in the chapter. Finally, the term 'critical period' concerns some specific bio-behavioral systems. What this implies for language learning is that not every aspect of language development is susceptible to CP effects. One task confronting research therefore involves identifying which aspects are so and which are not. In the section below, 'The Modular Nature of CP', we will take a closer look at this feature.

CPH in FLA and SLA

Since its postulation, the CPH has kindled a tremendous interest in its validity among language acquisition researchers. For decades, scores of theoretical and empirical studies have been undertaken; importantly, the bulk of them have yielded evidence in favor of the presence of the critical period in language learning. Even though the case is not closed on the CPH, as Scovel (2000: 216) put it, 'the belief in some version of the CPH presently represents the majority opinion'.

In FLA, evidence of the CP has come primarily from pathological cases. The oft-cited subjects are Genie and Chelsea (Curtiss, 1977, 1988, 1989). Genie was isolated, neglected and abused by her parents since she was a year and a half and until she was discovered by social workers at 13. The fact that she missed the critical period immediately brought her to the attention of researchers from a variety of disciplines, including psycholinguists who tried to restore her language ability. After seven years' immersion in a normal social interaction environment and receiving much external help from the researchers, Genie nevertheless exhibited very little progress in language development. Despite a significant growth in vocabulary and in pragmatic ability, her phonological and syntactic competence was said to not exceed that of a normal two-year-old. Results from dichotic listening tasks indicated that her linguistic ability was localized in the right hemisphere, despite the fact that she was right-handed and possessed an electroencephalographic characteristic of a left hemisphere dominant individual (Colombo, 1982). Her lack of linguistic development was rather uniformly taken as evidence for the CPH. Genie's case was almost paralleled by that of Chelsea, a deaf child born to hearing parents. Chelsea was not in any way abused but her parents had been misguided into the belief that she was mentally retarded and emotionally disturbed. Chelsea therefore did not receive any sign language input until she was 31 when she was found to be deaf. As a consequence of missing the entire CP, Chelsea showed little linguistic development even after years of late exposure to signed input.

Hence, in FLA, the critical period seems absolute. The question, then, is this: Is there also an absolute critical period in SLA? As mentioned, L2 ultimate attainment is characterized by general failure as well as inter- and intra-learner differential failure, which suggests, among other things, that in spite of lack of success, adult L2 learners are not total failures. As Oyama (1976: 279) puts it, 'anyone can learn *some* aspects of an unfamiliar tongue at any age'. Thus, a straightforward application of the CPH would be implausible. Eubank and Gregg (1999) claim that with adult L2 acquisition, the CP effects may be minor in scope, thus demanding refined examination. To date, on the CPH in SLA, two major speculations have been advanced: First, there is possibly a sensitive, rather than critical, period that is 'not an all-or-nothing phenomenon,' despite which 'adults can and do learn to speak new languages' (Oyama, 1976: 278; cf. also Long, 1990; Patkowski, 1980). In other words, there are no sharp discontinuities between acquisition within and beyond the sensitive period, but rather the relation is a roughly linear one. Second, such a sensitive period affects, differentially, different linguistic domains. As will be shown below, both speculations have gained considerable empirical support.

Early evidence of a sensitive period for L2 acquisition can be found in Oyama (1976), who tested 60 Italian-born male immigrants in the United States on their L2 acquisition of English phonology. The informants were divided along two independent variables – age of arrival (AOA) and length of residence (LOR) in the United States– and their pronunciation was scored from two taped speech samples collected individually from their reading of a short paragraph and account of a brief anecdote. In addition, a questionnaire was distributed to the same informants to gather information on their method of learning English, relative amount of use of native and second languages, attitudes and so forth. The data analyses, employing statistical methods for calculating variance and correlation, focused on the relationships among the two independent variables, the questionnaire variables and the accent measures. A linear relationship between age of learning and degree of accent was revealed: 'the youngest arrivals perform in the range set by the controls, whereas those arriving after about age 12 do not, and substantial accents start appearing much later' (1976: 272). Based on this finding, Oyama concluded:

> Age at arrival was a strong predictor of degree of accent, while length of stay had very little effect. Other practice and motivational factors were related to accent only by virtue of their correlation with age at arrival . . . a sensitive period exists for the acquisition of a nonnative phonological system. (1976: 261)

Thus, in this study, the evidence for a sensitive period is derived from the following fact: no sharp discontinuities were observed between the performance of the younger group and that of the older group; rather, the changes were gradual and linear.

How, then, is the term 'sensitive period' different from 'critical period'? According to Patkowski (1980: 449):

> The term 'critical period' refers to the notion that the age limitation is absolute in the case of first language acquisition. Theoretically, past the critical period, if no language has been acquired, there can be no learning of human language possible except for the learning of communication strategies dependent upon alternate cognitive mechanisms. The term 'sensitive period', on the other hand, refers to the fact that the age limitation on L2 acquisition is not absolute in the same sense as above. It is indeed possible to acquire a second language after the sensitive period, but it would theoretically not be possible to do so to the extent of attaining native-like proficiency and thus being able to 'pass for native'. In other words, the term 'critical period' is employed here in the case of first language acquisition because it is held that absolutely no linguistic proficiency in L1 is possible past the critical point (despite possible development of nonlinguistic systems of communication), while the term 'sensitive period' is used in the case of second language acquisition because the limitation is on the ability to acquire *complete* native-like proficiency in L2. (Emphasis in original)

Notice that, by differentiating the two terms, Patkowski does not simply clarify a terminological difference; he captures a conceptual difference as well in the application of the notion of CP in two cases – FLA and SLA. Of note also is the insight he provides onto the notion of failure and success: failure occurs only in the sense that L2 learners fail to pass off as native speakers while success is revealed by the fact that L2 learners are able to achieve varying degrees of L2 proficiency. As Patkowski explains it:

> The sensitive period notion holds only that absolute, native-like proficiency in all aspects of language (including vocabulary and syntax) is impossible to attain for the adult learner; it does not hold that extremely high, quasi-native levels cannot be attained in one or more areas. Furthermore, it must be insisted that what is referred to is the eventual level of proficiency attained after a sufficient period of exposure to and immersion in the target language under optimal sociolinguistic and affective conditions. (1980: 464)

It is important to note that for Patkowski, conclusions on L2 ultimate attainment can only be drawn from learners who have been learning in optimal exogenous and endogenous conditions (cf. Selinker & Lamendella, 1979).

The end of a sensitive period, for some, demarcates the threshold of fossilization. Lamendella (1977), for example, views the sensitive period as a period during which the potential for successful second language acquisition is enhanced, and after which fossilization far from TL norms is highly probable.

Granting the difference between a critical period and a sensitive period, in the remainder of this book, however, I shall use the two terms interchangeably. Such practice is largely in keeping with general discussions of the CPH in SLA (e.g., Johnson & Newport, 1989).[1] The point is that no matter which term is deployed, in the case of SLA, the notion holds that there exists a period of 'heightened sensitivity or responsiveness to specific types of environmental stimuli or input, bounded on both sides by states of lesser sensitivity' and that 'gradual increases to such [a period] or declines from such [a period] are expected to occur as well as variability from one individual to another' (Schachter, 1996a: 165).

Turning now to the second speculation (i.e., the CP concerns specific linguistic domains), the relevance of the CPH to SLA was first discovered in the realm of phonology. Scovel (1969: 250) should be credited for his pioneer work in this linguistic domain; he was the first to note that 'the maturational development of cerebral dominance is closely linked to the ability to acquire language', and that foreign accents appear when lateralization of cognitive, linguistic, and perceptual functions becomes permanent in the human brain at the age of about 12. The empirical basis for his position seemed strong:

> In sum, the collective body of evidence strongly implies that nature has endowed us with an innate releasing mechanism – the ability to program complex behavior like language to one hemisphere, so that the other can be free to program other complex tasks; that nurture allows this maturing linguistic system to respond to and learn from a community of language speakers (whether mono-, bi-, or multilingual); and that the timing of this interaction, at least for certain skills (e.g., sounding exactly like a native speaker), is preset by the advent of puberty. (Scovel, 1988: 154)

Such age constraints were considered by Scovel to be irreversible to the extent that even 'practice cannot make perfect what nature has already made permanent' (1988: 159).

Of interest, Scovel, in his early work in particular, staunchly advocated a narrow understanding of the CP, namely that the cerebral dominance accounts only for the obstruction of the sound patterns, not of the syntactic patterns of a language, because 'sound patterns are produced by actual motor activity and are thus directly initiated by neurophysiological mechanisms' and 'lexical and syntactic patterns lack any such "neurophysiological reality"' (Scovel, 1969: 252). He argued:

> Although most adults have great difficulty fully learning the syntactic patterns of a second language, there are many instances of adults learning the syntax of a second language completely and yet not being able to lose a foreign accent when speaking. Joseph Conrad, who learned English when he was eighteen, was able to write fluently and creatively in English after a few years practice. His prose demanded almost no grammatical editing, and yet his strong foreign accent prevented him from lecturing publicly in English. (1969: 247)

The validity of this argument,[2] as it turns out, has only been partially attested to by later studies. In terms of phonology, SLA research has accumulated a wealth of evidence suggesting that 'age at arrival was a strong predictor of degree of accent, while length of stay had very little effect' (Oyama, 1976: 261). In terms of lexical development, no CP effects have been observed so far.[3] Syntactic development, on the other hand, has also been found susceptible to CP effects, to which we now turn.

Patkowski (1980) was the first to note that age of arrival was equally a strong indicator of syntactic proficiency in SLA. He demonstrated that there is an age limitation on the ability to acquire full command of syntax in a second language. Sixty-seven immigrants who came to the United States at various ages and who had resided in the country for a minimum of five years were employed as informants, together with 15 native-born Americans as controls. Care was taken to ensure that the informants selected had all been exposed to near optimal learning conditions. That is, all the informants were 'highly educated and upwardly mobile' (1980: 451). Analyses of data (i.e., written transcripts of oral individual interviews) yielded the following findings:

> The population curve for the post-puberty group, with its normal characteristics, suggests the usual scatter of abilities which is often found in psychological and social research. The population curve for the pre-puberty group, however, strongly suggests that some special factor is at work and is the cause of such a skewed population distribution. Thus, even at a purely descriptive level, the distributional characteristics of the two nonnative groups are clearly consonant with the notion of a sensitive period for the acquisition of syntax in a second language. (1980: 454)

Patkowski thus provided evidence of a sensitive period for L2 acquisition of syntax. Reinterpreting Scovel's early work, he pointed out that 'results of Scovel's study demonstrate that accent is more easily perceived and judged than syntax, but not that nativelike syntactic proficiency is attainable by adults in a second language' (1980: 463).

Patkowski's findings are corroborated by Johnson and Newport (1989) who further demonstrate that L2 morphosyntactic development is maturationally constrained. The Johnson and Newport study, however, differs from the Patkowski study in several regards. First, unlike the Patkowski (1980) study that measured L2 spontaneous production through syntax rating, Johnson and Newport measured the underlying competence via sentence judgments. Second, the Johnson and Newport study tapped into the participants' knowledge of a wider variety of morphosyntactic structures (12 types altogether) of English grammar, thereby providing a better view of the relationship between age of exposure and the overall measure of English proficiency, as well as of the differential effects of age of exposure on various aspects of grammatical structure. Third, there was a wider range of ages of exposure examined, thus allowing a more precise approximation of the shape of the function relating age to attainment, particularly in terms of where the relationship plateaus or declines. Fourth, while Patkowski (1980) only calculated the overall correlations and group means, Johnson and Newport performed multivariate analyses to assess the relative contributions to ultimate attainment of age and other factors (affective, social and environmental). The two studies, nevertheless, complement each other well; together they provide a strong case for age-related limitation on L2 acquisition of morphosyntax.

Informants for the Johnson and Newport study were 46 native Chinese and Korean speakers of L2 English, varying in age of arrival in the United States from 3 to 39. They all had had at least five years of exposure to English[4] and an uninterrupted stay of at least three years in the United States. Age 15 was the dividing line between early arrivals (within the critical period) and late arrivals (beyond the critical period). The informants were tested on their knowledge of 12 types of morphosyntactic constructions via a grammaticality judgment task. Test stimuli (276 sentences) were orally recorded and played to each individual informant, and the results showed 'a clear and strong relationship between age of arrival in the United States and performance' ($r = -.77, p < .01$):

> Subjects who arrived in the United States before the age of seven reached native performance on the test. For arrivals after that age, there was a linear decline in performance up through puberty. Subjects who arrived in the United States after puberty performed on the average much more poorly than those who arrived earlier. After puberty, however, performance did not continue to decline with increasing age. Instead, the late arrival group, while performing on the whole more poorly than the younger arrivals, distinguished itself by having

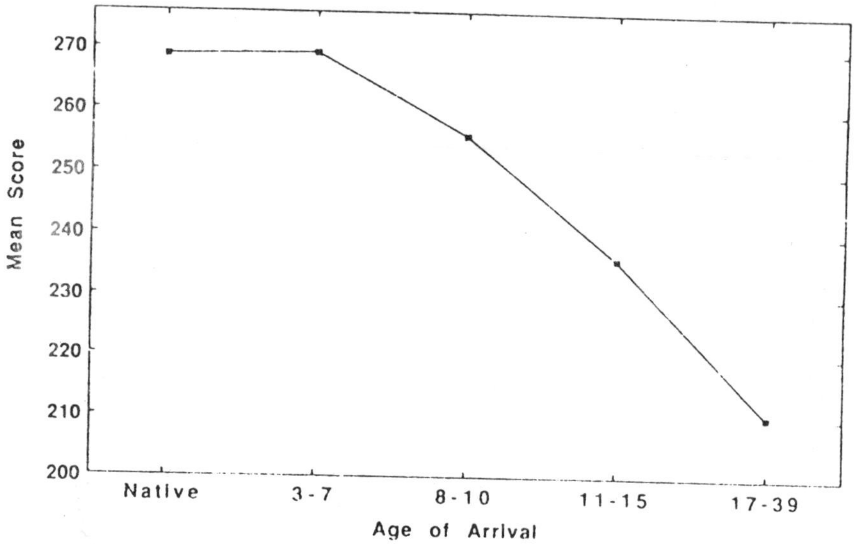

Figure 4.1 The relationship between age of arrival in the US and total score correct on a test of English grammar

> marked individual differences in performance, something which was not found in the earlier arrivals. (Johnson & Newport, 1989: 90)

Figure 4.1, reproduced from Johnson and Newport (1989), displays the scatterplot of test scores in relation to age of arrival for informants arriving in the United States before vs. after puberty.

As shown, learning within the critical period first reaches the ceiling, and then gradually declines from about age 7 on until adulthood; learning after the critical period does not exhibit continuous decline but rather a great deal of variance.

Of importance to note is that the Johnson and Newport (1989) study converges on three major findings with earlier studies by Patkowski (1980) and Oyama (1976). First, changes within the critical period are linear, and they gradually asymptote beyond the critical period. As Johnson and Newport (1989: 97) put it, 'there is a gradual decline in language learning skills over the period of an ongoing maturational growth and a stabilization of language skills at a low but variable level of performance at the final mature state'. Second, when the decline occurs over a number of years and is fairly high in the first place, the amount of exposure to language input – often equated with length of residence – ceases to produce any noticeable effect on learning as learners reach an asymptote. And third, there are vast individual variations among post-puberty learners in the level of ultimate attainment.

These findings have not only empirically verified Lenneberg's CPH in the context of SLA but also refined it to a significant extent. Among other things, they have modified a rectangular function in the relationship between age of acquisition and ultimate performance, as suggested in the earliest formulation of the hypothesis, into one characterized by linearity up through puberty and a subsequent lack thereof and great variability after puberty, pinpointed the age (i.e., 8) at which a decline in performance begins to occur within the critical period for L2 morphosyntactic development. Moreover, they have recognized that the age limitation on second language development is due largely to the biological maturation, and not to lack of exercise of the learning capacity during the critical period. Last but not least, the findings have demonstrated a heterogeneous variance in the ultimate performance of post-puberty learners. This heterogeneity of variance, as Johnson and Newport (1989: 96) note, underscores two simple but important points:

(1) Before age 15, and most particularly before age 10, there are very few individual differences in ultimate ability to learn language within any particular age group; success in learning is almost entirely predicted by the age at which it begins.
(2) For adults, later age of acquisition determines that one will not become native or near-native in a language; however, there are large individual variations in ultimate ability in the language, within the lowered range of performance.

This last point is of great relevance to understanding general as well as differential failure across L2 learners which we have sought to explain. Adult L2 learners, as predicted by both the earliest version and the refined version of the CPH, are destined to exhibit lack of success in their L2 development; complete native-like attainment (i.e., in all aspects of language) is impossible. It is in the latter sense that adult L2 acquisition is characterized by general failure. The well-noted heterogeneity of variance, on the other hand, marks inter-learner differential failure.

The Johnson and Newport (1989) study, though widely appreciated as providing unambiguous evidence of a CP for L2 morphosyntactic development, is not without its critics (see, e.g., Bialystok & Hakuta, 1994; Bialystok & Miller, 1999; Eubank & Gregg, 1999; Kellerman, 1995b). Kellerman (1995b), for example, raises doubts about the method, the materials used in the study and the way the data were interpreted. Concerning the method, he considers the binary choice response format of the grammaticality judgment task short of validity, noting 'one simply cannot know what is being judged in the sentence without supplementary information via think-aloud protocols, underlining or correction' (1995b: 220). He also expresses a concern about the test stimuli. That is, with some of the stimuli at least, there appears to be an intermingling of semantic and morphological considerations as well as of formal and functional considerations, and as such, they may potentially invoke multiple interpretations on the part of the testees. In addition, Kellerman challenges the almost exclusively biology based interpretation by Johnson and Newport of their data, suggesting that NL transfer can be a potential confounding variable leading to the results reported. Nevertheless, he points out that 'ascribing any variation in performance to L1-L2 differences would be of little value in this case since the language backgrounds of JN89's early and late arrivals were identical' (1995b: 224). As a direction for future research, he proposes a hypothesis for investigating the interaction between age and L1 influence:

> There is an interaction between L1 and L2 features and age of acquisition, such that learners attempting to acquire certain (but not all) features in the L2 which have no L1 equivalents must have acquired those features by the age of x_{12} or they will never acquire them. Features of the L2 with clear L1 analogues, on the other hand, can in principle be mastered whatever the age of onset of learning. (1995b: 229)

Though, to the best of my knowledge, there exists no empirical study as yet that directly tests this hypothesis, a similar line of consideration relating age with the distance between an L1 and an L2 has already been integrated in several recent studies (Bialystok & Miller, 1999; Birdsong & Molis, 2001; DeKeyser, 2000; Flege *et al.*, 1995). Bialystok and Miller (1999), for example, studied the grammaticality judgments by three groups of informants: native speakers of Chinese, native speakers of Spanish and native speakers of English, and they found that age was intricately tied up with other factors, one of which was the typological proximity between the L1 and the L2. Three specific findings from the study, all revealing an asymmetry of some sort, are particularly intriguing. The first pertains to the lack of difference in oral performance on the grammaticality judgment task between younger and older learners for the Chinese language group, but not for the Spanish group. A second finding is the presence of L1 effects on the performance of the Chinese group, but not the Spanish group. A third finding is that learners of all ages, from both language groups, showed a continued sensitivity to age of arrival for the oral task, but not for the written task. Yet most intriguing of all is the fact that there are more inconsistent than consistent findings across the two learner groups.

Collectively, these findings seem to compromise age as the sole predictor of child–adult differences in L2 proficiency. The authors, hence, point out that because of the close interaction of multiple factors, caution must be exercised in drawing any conclusions about CP effects. It is worth noting, however, that the Bialystok and Miller study, rather than concluding with a coherent explanation for child–adult differences in second language proficiency, leaves open a number of questions such as: How does age interact with L1 influence? Why is it that L1 influence is seen in case *X*, but not in case *Y*, when both *X* and *Y* involve approximating the same target language? Are L1 influence and age mutually exclusive? Can they overlap to affect L2 development? Evidently, further research on the relationship between age and L1 influence is warranted. Later in this chapter, we will look, at some length, at another attempt (Schachter, 1990) which explores the interaction between the two.

The Modular Nature of CP

From the preceding discussion, it becomes apparent that when applied to SLA, the notion of critical period is modular in nature. In other words, in lieu of a global critical period for all linguistic domains, there appear to be multiple critical or sensitive periods respectively for certain linguistic domains. So far, the general consensus is that CP effects, if any, would more profoundly impact on phonology and morphosyntax.[6] Lexicon and pragmatics, on the other hand, are relatively unaffected by delays in learning (for a recent account of the relationship between age and L2 acquisition of lexicon, see Singleton [1995]). As Eubank and Gregg (1999: 91) note:

> With these aspects of linguistic competence, we would expect to see fairly weak age effects, aside from the general decline in powers one attributes to senescence. Thus, in cases of significant adult failure to acquire these aspects of L2 competence, we would expect to find causes unrelated to a biological CP: limited input, insufficient motivation, and so forth.

Findings in support of such a view have accumulated over the past 20 years and are extending beyond their traditional source of behavioral studies. Weber-Fox and Neville (1999: 27), for example, present electophysiological evidence suggesting that 'the relation between age of immersion and linguistic judgment accuracy was not uniform across different types of language constructs; namely syntactic proficiency was more profoundly impacted than lexical (or semantic) judgment accuracy'. Further, they associate the reduced ability in late learners with reduced specialization in the left hemisphere and increased involvement of the right hemisphere.

One study which seems pivotal to any discussion of the CP's modular nature is that of Seliger (1978). In this study, pathological evidence was summoned from studies of patients of all ages suffering different kinds of aphasia to show that the process of brain lateralization is not a one-off event, but rather a continuous one (cf. Scovel, 1988), during which not only interhemispheric but also intrahemispheric localization take place. The implication of such an evolving biological process for language learning would be that 'there would be many critical periods, successive and perhaps overlapping, lasting probably throughout one's lifetime, each closing off different acquisition abilities' (1978: 16).

Seliger goes on to speculate:

> Owing to the loss of plasticity and the closing of critical periods for whatever language functions, the learner will not be able to incorporate some aspect of the second language. Such a situation would be true regardless of whether the language was being acquired in natural or formal learning environments. (1978: 16)

From this view, it necessarily follows that the language system created by adult L2 learners will be incomplete, exhibiting partial success.

In addition to lateralization, myelination is another neurological process that has been identified as possibly contributing to the multiple critical periods. Myelination, according to Pulvermüller and Schumann (1994), is not an all-or-none phenomenon, but rather develops gradually:

> The primary sensory and motor areas myelinate early, within the first 12 months, suggesting that neurons of primary cortices are the first to reduce their potential for making new synapses and for modifying established ones . . . higher-order association cortices (e.g., the prefrontal cortex and the angular gyrus) myelinate much later and even in the adult brain relatively few myelinated (glial wrapped) axons connect these regions of the left and right hemisphere . . . suggesting that even late in life they include a high number of unmyelinated neurons and show a high level of plasticity . . . Around puberty, all cortical areas, except perhaps the higher-order association cortices, have reached their full level of myelination. Accordingly, neurons in the perisylvian language cortex are left with reduced plasticity around puberty, the time after which language learning will lead to reduced grammatical abilities. (1994: 711)

Long (1990), after surveying a large number of critical period studies, very concretely suggests that the critical period for phonology begins to offset at age 6, but that for morphology and syntax it ends at age 15. This necessarily predicts less success for adult learners in acquiring native-like phonological competence but more in acquiring L2 morphosyntax.

The modular nature in the sense of 'multiple critical periods' is not only true of linguistic domains such as phonology and morphosyntax, but also of subsystems within each of these domains, as will be shown in the next section as we explore CP effects.

Critical Period Effects on Language Learning

Of the neurological processes that have been considered as underlying the critical period, lateralization appears to have received the most attention, since progressive lateralization of language functions to the dominant left hemisphere is widely taken to be concomitant with the gradual loss of neural plasticity.

Plasticity, in the eyes of many, is synonymous with sensitivity and flexibility. Scovel (1988), for example, defines it as the overall ability of the brain to program and process new patterns of behavior quickly and efficiently, and to relocate this ability to different areas of the brain should there be congenital damage or injury incurred after birth. High sensitivity to external stimuli is further correlated with success. Early learners are assumed to possess high sensitivity, and hence are successful in learning. Late learners (e.g., adults), on the other hand, have a lowered sensitivity – being less responsive to environmental influences such as input from the target language – and hence are less successful. As Eubank and Gregg (1999: 90) aptly put it, 'once the period is past, linguistic input ceases to have an instructional effect with regard to those aspects [of language]'. Of relevance to note, this proposition is consistent with findings from a number of recent neurophysiological experiments with early and late bilinguals that are conducted via Event-related Brain Potentials (ERPs), a technique for measuring electrical activity in different areas of the brain (see, e.g., Weber-Fox & Neville, 1999).

Loss of plasticity, however, is only a partial explanation for the physical reality of a critical period. As mentioned earlier, the existence of a CP hinges largely on the interaction between the innate neural mechanisms and the environmental stimulation. As Colombo (1982: 261) defines it:

> A critical period is a time during the life span of an organism in which the organism may be affected by some exogenous influence to an extent beyond that observed at other times. Simply, the organism is more sensitive to environmental stimulation during a critical period than at other times during its life.

In a similar vein, Eubank and Gregg (1999:67) assert:

> Connection between innate structure and peripheral stimulus is a necessary, albeit not sufficient, condition on CPs: CPs appear only where development of the mature state depends on a significant contribution of both the relevant neural architecture and peripheral exposure.

In many ways, the innate structure and the environmental stimulation are like two sides of one coin, and the constraints on language learning as a result of passing the critical period derive from the functioning, not of either side, but of both sides, of the coin. Just as maturational changes in the neural architecture may result in varying degrees of sensitivity to external stimuli – during the critical period learning is susceptible to alteration by external influences (Eubank & Gregg, 1999) – the type of external stimuli available to learners during the critical period can have permanent effects on their subsequent language development (cf. Eubank & Gregg, 1999; Schachter, 1996a). These effects, as Scott (1962; cited in Colombo, 1982: 261) points out, may take two forms: they may trigger the course of further normal development or produce 'an irrevocable result not modifiable in subsequent development' (p. 957).

The nature of the exposure to environmental stimuli during the sensitive period and its effect on subsequent learning is elegantly elaborated under Schachter's (1989, 1990, 1996a,b) Incompleteness Hypothesis, which posits:

> There is a maturational schedule for the development of certain principles and certain other properties of L1. Furthermore, this schedule results in sensitive periods before which *and after which* certain principles cannot be incorporated into a developing L1. If these principles have not been incorporated into a learner's L1 during the sensitive period, they remain forever unavailable for incorporation into an adult learner's developing L2. (Schachter, 1996a: 163; emphasis in original)

Situating her argumentation within a UG framework, Schachter contends that environmental stimulation is crucial not only for parameter setting, as generally recognized, but also for triggering certain universal principles. Following her line of reasoning, if a principle comprises a number of related properties and if these properties do not appear in the input which a learner experiences at the maturationally appropriate time, the principle will not subsequently form part of the learner's grammar of that language. A case in point is Subjacency (see, however, Bialystok & Miller, 1999; Juffs & Harrington, 1995 for counter-arguments), a principle constraining extraction rules at the level of S-structure, and whose function depends on other properties such as wh-movement, topicalization and so on. Using this principle as a test case for her Incompleteness Hypothesis, Schachter (1990) studied four groups of proficient L2 learners whose native languages are, respectively, Chinese, Korean, Indonesian, and Dutch, along with a group of native speakers of English. Grammaticality judgment tests were designed and administered to the informants to gauge the extent to which the English Subjacency constraints were acquired. Schachter's rationale was that 'if all groups show the same Subjacency effects in English that native speakers do, then it must be the case UG is still available for adult second language learning and completeness in second language grammar is possible; if not, then completeness cannot be included as a possible characteristic of adult second language acquisition' (1990: 91). Results from subsequent data analyses showed:

> Dutch speakers of English, whose native language operates as does English regarding Subjacency, performed as did native speakers of English on judgments of Subjacency violations. Korean speakers of English, whose native language shows no Subjacency effects, performed quite poorly on the same tests. Chinese and Indonesian speakers of English, whose native languages show partial overlap with English in Subjacency effects, are better at these tests than the Koreans and worse than the Dutch, indicating . . . that the more limited Subjacency effects in their native languages, while helpful, did not in general allow them to generalize to all possible effects in English. (Schachter, 1990: 116)

This finding led her to conclude:

> In the acquisition of the target language (TL) some data associated with the triggering of principle *P* is necessary, and if *P* is not incorporated into the learner's L1 (as appears to be the case with Subjacency in Korean), the learner will have neither language-internal knowledge nor initial state knowledge to guide her in the development of *P*. Therefore, completeness with regard to the acquisition of the TL will not be possible. The same holds true for parameter resettings not instantiated in the L1. (Schachter, 1996a: 171)

This is the so-called Incompleteness Hypothesis. It is worth noting that, at the same time it concerns a potential cause of incompleteness in adult L2 ultimate attainment, the hypothesis predicts differential success both at the inter-learner and intra-learner levels. One way to interpret this would be as follows: first, learners bring to the L2 setting different L1s which have differential instantiations of the UG principles and which thus may impact on their L2 learning differently, hence leading to inter-learner differential success; second, L2 learners, in the course of their L1 acquisition (i.e., during the critical period), may have had differential exposure to input that triggers various UG principles, and for this reason, may have commanded varying degrees of acquisition of the UG constraints associated with the principles instantiated in the L1. If this speculation turns out to be correct, then it would follow that what each L2 learner possesses is an idiolect of his or her mother tongue. This may sound like an overstatement and may seem, among other things, to be playing down the widely accepted argument that L1 ultimate attainment exhibits completeness or homogeneity as opposed to incompleteness or heterogeneity as has been widely claimed for L2 acquisition. Yet it may explain, at least in part, how an L1 selectively as well as differentially affects each individual L2 learner, thereby contributing to the inter- and intra-learner differential success in the L2. We will defer a more detailed discussion of this issue to the next chapter. On an incidental note, the above speculation may also provide insight into why there is rarely 100% convergence among native speakers' grammaticality judgments, a phenomenon which, though visible in most SLA empirical studies of grammatical competence that rely on a subset of native speakers to provide baseline data, has not yet received any serious attention.

Pivotal to the Incompleteness Hypothesis, it should be pointed out, is a broadened notion of maturation mirroring two perspectives: biological and linguistic. For Schachter, biological mechanisms undergo stages of maturation, and so do certain UG principles and parameters. These stages of maturation are, in fact, sensitive periods, which Schachter (1988, 1996) describes as 'Windows of Opportunity', bound on both sides by periods of lesser sensitivity to certain environmental stimuli. This assumption carries with it several implications. First, there can be critical periods within critical periods, both in biological and linguistic terms. Thus, we can envisage an overarching critical or sensitive period, biological in nature, for language learning in general, within which there exist multiple critical periods corresponding to the various linguistic domains (e.g., phonology, syntax, semantics and so forth) as well as to properties of language internal to the domains (cf. Singleton, 1995; Eubank & Gregg, 1999), as schematized in Figure 4.2.

Such a hierarchical structure is consistent with the modular view discussed earlier in the chapter. In Figure 4.2, the top 'CP' stands for a general CP for language learning; the CPs at the next level (middle), indicated by a smaller font, represent CPs for different linguistic domains (e.g., phonology, syntax, etc); and finally the CPs at the lowest level, indicated by the smallest font, represent CPs for different subsystems within each domain.

Returning to the implications of Schachter's conceptualization, the second one is that even during the critical period for a certain UG principle, if there happens to be a mismatch between the external stimuli (e.g., the

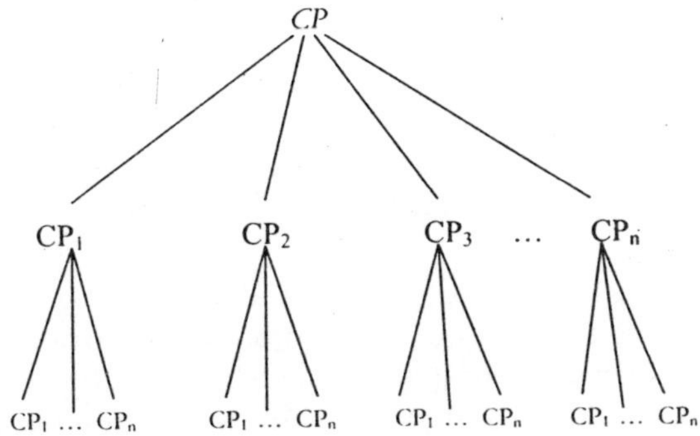

Figure 4.2 Critical periods within a critical period

absence of relevant triggering properties from the input for the learner), the principle will not become part of the developing grammar.

To recapitulate the Incompleteness Hypothesis: if the L2 learner brings to the learning setting an L1 that represents an 'incomplete' instantiation of UG principles and parameters, it will result in lack of completeness in his or her L2 grammar. This hypothesis is consonant with one of Scott's (1962) predictions mentioned earlier, namely that external stimulation during the critical period may produce 'an irrevocable result not modifiable in subsequent development' (p. 957). Although the Incompleteness Hypothesis was made from a UG perspective, thus pertaining only to the acquisition of UG-related features of the target language, it provides rich insights into L2 learning in general. In a non-technical sense, it suggests that linguistic features may experience maturation, hence the existence of Windows of Opportunity for acquiring them. Missing out on the opportunities will mean incomplete acquisition.[7]

Beyond the Incompleteness Hypothesis which delineates the ultimate *level* of L2 knowledge, Johnson *et al.* (1996) empirically examined the *nature* of that knowledge, as a function of late onset of learning. Giving the grammaticality judgment task of Johnson and Newport (1989) twice to 10 adult native speakers of Chinese and 10 native speakers of English, the researchers noticed that across the two testings, the adult learners of English showed 'a marked degree of inconsistency' (p. 335), while the native speakers' performance was highly consistent. This discrepancy was subsequently attributed to a knowledge base that is partially deterministic. Adult learners' knowledge, according to Johnson *et al.*, is composed of multiple types and sources of information, only some of which are deterministic in character. This part comprises learners' knowledge of English and their own rules. The remainder of the knowledge base comes from the interaction of the deterministic part with a number of 'probabilistic' sources such as varying accessibility of knowledge, response biases, practice effects and guessing, hence indeterministic in nature. Such a knowledge base was in turn considered to be an indication of late L2 learners using a different mechanism for learning than is used by younger learners.

Summing up, the effects of the critical period(s) on L2 learning can be broadly conceived of as three-fold: first, adult L2 learners, as a consequence of passing the critical period(s), will have low sensitivity to L2 input, hence a weak ability to benefit from exposure to input, even when it contains crucial properties for acquisition. Second, what is acquired as a result of the interaction between environmental stimulation and innate neurological mechanisms during the critical period will permanently impact, positively and / or negatively, on subsequent L2 learning. This predicts that L1 interference will necessarily occur in adult L2 learning. Third, as a function of lack of ability to benefit from natural exposure to input, adult L2 learners will take recourse to probabilistic strategies such as guessing, leading potentially to development of permanent indeterminate knowledge. As a major consequence of these factors working in tandem, adult L2 ultimate attainment is bound to feature incompleteness.

Summary

In this chapter, we examined the notion of 'critical period'. Functionally as well as conceptually, the critical period in the context of SLA has a number of characteristics. First, it is not absolute but rather a period of heightened sensitivity to environmental stimuli, within which L2 learning is successful and beyond which learning is *still possible but highly variable and less successful*. This period is biologically founded, hence endogenous in nature, but its function hinges on the interaction between innate neural processes and exogenous stimulation. Second, the sensitive period applies differentially to linguistic domains, and hence is modular in nature. Third, the sensitive period effects are intricately tied up with cognitive, affective and social factors, including, but not limited to, L1 transfer.

The brain-based account reveals much about the L2 learning ability (or lack thereof), and provides crucial insights into a universal lack of success across the majority of adult L2 learners. It alone, however, does not seem adequate for explaining inter-learner differential success. In other words, it does not explain why learners fossilize differentially *en route*. Yet when combined with a mind-based account (including, e.g., the process of cross-linguistic influence), as Schachter (1990, 1996) did, it provides a powerful means of understanding differential success and failure across adult learners (cf. Flege *et al.*, 1995).

Research on the CPH is not approaching its end, but rather continues to proliferate as a rich source of speculation and empirical verification. What, then, is to be further researched? Recent attempts appear to center around two major tasks: (1) teasing apart variables that may confound with age (see, e.g., Moyer, 1999); and (2) looking into the interaction between age and other factors, not the least of which is L1 transfer. Additionally, there is a growing number of experimental studies that seek neurophysiological evidence for the CPH rather than behavioral reflexes, as has been true for most age-related studies thus far. Issues that remain to be addressed include, among others, the measurement of ultimate attainment. Since child–adult differences are most visible when ultimate attainment constitutes the focus of examination (Patkowski, 1980, 1990), it is necessary to establish, through reliable and valid methods, that the informants have indeed reached the level of ultimate attainment, rather than to assume that this is so via some arbitrary yardstick (e.g., five years of residence in the country of the target language). Longitudinal (long-term) studies are warranted to determine if the informants have indeed reached an asymptote. Moreover, the scope of the linguistic features investigated needs broadening; multiple tasks involving a variety of linguistic features should be employed rather than singular tasks focusing on a narrow set of features, to enhance the validity of the studies and the generalizability of their findings (for a recent study in this direction, see Flege & Liu, 2001). Yet another standing issue is the conception of ultimate attainment. As argued in this book, ultimate attainment is not a monolith. In line with the modular view on the critical period in SLA, there can exist differential ultimate attainments, with some successfully reaching the target and others falling short of it. Hence in investigating ultimate attainment, success and failure are *both* to be expected. This conception would, among other things, call into doubt a considerable amount of available empirical evidence refuting the Critical Period Hypothesis.

Notes

1. As Johnson and Newport (1989: 61) note, a broad use of the term 'critical period' 'may avoid prejudging what the degree or quality of such maturational change may be (e.g., is it a sharp qualitative change or a gradual quantitative one?) and what the nature of the underlying maturational mechanism may be (e.g., is it a change in a special language faculty or a more general change in cognitive abilities?)'.
2. Seliger (1978: 13) offers the following three reasons for researchers wanting to associate the concept of CP with only phonological acquisition: First, since phonological production can be elicited as a physically measurable response,

phonological errors are more easily identifiable. Second, the phonological system is the most studiable of the finite subsystems of a language, and its parts are the most easily identified and described. Third, there is not yet any way to measure completeness of acquisition of any other aspect of language, such as syntactic or semantic features. Since these other subsystems are so vast and complex compared to the finiteness of a phonology, incomplete acquisition in syntax and semantics may exist without consequences in performance; given the size of these subsystems and possible employment of avoidance strategies, the likelihood of errors occurring is greatly reduced.

3. By 'lexical development', I mean the development of content words.
4. In their study, Johnson and Newport equated age of arrival with age of exposure to the target language.
5. Kellerman's (1995b: 230) original footnote: 'Fill in your own favored upper bound for the CPH'.
6. There is yet limted evidence of a critical period for semantics. An oft-quoted study on this topic is Coppieters (1989).
7. See, however, Eubank and Gregg (1999: 78) for some arguments to the contrary, one of which is that 'the mature state of a neural region is not totally incapable of alteration by altered peripheral exposure'.

Chapter 5

A Macroscopic Analysis: Native Language Transfer

Through exploring CP effects on L2 acquisition we have gained the understanding that age can act in concert with native language influence in manufacturing incomplete attainment in adult L2 acquisition (cf. Birdsong, 1999; Harley & Wang, 1997; Odlin, 1989). Birdsong (1999: 17) points out that 'the CP driven loss of ability and L1 interference are so intertwined that they are hard to separate in the context of SLA, due to the coincidence of the two milestones,' and suggests that the two be traced as jointly underlying adult learners' lack of ability to learn a new language.

L2 research over the last several decades has made available considerable evidence showing L1 as a strong competing causal factor of age-related differences in L2 ultimate attainment. To mention but one recent study, Flege *et al.* (1995), in their investigation of child–adult differences in L2 phonological acquisition, found that the pre-existent phonetic categories in the adult L2 learners' L1 may restrict their perception of L2 phonetic input. The impact of the L1 on L2 learning appears to be strong and has, in fact, led some researchers to go so far as to claim that 'the price we pay for successful L1 acquisition is the inability to acquire an L2' (Eubank & Gregg, 1999: 92). Given this strong proposition, it would only seem necessary and appropriate that we dwell on the transfer issue in this chapter, in a more complete pursuit of a macroscopic analysis of failure.

A central component of cross-linguistic influence, native language (L1) transfer has been a perennial issue in SLA research. Despite decades of controversies, however, certain generalities that were drawn in the early days of SLA research are still widely accepted today. One such generality was that the L1 constitutes the initial point of L2 acquisition (e.g., Corder, 1967, 1983; Nemser, 1971; Selinker, 1972), and this very same view is still held by many current researchers (e.g., Bialystok, 1994; Carroll, 2001; MacWhinney, 2001; Schwartz & Sprouse, 1996), though from perspectives different than those of the early researchers. Schwartz and Sprouse (1996: 41), for example, propose, within UG concerns, a Full Transfer / Full Access model that stipulates that 'the initial state of L2 acquisition is the final state of L1 acquisition'. In their view:

> All the principles and parameter values as instantiated in the L1 grammar immediately carry over as the initial state of a new grammatical system on first exposure to input from the target language (TL). This initial state of the L2 system will have to change in light of TL input that cannot be generated by this grammar; that is, failure to assign a representation to input data will force some sort of restructuring of the system ('grammar'), this restructuring drawing from options of UG (and hence the term 'Full Access'). (Schwartz & Sprouse, 1996: 41)

On this view, L2 learners initially and immediately utilize their L1 system ('grammar') and will continue to do so until that system fails to assign a representation to the L2 data.

From a cognitive processing perspective, Bialystok (1994: 163) asserts:

> The mental representations developed in the course of first language acquisition provide the starting point for the representations that will be developed for the second language. Similarly, the attentional procedures developed for processing a first language are the basis for building up the new procedures needed for the second. Structural differences between languages such as where the verb is positioned and how predication is expressed require different forms of attentional control. The second language learner begins with a more highly analyzed conception of language and more well-developed procedure for directing attention than does the child learning a first language. Yet both learners are faced with the problem of building up the representations and selective attention through analysis and control that are required to function in the specific language.

Thus, following Bialystok, adult L2 learners would initially resort to an L1-based knowledge creation mechanism (known as 'analysis') and a knowledge processing mechanism (known as 'control'), and L2 development, subsequently, involves switching from the L1 version of analysis and control to the L2 version.

Because L2 learners are considered to use their L1 as a point of departure, it has also been suggested that the typological proximity between an L1 and an L2 may determine the degree of ease or difficulty in acquiring the L2 (e.g., Lado, 1957; Schachter, 1996a). Following from this position, adult L2 learners are not 'equipotential' (Schachter, 1996a) for language acquisition in the same way as child L1 learners are. As Schachter (1996a: 161) has stated it:

> The adult's knowledge of a prior language either facilitates or inhibits acquisition of the L2, depending on the underlying similarities or dissimilarities of the languages in question. An adult speaker of English will require considerably less time and effort to achieve a given level of ability in German than in Japanese because the similarities between English and German, at all levels, are much greater than those between English and Japanese, and the adult's prior knowledge of English influences subsequent acquisition. This contributes to differences in completeness . . . The closer two languages are in terms of syntax, phonology, and lexicon, the more likely it is that higher levels of completeness can be reached.

This conception pinpoints, among other things, the fact that L2 learners from different L1 backgrounds, while approaching the same target language, may bring to the L2 learning task differential readiness, a variable that may affect the quality of their ultimate attainment.

In a similar vein, but tying transfer to age, Bialystok and Miller (1999) claim for an asymmetry in L1 effects in circumstances in which the L2 has a morphosyntactic category not found in the L1:

> Younger learners should readily construct the new L2 category, whereas older learners should have limited success at best. Older learners have neither access to language acquisition mechanisms nor knowledge of the structure, so these categories are presumably difficult to learn. For categories that correspond across the two languages, older learners could profit from the similarity while younger learners may use either analogy with the similar L2 construction, or guidance from language acquisition mechanisms, or both, to master the category. For similar categories, therefore, the gap between older and younger learners would be narrowed , but for reasons that are not necessarily clear. (1999: 130)

Bialystok and Miller thus predict that where there is L1–L2 structural congruence, the L1 will play a facilitative role in L2 learning and there will be little discrepancy in the L2 outcome between child and adult L2 learners, but that where there is L1–L2 structural disparity, the L1 will become a hindrance and there will be noticeable discrepancy in the L2 outcome between child and adult learners (cf. Kellerman, 1995a). Such a prediction is in a way reminiscent of the early Contrastive Analysis Hypothesis (Lado, 1957), which associates difference with difficulty and similarity with ease. Yet clearly, Bialystok and Miller have gone beyond that understanding by further associating difference with child–adult divergence on the one hand, and similarity with convergence on the other, vis-à-vis L2 ultimate attainment.

Thus, current L2 research not only has reinforced the earliest view but also substantiated it by suggesting, among other things, that a learner's L1 may potentially have an impact on his or her L2 ultimate attainment.

In the following sections, we will look specifically into L1 transfer as a source of hindrance to L2 learning.[1] We will first focus on manifestations of language transfer as a conscious, idiosyncratic, and selective process, and then on transfer as part of a general mechanism driving L2 learning. Accordingly, issues will be discussed in the following sequence: (1) transfer-inspired delay in L2 learning, (2) 'transfer to somewhere' and 'transfer to nowhere', (3) transfer of 'thinking for speaking', and (4) L1 preprogramming.

Transfer-inspired Delay in L2 Learning

Building on the insight from researchers in the 1960s and 1970s that L1 transfer may delay learning, Zobl (1980) posits two types of errors in interlanguage development, developmental errors and transfer errors. Both are considered of a common genesis in that they both arise from the processing of properties of L2 input, yet only transfer errors are thought to be able to 'retard subsequent restructuring' (1980: 469). Zobl's argument goes as follows:

1. Structural properties of the L2 which give rise to developmental errors may also activate influence from the learner's L1 when an L1 structure is compatible with the developmental error.
2. General language acquisition principles promote transfer when an L1 structure more closely conforms to the linguistic parameters of the developmental acquisition principle than [to] the L2 structure to be acquired.
3. Although there is a crucial degree of overlap between developmental and transfer errors with respect to the factors involved in their genesis, transfer errors may prolong restructuring of the rule underlying the error. It is hypothesized that this tendency toward fossilization results from the use of a common rule in a mature linguistic system (the L1) and in a developing linguistic system (the L2 developmental stage [which] the learner has attained). (1980: 470)

This account not only outlines for us conditions under which transfer errors may be brought into existence, but more importantly, it pinpoints the cause for the persistence of transfer errors, namely, an L1 rule overlapping with a universal developmental feature (see also the Multiple Effects Principle proposed by Selinker & Lakshmanan [1992]).

'Transfer to Somewhere' and 'Transfer to Nowhere'

In much of his work on language transfer, Kellerman maintains that transfer is a strategy which learners tend to fall back on as a means to compensate for their lack of L2 knowledge. In his early work (1977, 1978), Kellerman identified two criteria that learners use to determine what is transferable, namely that a form which, in the learner's perception, is both unmarked and semantically transparent in the native language can be transferred. Two observations can be made on these criteria. The first is that they are largely derived from studies of transfer in a context where the L1 and the L2 are typologically similar. The second is that the criteria are subject to learners' perception of similarities (or lack thereof) – as opposed to the factual (objective) similarities – between the two languages. Indeed, similarity based transfer marks much of the early L2 research on L1 transfer, and has led to the formulation of a number of transfer principles. A case in point is Andersen's (1983) *transfer to somewhere* principle, in which he explicitly postulates two general conditions for transfer to occur (cf. Zobl, 1980):

> A grammatical form or structure will occur consistently and to a significant extent in the interlanguage as a result of transfer *if and only if* a) natural acquisitional principles are consistent with the L1 structure or b) there already exists within the L2 input the potential for (mis)generalization from the input to produce the same form or structure. (Anderson, 1983: 182; emphasis in original)

In simplified terms, the two conditions are (a) that there should be a place in interlanguage development or use for holding the transferred form (a 'place-holder', so to speak); and (b) that in the L2 input, there should be something that induces the learner to the belief that it is the counterpart of the form being transferred from the L1.

Quite obviously, the 'transfer to somewhere' principle characterizes transfer as a rather conscious process; transfer is considered to be primarily a strategy employed by learners not only to fill gaps in L2 knowledge but also to free up attentional capacity for other aspects of an ongoing communicative task (Kellerman, 1995a).

As pointed out earlier, however, these early thoughts on language transfer are primarily founded on analyses of data from typologically similar languages. If cross-linguistic similarity is the driving force behind language transfer, then it would seem logical to argue that where there is no perceived similarity, there should be no transfer (cf. Kellerman, 1995a). This argument, however, would not bear up under scrutiny. For one thing, it is not consistent with the general observation that transfer nonetheless occurs in L2 learners whose L1s are typologically distant from the target language. The two examples below suffice to show that transfer can occur in both cases (i.e., where the two languages are typologically close or distant), though the content of transfer in one case differs from that in the other.

[5–1a] Italian (L1):
a causa di
on account of, owing to

[5–1b] Portuguese (L2):
por causa de
because of, owing to

[5–1c] Italian–Portuguese interlanguage:
*a causa de

[5–2a] Chinese (L1):
A: ni3 zuo2tian1 mei2you3 qu4 na4li shi4 ma?
You yesterday not go there right Q
You did not go there yesterday, right?
B: dui4, wo3 mei2 qu4.
Right I not go
Right, I didn't go.

[5–2b] English (L2):
A: You didn't go there yesterday, did you?
B: No, I didn't.

[5–2c] Chinese–English interlanguage:
A: You didn't go there yesterday, did you?
B: *Yes, I didn't.

[5–1a–c] represent a typologically close context, with [5–1c] showing surface syntactic transfer due to the syntactic and semantic similarity between the L1 and the L2. [5.2a–c], on the other hand, represent a typologically distant context, with [5–2c] manifesting transfer of an L1 expression of agreement with a negative statement, a phenomenon known as transfer of L1 'thinking for speaking', which we shall dwell upon shortly. Without enumerating instances of transfer from typologically distant L1s, suffice it to say at this point that similarities across languages may lead to transfer, and so may differences (cf. Odlin, 1989).

The latter view is by far best pronounced in Kellerman's (1995a) 'transfer to nowhere' principle:

> There can be transfer that is not licensed by similarity to the L2, and where the way the L2 works may very largely go unheeded; hence transfer to nowhere . . . [T]his principle does not so much refer to differences in grammatical form as to differences in the way languages predispose their speakers to conceptualize experience. (1995a: 137)

The 'transfer to nowhere' principle, aside from claiming that transfer can come about through differences, recognizes yet another feature of transfer, namely that transfer can be an unconscious process. In distinguishing 'transfer to nowhere' from 'transfer to somewhere' and, at the same time, uniting these two principles, Kellerman points out (1995a):

> Andersen's *transfer to somewhere* principle is about the acquisition of the means of linguistic expression. ***Transfer to nowhere* is about the conceptualization that fuels the drive towards discovering those means.** In fact, Andersen's transfer to somewhere is a heuristic designed to make sense of the L2 input. It assumes some sort of awareness on the part of the learner of the ability to map the L1 onto the L2.
>
> . . .
>
> Most of the evidence so far amassed about the provenance of [cross-linguistic influence] seems to support the transfer to somewhere principle, but it is claimed here that there are other ways that the first language can influence the second at a level where cognition and language touch. **These language-specific ways of dealing with experience lead to *transfer to nowhere*.** In this sense, learners may not be able to capitalize on cross-language correspondences because some types of 'thinking for speaking' may be beyond individual awareness. (1995a: 142; emphasis [bold] added)

Thus, the difference between transfer to somewhere and transfer to nowhere boils down to this: the former involves conscious transfer of L1 surface linguistic features, whereas the latter is an unconscious process whereby L1 mediated conceptualization finds its expression in the interlanguage – a phenomenon known as 'transfer of thinking for speaking'.

Transfer to nowhere, when occurring at the discourse level, may result in a distinct discourse accent. As an illustration, let us look at an excerpt of Africanized English taken from Achebe (1966; cited in Kachru, 1990):

> [5–3a]
> I want one of my sons to join these people and be my eyes there. If there is nothing in it you will come back. But if there is something then you

> will bring back my share. The world is like a mask, dancing. If you want to see it well, you do not stand in one place. My spirit tells me that those who do not befriend the white man today will be saying 'had we known', tomorrow.

The discourse accent of this passage becomes apparent when compared with the following 'Englishized' version:

> [5–3b]
> I am sending you as my representative among these people – just to be on the safe side in case the new religion develops. One has to move with the times or else one is left behind. I have a hunch that those who fail to come to terms with the white man may well regret their lack of foresight. (1990: 162)

From [5–3a] and [5–3b], we can see how different thought patterns have resulted in different language designs (Kachru, 1990; see also Hartford, 1993).

In adult second language acquisition, transfer of L1-based thinking for speaking appears to transpire regardless of any L1 and of its proximity to the target language. A case thereof is reported in Han (2000). From a two-year longitudinal corpus of L2 – written English data produced by two adult native speakers of Chinese, a language known to be typologically distant from English, Han found that the informants – their high level of English proficiency notwithstanding – persisted in producing 'pseudo-passives',[2] examples of which are given below in underlined format in [5–4] through [5–8]

[5–4] They told me that the attractive offer will be sent to me a bit later since <u>what I sent to them have not received</u>. (F: writing to friend / 28-Feb-1996)

[5–5] Thank you for your paper which you sent me on 22/02/96. Since you did not address the postcode (SW7 2BY), and so it arrived just this morning. <u>The letter about graphics file has not received</u>. (F: writing to friend/28-Feb-1996)

[5–6] Hello, Dear X, <u>Your letter of 17/04/96 has just received</u>. Thak you very much. I guess that the letter may be enough for the visa use. This letter will be delivered to Australia Embassy tomorrow. (F: writing to future employer/24-Apr-1996)

[5–7] After two months's study, I feel that the structural analyses of composite material (polymer (pure or fiber-reinforced)) is a very difficult and challeging field for computational mechanics worker. The correct modelling will be invovled with anisotropic, finite strain plasticity and strain-rate and temperature effect. Futhermore, the material properties is coupled with processing. Fanta's software can use to model processing procedure properly for injection moulding components. (F: writing to customer/23-Sept-1996)

[5–8] Though I have not learnt much about it, Bates' suggestions (May, 1995) about enhancement on this issue impressed me deeply. His viewpoints are absolutely right and should be stressed again (I do not know whether these problems have solved in the newest release) (F: writing annual report/ 3-Oct-1996)

The pseudo-passive structure, as suggested by Schachter and Rutherford (1979; see also Rutherford, 1983), is a direct reflex of the function and surface syntax of the informants' L1, i.e., Chinese, which licenses discourse-related omission of subject and topic-related omission of a pronoun (see also), as schematized below:

Topic	–	Comment
↓		↓
{ what I sent to them }		{have not received.}
⇑		⇑
{wo jigei tamen de dong xi}		{hai mei shoudao}
I send them poss thing		*still not receive*

What I sent to them [?] have not received [**it**].

Interestingly, the L1 topic-comment prominence found its expression not only in the pseudo-passives, but in the informants' use of target-like passives as well. An example is given in [5–9]:

[5–9] What I can do for you is to give you a list of professors or lecturers who are active in academic circles. You can contact them directly. The list will be sent to you later (next week or slightly later). (F: writing to friend/29-Mar-1996)

Here, the target-like passive (i.e., *The list will be sent to you later.*) was utilized for executing the same L1 topic-comment function as in the pseudo-passive:

Topic	–	Comment
↓		↓
{The list}		{will be sent to you}.

Syntactically, the target-like passive is a higher-order form, i.e., the more syntacticized form, of the pseudo-passive. The fact that the informants used the passive construction as a vehicle for L1 discourse functions is indicative of the persistence as well as of the profundity of the L1 influence.

Transfer of the L1-based thinking for speaking is not limited to L2 learners of the L1-Chinese background. In his corpus of L2 written English produced by Japanese speakers who were at the advanced level of English proficiency, Zobl (1989) discovered that they mapped the syntactic representations of English onto the discourse-pragmatic representations of Japanese, and further that they overproduced certain English structures to serve the L1 discourse constraints. Similarly, Trévise (1986) reported overuse of topicalization structures in English by Francophone speakers. Influenced by the topic prominence character of their native language, these learners specifically overused structures corresponding to left-dislocations, right-dislocations, and 'c'est . . . que' in French. Overuse of a given structure, according to Seliger (1989: 33), is often associated with an 'inability to acquire the semantically constrained distributional rules concerned with the selection of a particular form from among other options' offered by the target language. Needless to say, this inability, in the view taken here, results, at least in part, from L1 transfer.

Interestingly but not surprisingly, transfer of the above kind has also been attested in child SLA. Harley and King (1989, cited in Lightbown, 2000), for example, noted that English-speaking children in French immersion classes tended to follow the English pattern in their use of French verbs. They, for instance, used 'aller en bas' ('go down') in contexts where 'descendere' would have been used by native speakers of French. They did so in spite of the fact that English and French differ markedly from each other in that in English, prepositions or adverbials are used in conjunction with verbs to signal the direction of the motion, whereas in French, the direction of motion is often entailed in the verb itself.

While production is often where thinking-for-speaking effects are strong, it is by no means the only place where such influence exists. Spada and Lightbown (1999) provided some pertinent evidence in the domain of sentence interpretation. Their informants, French-speaking students learning English, readily accepted questions in which the sentential subject is a pronoun (e.g., *Can you play outside?*), but not those in which the subject is a noun (e.g., *Can the children speak Spanish?*). This is attributable to a subtle influence of the L1: In French, not in English, inversion in questions is allowed when the subject is a pronoun (e.g., *Peux-tu venir chez moi?*), but is prohibited when the subject is a full noun (e.g., **Peut-Pierre venir chez moi?*).

Given the centrality of thinking for speaking to the transfer-to-nowhere principle and the well-attested transfer of L1 thinking for speaking in L2 acquisition, a better understanding of its impact on L2 learning is warranted. In the next section, therefore, we take a closer look at the nature of the construct.

Transfer of 'Thinking for Speaking'

The term 'thinking for speaking' was originally proposed by Slobin (1996: 75) to refer to 'a special kind of thinking that is intimately tied to language – namely, the thinking that is carried out, on-line, in the process of speaking', and it was based on the classic assumption of linguistic relativity and determinism in the Whorf-Sapir tradition:

> Languages differ from one another; thought and language are inseparable; therefore each community embodies a distinct world-view. (1996: 70)

One corollary of this view is that 'children who learn different languages end up with different conceptual structures'(Slobin, 1996: 70).

In their investigation of how thinking for speaking differs for speakers of different languages, Slobin and his associates carried out a cross-linguistic study of picture narration by English, Spanish, Turkish, Hebrew, German child and adult speakers. The analysis of the grammatical organization of the narratives provided by the informants demonstrated that by the age of three or four, the children acquiring different languages had already been influenced by the grammatical categories of those languages used in verbalizing events.

In a separate experiment (also cited in Slobin [1996]) that involved pre-school (three to five-year-old) and school (nine-year-old) children and adults of different native languages, i.e., English, German, Spanish, and Hebrew, Slobin and his colleagues elicited informants' descriptions of several scenes. This time their focus was on expressions of temporal and spatial relations. It was found that even the pre-schoolers displayed language-specific patterns of thinking for speaking. Slobin hence suggests that, in acquiring each of the languages, the children were guided by the set of grammaticized distinctions in the language to focus on features of events while speaking.

Importantly, with respect to second language acquisition, Slobin (1996: 89) asserts that 'the way one learns a language as a child constrains one's selectivity to what Sapir called "the possible contents of experience as experienced in linguistic terms",' and further, that difficulty can arise where ways of thinking for speaking differ between a first and a second language:

> For example, native French speakers have no trouble with the Spanish imperfective, since they have a similar category in French; but the progressive and perfect pose problems to them, since these are not French ways of looking at events. Turkish speakers have difficulty with definite and indefinite articles in learning to speak Spanish, English, and German, since there are no definite articles in Turkish. German speakers of English use the progressive where they should use simple present, although Turks do not make this error in English, since Turkish uses progressive aspect and German does not. Spanish learners object that we make too many obscure distinctions with our large collection of locative prepositions and particles. And so on.

Abstracting from these examples, Slobin thus argues:

> Each native language has trained its speakers to pay different kinds of attention to events and experiences when talking about them. This training is carried out in childhood and is **exceptionally resistant to restructuring in adult second-language acquisition**. (1996: 89; emphasis added)

Aspects of this training that are most resistant to restructuring, according to Slobin, are grammaticized categories that are independent of 'our perceptual, sensorimotor, and practical dealings with the world'(p. 91), such as aspect, definiteness, and voice.

Put simply, the fact of having acquired a first language prior to a second language equips an L2 learner with a mature system of thinking for speaking (i.e., a language-specific system for verbalizing one's conceptualization of experience in a particular way). Such a system would, then, accompany the learner throughout his or her journey of L2 learning. Although it is not yet known to what extent such a system is open to modification *en route* (for recent studies , see Jarvis, 1998; Pavlenko & Jarvis, 2001), one consequence nevertheless seems inevitable: the thinking-for-speaking system, once established, would be difficult to undo completely. As Wilhem von Humboldt (1836: 60) aptly put it:

> To learn a foreign language should . . . be to acquire a new standpoint in the world-view hitherto possessed, and in fact to a certain extent this is so, since every language contains the whole conceptual fabric and mode of presentation of a portion of mankind. But because **we always carry over, more or less, our own world-view, and even our own language-view, this outcome is not purely and completely experienced**. (emphasis added)

Following this line of reasoning, we can hypothesize, for our concern with fossilization, that as long as there are residues of this conceptual system in the L2 learning process, the interlanguage competence will never be completely target-like.

To push our argument further, if the L1-based thinking for speaking does indeed predispose L2 learners to conceptualize, in L1-related frames, experience that is contextualized and mediated in the L2, and if the resultant conception influences the learners' perception and assimilation of L2 input, as argued by Slobin and others, then it would seem reasonable to claim that an L1 *preprograms* L2 learning such that it determines the developmental as well as the ultimate outcome of L2 learning. The notion of 'preprogramming' is explored in the next section.

Preprogramming

What exactly is *preprogramming*? When an L1 preprograms L2 learning, the L1-embodied conceptual system guides an adult learner's processing and assimilation of the L2 input.[3]

Explicit and implicit claims on *preprogramming* abound in the L2 literature. In the prediction of Slobin (1996), the L1 grammaticized categories which go beyond our perceptual, sensorimotor, and practical dealings with the world would be carried over into L2 learning, thus obstructing a complete mastery of the L2. Schachter (1996b: 86) draws the conclusion, within UG concerns, that 'whatever principles constrain the L1 will also constrain the L2, since the learner will rely on prior knowledge in the development of a new L2 grammar'. Similarly, Carroll (2001: 196) notes that 'learners map L2 stimuli onto L1 categories wherever they can'.

To illustrate how *preprogramming* functions to determine the shape of an interlanguage, in the remaining part of this section we will tale a look at two studies: Schwartz and Sprouse (1996), which examines L1 influence at the early stage of L2 acquisition, and Sorace (1996), which examines L1 influence on the end-state of L2 grammar. Representing two extreme stages of the course of L2 development, both studies, as we will see, are highly revealing about how the L1 can bias L2 acquisition.

The Schwartz and Sprouse (1996) study

In Schwartz and Sprouse (1996: 41–42), the initial state characterized by full transfer is considered partially responsible for the course of interlanguage development:

> The course that L2 development takes is determined in part by the initial state, in part by input, in part by the apparatus of UG and in part by learnability considerations.

> ...
>
> The final states of L2 acquisition do not systematically replicate the final state of L1 acquisition, precisely because the constraints on the processes (i.e., UG and learnability principles) are constant, whereas the initial states are distinct.

In supporting their position, Schwartz and Sprouse refer to their 1994 longitudinal case study of an adult L1-Turkish speaker named Cevdet acquiring L2 German, where they found, among other things, an interesting developmental pattern in regard to finite verb ($V_{[+F]}$) placement in matrix clauses in the informant's interlanguage:[4]

Stage 1
(X)S$V_{[+F]}$O
jetzt er hat Gesicht [das is falsches Wagen]
now he has face that is wrong car
'now he makes a face (that) that is the wrong car'

Stage 2
(a) (X)S$V_{[+F]}$O
in der Turkei der Lehrer kann den Schüler schlagen.
in the Turkey the teacher can the pupil beat
'in Turkey the teacher can hit the pupil'
(b) X$V_{[+F]}S_{[+pron]}$
dann trinken wir bis neun Uhr
then drink we till nine o'clock
'then we will drink until nine o'clock'

Stage 3
(a) (X)S$V_{[+F]}$O
spater der Charlie wollte zum Gefängnishaus
later the Charlie wanted to-the prison
'later Charlie wanted to go to the prison'

(b) X$V_{[+F]}S_{[\pm pron]}$
das hat eine andere Frau gesehen
that has an other woman seen
'another woman saw that'.
(Schwartz & Sprouse, 1996: 43)

Such a developmental pattern is not a direct reflection of the canonical word order in Cevdet's L1, which is OV. Nevertheless, Schwartz and Sprouse (1996) assume, after Vainikka and Young-Scholten (1994), that

Cevdet passed through the stage where he did produce L1-based verb-final clauses. Taking the Stage 1 sentences as manifesting the restructured word order, they reason that, as Cevdet's understanding of the meaning of the input developed, he would find his L1 system insufficient to enable him to assign a representation to the input sentences, and that he would, subsequently, have to restructure his representational system on the basis of the UG-licensed options. In Cevdet's Stage–1 sentences, there appeared to be two notable types of restructuring: (a) that the verb was fronted; and (b) that the subject always preceded the finite verb. To account for these changes, Schwartz and Sprouse (1996) postulate the L1 Turkish grammar, making use of the C position, and of the mechanism for nominative case assignment:

> [I]nput forces the verb to raise (from V to I) to C; the Case Filter requires the subject to move (from [Spec, VP] to [Spec, IP] to [Spec, CP]), since the only mechanism for nominative case assignment in the L1 is Spec-Head agreement. (1996: 46)

Another noteworthy fact is that at Stage 1, Cevdet also produced V3 sentences, i.e., $XSV_{[+F]}O$, which is an indication that he allowed adjunction to CP. In fact, as we will see from his utterance patterns at Stages 2 and 3, he never appeared to relinquish such an option.[5] This use of CP-adjunction, in the speculation of Schwartz and Sprouse, is likely to be a carry-over from the L1-Turkish.

Cevdet's Stage–2 sentences showed not only $(X)SV_{[+F]}O$ pattern of the first stage, but also a new pattern, i.e., $XV_{[+F]}S_{[+pron]}\ldots$, accounting for 32% of all utterances containing a pronominal subject compared to 0% in the first stage. Moreover, the utterances in which the verb preceded a nonpronominal subject were virtually absent (1/120). Schwartz and Sprouse take this to suggest that Cevdet did not have a real V2 grammar, and that Stage 2 was an enhanced intermediate stage in Cevdet's grammar. They further account for the asymmetric $XV_{[+F]}S_{[pron]}$ pattern, after Rizzi and Roberts (1989), in terms of a UG-licensed incorporation mechanism:[6]

> At the second stage, then, pronominal subjects (and only pronominal subjects) can incorporate (from [Spec, AgrP]) into the verb. Nonpronominal subjects are assigned case as before, namely, under Spec-Head agreement inside CP. (1996: 48)

Although the $XV_{[+F]}S_{[+pron]}$ pattern at this stage of Cevdet's interlanguage appeared to match that in German,[7] i.e., the target language, Schwartz and Sprouse point out that 'the analysis this pattern receives is distinct in the two'(1996: 48), thus suggesting the existence of covert deviances, despite the surface identity.

Cevdet's Stage–3 utterances, while further exhibiting the persistence of $(X)SV_{[+F]}O$, showed an extension of $XV_{[+F]}S_{[+pron]}$ to non-pronominal subjects, i.e., $XV_{[+F]}S_{[\pm pron]}$, hence suggesting continued development. For $XV_{[+F]}S_{[-pron]}$, Schwartz and Sprouse posit that by Stage 3, Cevdet had added to his grammar the government option mechanism:

> The verb in C governs IP, and hence the specifier of IP. Thus, it is only at Stage 3 that (nonpronominal) subjects need not move to [Spec,CP] in order to get nominative case. (1996: 48)

Cevdet's retention of $(X)SV_{[+F]}O$ throughout the three stages, on the other hand, is suggestive of the persistent influence of the L1 grammar on his L2 mental representations. Such influence is reinforced, in Schwartz and Sprouse's view, by the learnability problem that 'there seem to be no input data that could force the delearning of adjunction to CP', meaning that 'while all the main-clause data to which Cevdet is exposed will be V2, Cevdet will not hear any utterances indicating that V3 is ungrammatical' (1996: 49). It is predicted that '$XSV_{[+F]}$ . . . is a prime candidate for fossilization . . . In regard to the strict V2 constraint, Cevdet's Interlanguage will never mirror that of the TL, German' (1996: 49).[8]

In sum, Schwartz and Sprouse's study has offered us the compelling insight that when a learnability problem (i.e., when there is no disconfirming positive evidence) coalesces with the initial state effect (i.e., L1 transfer), the UG-licensed options cannot be activated, in which case restructuring will not be possible, and fossilization is likely to develop.[9]

The Sorace (1993) study

While Schwartz and Sprouse focused on the function of the initial state (i.e., full transfer of the final state of L1 acquisition) in L2 acquisition, Sorace (1993) looked into the L2 'end state', that is, L2 ultimate attainment.

Selecting L2 acquisition of unaccusativity[10] as the domain of inquiry, and employing near-native speakers as informants and native speakers of Italian as controls, Sorace examined the mental representations of several properties of unaccusativity in L2 Italian by native speakers of French and of English. In her study, the near-native informants were considered to have reached 'the most advanced stage of second language acquisition' (1993: 23) whose ultimate attainment was characterized by incompleteness or divergence.

'Incompleteness' and 'divergence' were defined as follows:

> The incomplete grammar, lacking a given L2 property *P*, would lead to

random, inconsistent, in short indeterminate judgments about *P*, whereas the divergent grammar, since it incorporates an alternative representation of *P*, would lead to determinate judgments that are consistently different from native judgments. (1993: 24)

The study investigated the following unaccusative properties:

1. *Essere*-selection[11] with five classes of unaccusative verbs in Italian along the Unaccusative Hierarchy:
   1) change of location, e.g.
      a. Maria **è venuta** alla festa da sola.
      Maria came to the party alone.
      b. *Carla **ha venuto** al cinema con noi.
      Carla came to the cinema with us.
   2) Continuation of state, e.g.
      a. Paola **è rimasta** da me fino a tardi.
      Paola stayed at my place until late.
      b. *Maria **ha rimasto** a Roma tutto l'inverno.
      Maria stayed in Rome throughout the winter.
   3) Existence of state, e.g.
      a. I dinosauri **sono esistiti** milioni di anni fa.
      Dinosaus existed a million years ago.
      b. *Gli unicorni non **hanno** mai **esistito**.
      Unicorns never existed.
   4) Transitive alternant, e.g.
      a. I pezzi **sono aumentati** del 20%.
      Prices increased by 20%.
      b. *Le tasse **hanno aumentato** del 10%
      Taxes increased by 10%.
   5) Unergative alternant, e.g.
      a. Paola **è corsa** in farmacia.
      Paola ran to the chemist's.
      b. *Maria **ha corso** a casa dei genitori.
      Maria ran to her parent's house.

2. Obligatory auxiliary change in restructuring constructions with Raising verbs, where the clitic 'climbs' to the main verb, e.g.,
   a. *Alla mia festa, Maria non ci **ha potuto** andare.
   To my party, Maria couldn't go.
   b. A scuola, mia figlia non ci **è potuta** venire.
   To school, my daughter couldn't come.

3. Optional auxiliary change in basic restructuring construc

tions, e.g.

a. Maria non **ha potuto venire** alla mia festa.
Maria couldn't come to my party.

b. Mia figlia non **è potuta venire** a scuola.
My daughter couldn't come to school.

4. Optional auxiliary change in restructuring constructions with Raising verbs, where the clitic remains attached to the embed ded verb, e.g.,

a. Alla mia festa, Maria non **ha potuto andarci**.
To my party, Maria couldn't go.

b. A scuola, mia figlia non **è potuta venirci**.
To school, my daughter couldn't come.

(Sorace, 1993: 34; emphasis added)

Using the Magnitude Estimation Technique,[12] Sorace elicited the informants' judgments of the acceptability of a set of sentences containing the above syntactic and semantic properties of Italian unaccusativity. Figures 5.1,5. 2, 5.3 and 5.4, reproduced from Sorace (1993), illustrate the performance of each group of informants.

Sorace summarized the results as follows:

1. The intuitions of near-native speakers are on the whole different from native Italian intuitions;
2. Both French and English near-natives are sensitive to the semantic categories along the Unaccusative Hierarchy;
3. The judgments of the two groups of near-natives are clearly different with respect to the syntax of restructuring: while the French subjects have determinate (though not always native-like) intu-

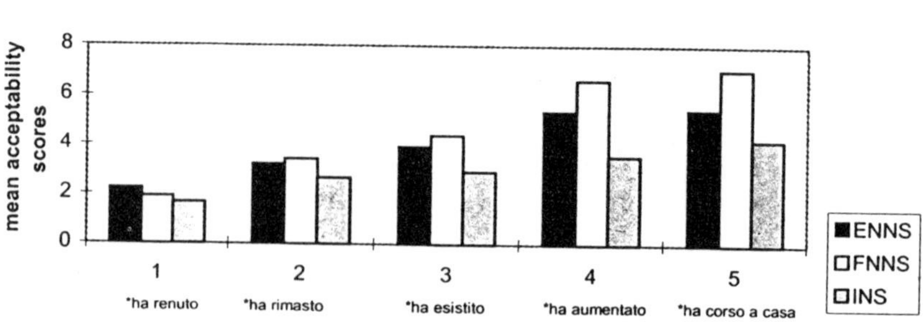

Figure 5.1 *Avere* with unaccusative verbs: native and near-native judgments
Notes: INS = Italian native speakers; FNNS = French near-native speakers; ENNS = English near-native speakers.

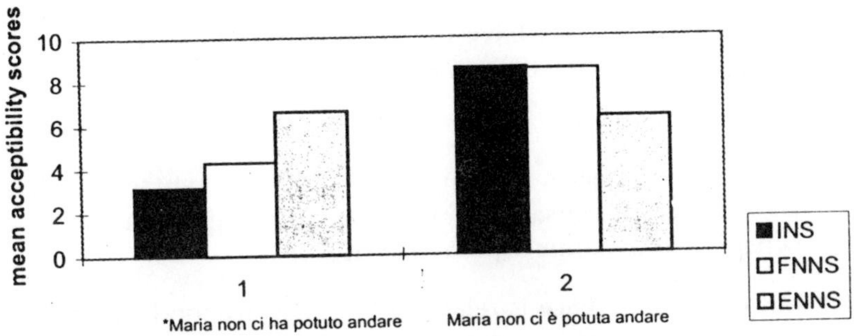

Figure 5.2 Obligatory auxiliary change under clitic-climbing

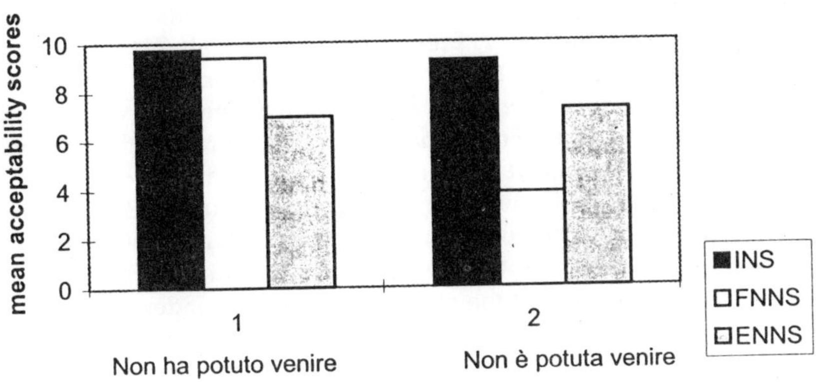

Figure 5.3 Optional auxiliary change under restructuring/basic

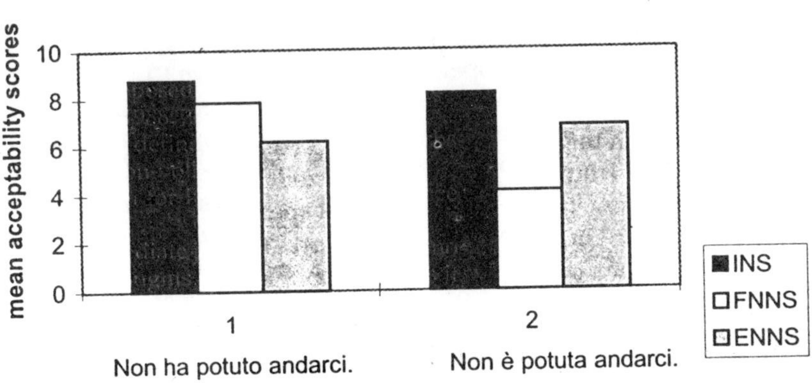

Figure 5.4 Optional auxiliary change under restructuring/no clitic-climbing

itions about the syntactic phenomena related to restructuring, the English subjects have indeterminate intuitions about the whole range of them. (1993: 37)

In brief:

> The French subjects are sensitive to both the syntactic and semantic aspects of unaccusativity, whereas the English subjects are only sensitive to semantic aspects. (1993: 37.)

Crucially, this difference is relatable to the corresponding features in the respective L1s. As Sorace notes:

> 1. French has a system of auxiliary selection that is in parametric variation with the Italian system. Its class of unaccusative verbs coincides with the Italian class and exhibits similar syntactic behavior. However, French requires *être* almost exclusively for verbs belonging to the two core categories at the top of the Unaccusative Hierarchy, and *avoir* for all the other verbs that select *essere* in Italian. French has clitics, but no restructuring constructions, although it used to have them at a previous stage of its historical evolution. One can therefore argue that French presents partial instantiation of the properties under investigation.
> 2. English has a semantic class of unaccusative verbs but does not instantiate any of the syntactic properties under investigation. It has no system of auxiliary selection and no clitics. One can therefore say that English shows virtually no instantiation of the properties in question. (1993: 35)

However, the influence of L1, Sorace maintains, acted on L2 learning in an indirect rather than a direct way; what was transferred into the interlanguage by the French-speaking and English-speaking informants was not so much the specific properties of their respective L1 unaccusatives as the overall representations of unaccusativity in each language. This is further argued on the grounds that if direct transfer had occurred, the L1-French speakers would have overgeneralized *avere* to the construction of clitic climbing as well, and the L1-English speakers would have adopted *avere* in all three constructions in question. To what, then, should the ultimate difference between the L1-French speakers and the L1-English speakers be attributed? According to Sorace (see also Gass, Sorace, & Selinker, 1999), the difference can be explained by the overall typological similarity between French and Italian and the lack thereof between English and Italian. Due, particularly, to the fact that unaccusativity in French, as in Italian, is a syntactic (rather than semantic) phenomenon, but not so in

English, it was, on the whole, easier for the L1-French speakers than for the L1-English speakers to acquire Italian unaccusativity.

For our purposes, it is important to note that the fact that in their ultimate attainment, even the near-natives displayed features that were consistent with features of their L1 but deviant from the target language points not only to the permanence, but also to the nature, of L1 influence. L1 preprograms L2 learners such that it determines the selectivity of their perception and assimilation of the L2 input. As Sorace (1993) aptly notes:

> The use they have made of evidence in the input to modify their interlanguage grammar has been selective, despite the ample availability of positive evidence . . . the relevance and the salience of positive evidence may be a matter of degree and . . . other things being equal, some learners may be in a more favorable position to *notice* the relevance of the L2 input and to incorporate it in their developing grammar
>
> . . .
>
> The propensity of certain learners to notice, or fail to notice, the occurrence of a given property *P* in the L2 input appears to be related to the status of the learner's native language with respect to that property . . . Depending on the crosslinguistic characteristics of such a subsystem and on its degree of typological consistency with the L2, a given L1 may represent a more or less favorable starting point for the acquisition of *P*. (1993:. 43–44; emphasis in original)

From this line of reasoning, we can infer that the L1-driven propensity will ultimately lead to incomplete L2 attainment. Given the sizable collection of evidence – similar in nature to the findings discussed above – now available in the SLA literature, we can safely argue that knowledge of an L1 is in and of itself a potent source of fossilization in adult L2 learning, and hence a source of the observed general lack of success across the L2 learning community.

Summary

In this chapter, we discussed several important notions pertaining to L1 influence on adult L2 learning, including the L1 function of delaying L2 learning, the 'transfer to somewhere' (Andersen, 1983) and the 'transfer to nowhere' (Kellerman, 1995a) principles, transfer of 'thinking for speaking', and L1 preprogramming, all of which shed crucial light on the general failure witnessed across adult L2 learners. As Schachter (1990, 1996) has pointed out, what knowledge of an L1 does to L2 learning is that it places cognitive constraints on the learners' perception of, and sensitivity to, L2 input, the outcome of which can only be an incomplete mastery of the target language. L1 transfer, along with the CP effects discussed in the preceding chapter, seems to offer a sufficient explanation for the general lack of success in adult L2 learning: Together, they impose bio-cognitive constraints on L2 learning which, pervasively as well as profoundly, curtail the ability to fully attain target-like competence.

Notes

1. For our purposes, we are only looking at the interference aspect of transfer, which should not be taken as suggesting that an L1 has no facilitative role to play in L2 learning. In fact, as Bialystok and Miller have suggested, depending on the similarity and difference between the L1 and the L2, the L2 ultimate outcome may partially converge to the target language and partially diverge from it.
2. The structure is often considered by L2 instructors to be a malformed passive, hence 'pseudo-passive', as its intended meaning is taken to be that of an English passive. For example, '*New cars must keep inside*' is interpreted as meaning '*New cars should be kept indoors*' (Yip, 1995).
3. This is different from saying that the L1 can determine the developmental sequence for a particular learner's interlanguage.
4. The L1, Turkish, is verb-final, and the target language, German, has SOV as an 'underlying order', but with the overlay of the V2 phenomenon in matrix clauses.
5. Sprouse (personal communication, 1997) comments: 'Cevdet never relinquishes optional adjunction to CP (there is nothing in the input that shows him that he needs to) and thus he never acquires a fully German-like grammar – as far as we can tell from the corpus'.
6. Rizzi and Roberts (1989) invoked the incorporation mechanism to explain a similar asymmetric pattern in French.
7. In German, both pronominal and nonpronominal subject can be postverbal.
8. Schwartz and Sprouse's prediction is made on the basis of the assumption that 'negative data cannot ever effect the restructuring of grammar'(p. 49).
9. Hale (1988), in commenting on the use of 'small pro' by an Italian linguist in his L2 English, noted: 'Examples of this sort suggest that certain L1 parameter settings may be extremely difficult to eradicate from an acquired L2, at least at the level of integrated linguistic competence (as opposed to conscious intellectual understanding of surface grammatical facts)' (1988: 201)
10. This covers unaccusative verbs which, loosely defined, are intransitive verbs that indicate change of location or state with non-volitional control.
11. For an accessible account of auxiliary selection for Italian unaccusatives, see Sorace (1993).
12. This is a timed procedure which requires immediate judgments and leaves no time for metalinguistic reflection or second thoughts. The technique 'makes it possible to measure variability in acceptability judgment directly, which has the advantage of producing interval scales that can then be properly analyzed by parametric statistics' (Sorace, 1993: 36).

Chapter 6

A Microscopic Analysis: Some Empirical Evidence

In the previous two chapters, I explored two major constraints (i.e., biological and cognitive) on adult L2 learning, in attempts to account for the general lack of success. I made the point that the bio-cognitive constraints control the ability to acquire an L2 and subsequently the ultimate degree of success. What also seemed clear from that discussion, however, was that these constraints were limited in their capacity to explain inter-learner and intra-learner differential failure.

This chapter is therefore purported to examine the latter through a microscopic analysis of failure. A major argument to be advanced is that within the general confine of bio-cognitive constraints, other factors – social, cognitive, environmental and psychological – may operate, independently or in tandem, leading to differential failure at both an inter-learner and an intra-learner level. First, by putting under scrutiny a number of empirical studies, I will (1) show evidence of local fossilization, (2) evaluate the major methodological approaches to researching fossilization; and (3) highlight the modular nature of fossilization. Then, I will present and discuss some linguistic structures that have been generally considered prone to fossilization. Finally, I will discuss the Multiple Effects Principle (MEP; Selinker & Lakshmanan, 1992) as a potential explanation for inter- and intra-learner differential failure.

Some Empirical Studies

Over the years, researchers who attempted empirical investigations of fossilization have generally adopted either of the two perspectives: a *product perspective* or a *process perspective*. In the product perspective, fossilization has been assumed, and the informants labeled, from the outset, 'fossilized', with the subsequent research effort being to confirm fossilization in such learners. Usually this is done through a 'defossilization attempt': if the attempt is unsuccessful, it is thought to provide evidence that the informants are indeed fossilized. A *process perspective*, on the other hand, usually relies on a longitudinal, or sometimes, pseudo-longitudinal, study for establishing what is fossilizable.

On the whole, researchers have looked to *persistence* and *resistance* as major indicators of fossilization, even though there is yet a lack of agreement on what *persistent* and *resistant* actually mean. They, consequently, set out to look for different phenomena. Some have sought stabilized deviant interlanguage forms, others have looked for typical errors across learners with the same L1, and still others have collected the remaining errors in the interlanguage of the advanced learners in the belief that what remained should be the most persistent and are therefore the most likely candidates for fossilization.

Empirical studies to date have typically adopted one, or a combination of more than one, of the following methodological approaches: (1) longitudinal; (2) typical-error; (3) advanced-learner; (4) corrective-feedback; and (5) length-of-residence (LOR). In the remaining part of this section, we take a look at each of them in turn.

The longitudinal approach

To illustrate this approach, two studies are reviewed here: one conducted about 25 years ago by Schumann (1978a), offering the first documented case of fossilization,[1] and the other performed more recently by Lardiere (1998a). Differences in their theoretical orientation notwithstanding, in terms of methodology, the two studies have much in common in that both are longitudinal, and that both invoke a quantitative measure for showing the persistence of the interlanguage structures studied.

Schumann (1978a) reported on a 10-month longitudinal study of an adult native speaker of Costa Rican Spanish named Alberto. Alberto was 33 years old at the time of the study and had stayed in the U.S. for four months. Before he came to the U.S., he had had six years, two to three hours a week, of instructed learning of English. At the beginning of the study, 'he could speak only a few words and phrases in English' (1978a: 6). His use of English in the U.S. was limited to work and shopping.

The data studied comprised 20 tapes of recordings of spontaneous conversations between Alberto and the researcher, as well as supplementary data elicited through conversations and experiments. The linguistic focus of the data analysis included the English auxiliary and its related structures, the negative, and the interrogative. Throughout the 10-month period, Alberto was said to have shown little development in these areas. Regarding Alberto's acquisition of the negative, for instance, Schumann reported:

> During the ten month period of our research Alberto either never learned to place the negative after the auxiliary or he resisted doing so. Instead, he consistently placed the negator before the verb and did not move it behind the first auxiliary element as required in English. (1978a: 21)

In Schumann's study of Alberto, lack of development is shown by comparing, statistically (in the form of percentages and frequencies), his development during the 10 months with that of five other informants. For instance, in examining Alberto's acquisition of yes/no question inversion, the frequency of his target-like production in obligatory contexts was compared to that of the other five informants:

Alberto	5%	(11/213)
Cheo	19%	(31/161)
Jorge	37%	(74/202)
Marta	43%	(99/227)
Dolores	55%	(195/352)
Juan	56%	(108/192)
		(1978a: 29)

Note that for Schumann, lack of development meant not only stabilization but also less development in a comparative sense:

> When Alberto was compared with the other five subjects in terms of negative, interrogative and auxiliary development, he was found to have considerably less growth in these structures than the other subjects. (1978a: 113)

In order to account for Alberto's persistent lack of development, Schumann explored several factors, and he eventually isolated social and psychological distance as the prime cause (see Chapter 3, p. 00).

While Schumann's longitudinal study spanned 10 months, Lardiere's study had a far longer time span which enabled her to compare the informant's performance at different points over time with significant intervals in between.

Lardiere (1998a) reported on an eight-year longitudinal case study of an adult L2 learner of English. Her informant, Patty, whose L1 was Hokkien and Mandarin Chinese, had lived in the U.S. for 18 years prior to the study. Out of these 18 years, she was totally immersed in the English-speaking environment for 10 years. Data came from three audio-recorded conversations[2] with Patty. The first and second recordings were eight years apart; and the second and third recordings were two months apart.

One of Lardiere's primary motives for the study was to question a methodological overreliance, following the Weak Continuity approach,[3] on the criterial production rates of inflectional morphology as 'evidence' for positing underlying syntactic representations in the interlanguage grammar. For this purpose, she examined the informant's pronominal case marking and past tense inflectional morphology across the three recordings. A quantitative analysis of the informant's past tense marking in finite obligatory contexts showed that Patty had 'remained unchanged over the eight years, despite massive exposure to target-language input by native speakers in a virtually exclusively target-language environment' (1998a: 17). In contrast, her mastery of pronominal marking was perfect, as evident from a quantitative analysis of the nominative forms that she used as subjects of finite clauses.

In sum, both aspects of Patty's IL grammar reached a steady state, with one successfully meeting the target and the other falling short of it. Lardiere's explanation for the differential success was as follows: 'Case marking on pronouns in English is simple and invariant, allowing for a direct mapping as a function of "finiteness"', whereas tense marking in English is not, because 'the choice of how and where to spell out verbal inflection (e.g. 'affix-hopping') interacts in a somewhat complicated way with modality, (im)perfectivity and negation' (1998a: 23).

It is worth mentioning that based upon her further analyses of the same database, Lardiere (1998b, 2000) subsequently argued for a dissociation between the development of inflectional affixation and syntactic knowledge of formal features, and that L2 learners' syntactic knowledge may outpace their production of overt verbal morphology. Under this view, Patty's fossilized marking of past tense is attributable to a computational capacity problem rather than a deficiency in syntactic knowledge. That is, Patty had a correct understanding of past-tense marking yet was unable to produce them correctly under some conditions of real time language use (see, however, Hawkins [2000] for a different argument).

The typical-error approach

In the fossilization literature, we also find studies using a typical-error analysis approach whereby errors that are characteristic of learners with the same L1 background are studied, usually across different proficiency levels. Kellerman (1989) is a case in point.

The major concern of Kellerman (1989) is the linguistic features that give rise to the syntactic accent of Dutch-English interlanguage. Two assumptions appear to have underlain the study. First, errors that typify a whole community of L2 learners with homogeneous L1 background are the strongest candidates for fossilization; second, errors that are not only common to that community but also stay with its most advanced members are indicative of fossilization.

Kellerman based his argument, among other things, on an empirical study conducted by Wekker *et al.* (1982) of a typical error in Dutch English that involves using 'would' in the protasis of hypothetical conditionals:

> [6–1] If I *would* be able to live all over again, I *would* be a gardener. (1982: 110)

Wekker *et al.*'s study investigated the performance of Dutch learners of English on non-past and past hypothetical conditional sentences in Dutch and English under experimental conditions. Informants were first, second, and third year university students and were considered advanced. The study was pseudo-longitudinal in that learners clearly at different proficiency levels were used as informants to provide a diachronic view of the interlanguage structure under scrutiny. Results obtained through an analytic procedure called *shift analysis*[4] indicated that all groups of informants had had at least some tendency to select +/+[5] as the English target, irrespective of their choice in Dutch' and that 'even third year students do not behave like native speakers' (1982: 100). The fact that even the most advanced learners persisted in the typical error was, for Kellerman, evidence of the tendency to fossilize.[6]

Kellerman (1989) made an attempt to explain the fossilized structure. Looking into the relevant evidence in world languages as well as in first language acquisition, he concluded that the fossilized structure was a function of the intersection of multiple tendencies: (1) avoidance of directly transferring the modal meaning of Dutch past tenses to English past tenses; (2) avoidance of structural ambiguity; and (3) creation of a structural symmetry. Of note is that these tendencies interacted with the native language:

> The Dutch structure as perceived by the learner provides the environment in which these tendencies become apparent. (1989: 111)

Although both +/+ and –/+ are permissible in Dutch, the learners chose to transfer the default structure, +/+ into their interlanguage. Native language influence was said to have taken a subtle form here: instead of transferring what they perceived as the marked model meanings of the Dutch past tenses (i.e. –/+) to their formal English equivalents, the learners opted to reallocate the model meaning to the explicitly hypothetical morpheme *would*, which is the equivalent of Dutch *zouden*. The role of the native language was thus to 'constrain the form that the developing interlanguage may take rather than to provide a structure for copying over into the L2' (1989: 102).

In Kellerman's study, the cross-linguistic influence was considered psycho-typological. This influence, however, as we will see in Schouten (1996), can also be functional.

Schouten's (1996) study, another attempt at understanding causes of the typical error, was motivated by the following two research questions:

> 1) Why is it exactly that this error is so persistent while other aspects of grammar are acquired much more easily?
> 2) To what extent does the mother tongue influence the fossilization process and to what extent do general principles like markedness and semantic disambiguation play a role? (p. 223)

The study gained a crucial insight from examining a Dutch corpus of 1000 hypothetical conditionals, namely that in Dutch, although both +/+ and −/+ are permissible, one form is often highly preferred over the other, depending on factors like time frame (future/present/past), clause order, and nature of the verb (strong/weak).

In order to find out whether the L1 use of +/+ and −/+ had a corresponding effect on the Dutch-English interlanguage, Schouten administered a written test to Dutch learners of English. The test had a similar design to the two experiments reported in Kellerman (1989), and was administered, first in Dutch and two weeks later in English, to advanced Dutch learners of English at three levels of proficiency: secondary school students, and 1st year and 3rd year university students of English. The following results were obtained:

> The distribution of the different forms in Dutch was to a large extent mirrored in English; i.e. where in Dutch the *would* equivalent was used, the number of *if... would* errors increased in English, and where a past tense in the if-clause was favored in Dutch, fewer mistakes were made in English. Apparently cross-linguistic influence does play a role here and the fossilization of *if... would* seems to be limited only to a sub-set of conditional types. (1996: 223)

Note that like Kellerman (1989), Schouten also constructed a pseudo-longitudinal perspective in his study for obtaining evidence of fossilization.

The advanced-learner approach

Similar to the pseudo-longitudinal approach that uses advanced learners as the major source of information on fossilization, the advanced-learner approach, as the name suggests, studies very advanced learners, usually, the so-called 'near-native speakers'. The underlying assumption is that 'the differences from native speakers are presumably limited, and therefore easier to study' and that 'the few deviances from the native norm that do exist should be more certain candidates for inclusion in the category of fossilization' (Hyltenstam, 1988: 70).

The Hyltenstam (1988) study was, in fact, the first in the literature that dealt with lexical fossilization, and it addressed two questions: (1) Are there any differences between near-native and native speakers in the variation, density and specificity of their lexicon in literacy-related language use? (2) Are the near-native speakers different from the native speakers in the quality and quantity of lexical units that deviate from the native norm? Thirty-six students at the Swedish *gymnasieskola* (senior high school level) served as informants. Among them, 24 speakers were bilingual: 12 in Finnish and Swedish and 12 in Spanish and Swedish; then there were 12 monolingual Swedish speakers who served as controls. The 24 bilinguals were considered to be near-natives on the grounds that they could pass as native speakers of Swedish in everyday conversation; that they used their first language on a daily basis; and that they represented the whole range of grade levels.

Oral and written data were collected for both languages from each bilingual informant, and were subjected to quantitative and qualitative analyses. Specifically, such quantitative measures as *lexical density*, *lexical variation*, and *lexical sophistication* were used to estimate the lexical characteristics of the three groups, and the qualitative measure of *lexical error analysis* was used to analyze two main error types: *approximations* to a target lexical unit, and *contaminations* of two or more such units. The results showed insignificant differences between the three groups in the density, variation and specificity of their lexicon – 'the vocabulary, as it is used in the literate tasks in this investigation, seems to be as large, as varied and as sophisticated in the bilingual groups as in the monolingual group' (1988: 79). However, significant differences were found between the bilingual informants and the monolingual informants in terms of the frequency of errors and the distribution of error types. Hyltenstam thereby concluded that the results had some bearing on fossilization. In his view, the informants who were near-natives were in an 'end state' (Klein, 1986), and the lexical deviances that remained in their interlanguage must have fossilized. Yet he also conceded that the credibility of his claim was limited, urging that longitudinal studies of near-natives be conducted 'to see whether fossilization features really are fossilized, or if they disappear with time, although at a very slow rate' (1988: 82).

Driven by a similar conviction, namely that advanced learners' interlanguage provides the best index of fossilization, Lennon (1991) studied errors in advanced interlanguage, but unlike Hyltenstam's, his study had a six-month duration and focused on one advanced learner who was having her first exposure to the L2 community. Lennon claimed that a study of one learner could lead to an in-depth knowledge of the interlanguage system, and stressed that it was necessary to conduct longitudinal studies to establish 'under what circumstances fossilization may set in' (1991: 131).

Set against the background of the paradoxical issues of 'transitional competence' and 'error fossilization', the study sought to address two questions:

(1) To what extent were errors eliminated?
(2) To what extent might there be evidence for the onset of fossilization?

The informant for the study was a 24-year-old German learner of English named Andrea. The study was conducted at the time when Andrea came to the University of Reading in England to do postgraduate study. Data consisted of 15 unstructured interviews between the researcher and the informant, and the analysis centered around the following five areas where 'Andrea appeared to make systematic and regular errors' (1991: 133):

1. adverb order with reference to 'only' and 'already'
2. 'there is/there are'
3. 'have got'
4. use and overuse of 'always'
5. future time forms (1991: 129)

The data analysis showed that, on the one hand, 'in the cases of 2), 3), and 4), the informant's interlanguage is dynamic and moving towards native speaker norms,'[7] but that data in the area of 5), on the other hand, offered very strong evidence that 'some sort of fossilization may be operating' (1991: 142). It is interesting to note the kinds of behavior that Lennon registered as indicative of fossilization:

> In the data there is no evidence over the period studied that Andrea has improved in her erroneous use of simple present forms for future meaning and her consequent non-use of other forms, especially continuous forms. There is some evidence of fossilization of error here, particularly as she seems to regard the simple present as a free alternative to correct forms and to be insensitive to interlocutor input. There is no evidence of hypothesis testing or grammar modification on her part. Simple present as a frequent future form seems to have become part of her competence, no doubt influenced by the grammar of her L1. (1991: 145)

Lennon thus identified several indicators of fossilization in Andrea's interlanguage, including no improvement over time, insensitivity to input, and no grammar modification. What is also worth noting is that the study provides evidence for progress and halt of progress co-occurring in the same interlanguage, thereby displaying intra-learner differential success/failure.

The corrective-feedback approach

A question that appears to confront any fossilization study is: How can one establish that for a given learner, fossilization is a permanent condition and not merely a temporary cessation of learning? Selinker and Lamendella (1979: 373) suggest that 'the conclusion that a particular learner had indeed fossilized could be drawn only if the cessation of further IL learning persisted in spite of the learner's ability, opportunity, and motivation to learn the target language and acculturate into the target society'. Following this proposition, any studies of fossilization ought to find ways to grapple with two issues: first, to demonstrate that a certain interlanguage structure has ceased to develop; and second, to find out whether or not cessation of progress has occurred despite the learner being in both an internally and externally favorable position to learn.

To tackle the first issue, in addition to the approaches described above, researchers have also resorted to the L2 learner's reaction to corrective feedback as a means of determining whether or not learning has ceased to develop. In Kellerman (1989), for example, it was not only a typical error in Dutch-English interlanguage community but also an error which seemed to have been immune to the pedagogic intervention that was made the linguistic focus for investigating fossilization (see also Schouten, 1996).

To investigate the second issue, researchers often choose to study learners who have lived in the target language environment for some time. Their premise is that the length of residence is correlated with the amount of exposure to the target language, hence a good indicator of the learning environment. Five years of residence in a country where the TL is spoken is therefore equated with five years of exposure to the TL, and has in actuality been widely adopted as an index of L2 ultimate attainment (see, e.g., Johnson & Newport, 1989; Johnson *et al.*, 1996; Patkowski, 1980; Selinker, 1985). According to Patkowski (1980: 451), five years is a way to ensure that 'participants had had ample time to acquire their second language'.

In her investigation of fossilization, Thep-Ackrapong (1990), using a combination of corrective feedback and length of residence, studied an ethnic Chinese Vietnamese refugee student at an American university for a year and a half. The informant, named Lin, was assumed to be fossilized from the outset based on the observation that 'she made many errors in all aspects of language performance though she had been studying and exposed to English in the United States for over six years' (1990: 109). Focusing on the infinitival complements and the related structures, which Lin was reported to consistently have trouble with, Thep-Ackrapong tutored her for one semester by means of providing explicit rule explanation and corrective feedback, and subsequently observed if any progress was made on Lin's part. Data collected at three times over a year and a half (i.e., before and after the tutoring session and a year afterwards) indicated that the tutoring had had little effect on Lin's use of the linguistic structures. In other words, her errors persisted despite the pedagogic intervention. For the researcher, this result confirmed that Lin was a fossilized learner, and the lack of progress was in turn attributed to her lack of ability to analyze and synthesize linguistic elements.

While Thep-Ackrapong (1990) used a combination of LOR and corrective feedback in diagnosing fossilization, Mukattash (1986) examined solely the effect of corrective feedback on typical errors in Arabic-English interlanguage. Eighty fourth-year English majors in the Department of English Language and Literature at the University of Jordan served as informants. The study took place at a time when they were taking a course of contrastive analysis, during which

> they were made aware of the major grammatical error-types which characterized the interlanguage of Jordanian / Arab learners, as well as of their possible causes. Furthermore, they were trained to describe and justify grammatical errors produced by less proficient E.F.L. Jordanian learners. (1986: 187)

The data came from the two written assignments the informants completed respectively in Weeks 10 and 16. Major errors from the first piece of written work were then compared with those in the second. It was noticed that a great number of errors had persisted. These errors were said to have been discussed in some detail in the classroom before the informants handed in their second piece of written work. The errors included conflation of simple past tense with the simple present, the conflation of aspect such as using the non-perfective instead of the perfective, Be-deletion, and using active instead of passive voice. An example of each, reproduced from Mukattash (1986), is given below:

[6–2] CA *failed* to give us a comprehensive comparing between L1 and L2.
[6–3] CA *did not prove* until now that it is workable and adequate.
[6–4] Linguists found that not all the differences between the languages e^8 necessary to result difficulty.
[6–5] If the learner *exposed* to L, he will learn it.

All these errors were, according to Mukattash, directly or indirectly ascribable to the influence of L1 Arabic. Furthermore, they were fossilizable because of their high frequency of occurrence.

Despite the short duration of the study, the data collected at two different points in time over a period of 16 weeks nevertheless allowed Mukattash to draw some conclusion on the persistence and resistance of the L1 influenced errors and on the effect of corrective feedback: 'There is not much value in explicit and systematic error correction in the case of advanced adult foreign-language learners' (1986: 201).

The length-of-residence approach

In some empirical studies LOR is employed as a singular criterion for determining fossilization, and as such, fossilization is assumed as opposed to established through longitudinal tracking of progress. An example can be found in Washburn (1991: v), the focus of which was 'to identify some characteristics of linguistic behavior that distinguishes fossilized nonnative speakers from those who are still learning'.

Using primarily 'five years' as the cut-off point,[9] Washburn divided her 18 informants, who were undergraduates at a large public university in the U.S., into two groups which she respectively labeled 'fossilized' and 'nonfossilized'. Within a Vygotskian theoretical framework, she devised a number of tasks, including grammaticality judgments, imitations, short-term learning, and picture narration, all of which were purported to be linguistically and cognitively challenging. Data, comprising recordings of structured interviews between the researcher and the informants, and the informants' oral performance on the tasks, were collected to test several hypotheses, an example of which is that 'On the short term learning task, the nonfossilized subjects will learn (become able to learn) to produce the task utterance more accurately and efficiently than the fossilized subjects, as measured by the number of turns needed and the maintenance of accuracy of form' (1991: 78). Subsequent data analyses showed that some of the hypotheses were indeed supported but some were not. In regard to the hypothesis just mentioned, for example, it was strongly supported. It is important to note, however, that because fossilization was assumed in Washburn's study, any evidence that ran counter to her hypotheses would not shake her belief that the fossilized group were indeed fossilized, and the lack of support from the data was instead attributed to difficulty in accessing the required cognitive processes.

Critique of the Methodologies

As is clear from the preceding review, over the years researchers have attempted various means when determining fossilization. Kellerman (1989), for instance, viewed a typical error as an indicator of fossilization, and, to demonstrate that this was so, he invoked pseudo-longitudinal evidence. While a typical error does indeed show the pervasiveness of an interlanguage structure within a particular interlanguage learning community, this way of demonstrating fossilization has a drawback as far as the use of pseudo-longitudinal evidence is concerned. Being cross-sectional, the pseudo-longitudinal evidence can only produce a general picture, not a specific one, of what is going on in each individual's interlanguage. It therefore either reduces the credibility of the typical error as an indicator of fossilization in every L2 learner's interlanguage, or falsely implies that the typical error would fossilize in every learner within the same interlanguage community. As long as L2 learners can be found in that community whose interlanguage shows no sign of the typical error, it would significantly weaken the researcher's general claim that the error is fossilizable. Fossilization, in the view of many (Nakuma, 1998; Selinker, 1992), is an idiosyncratic process. In a nutshell, the use of pseudo-longitudinal evidence seemed effective in revealing the genesis of the interlanguage construction, but weak in revealing individuality.

Some researchers (e.g., Hyltenstam, 1988) turned to advanced learners or near-native-speakers for evidence of fossilization. Their rationale was that whatever remained in the interlanguage of this group had been subject to long-term stabilization and changed the least (see also Selinker & Lakshmanan, 1992). This kind of reasoning, however, leaves itself open to two sorts of questions: (1) If these advanced learners have succeeded in moving so close to the target language, why is it not possible for them to move even closer? (2) In the absence of any longitudinal evidence, how sure are we that the deviant features are products of long-term stabilization rather than of recent restructuring?

Other researchers used corrective feedback as a diagnostic of fossilization (e.g. Thep-Ackrapong, 1990; see also Lin, 1995; Lin & Hedgcock, 1996). Implicit in these studies was the assumption that corrective feedback is a uni-dimensional, rather than a multi-dimensional process. Consequently, it was always the learner's performance following the corrective feedback, not the corrective feedback itself, that was put under scrutiny. This can be problematic because in the feedback process, a number of factors such as the explicitness, the timing and the learner's interpretation may interact to determine its effect (for recent studies of learners' response to corrective feedback, see Han, 2001b; Mackey *et al.*, 1995). Thus, if L2 learners do not respond to corrective feedback in the way the teacher/researcher desires, it is possible that the feedback provided is flawed.

Another criterion researchers have often resorted to for identifying 'fossilized learners' is length of residence (e.g., Thep-Ackrapong, 1990; Washburn, 1991). In this connection, it is also worth noting that recent SLA research has seen increased use of LOR in conjunction with age of arrival

(AOA) to index L2 ultimate attainment and age effects in SLA (for a recent collection of studies, see Birdsong, 1999). Both LOR and AOA[10] have a limited scope of application, however, as they confine research to informants who reside in the target-language environment. Moreover, research based on LOR raises a fundamental question: In the absence of longitudinal evidence, how can we be sure that an interlanguage form has stabilized? LOR presupposes the knowledge of the time it generally takes for acquiring an L2, and we know for sure that this knowledge does not yet exist with regard to L2 acquisition. Klein (1993: 115) has suggested that 'duration of stay is an uninteresting variable,' and that 'what matters is the intensity, not the length of interaction'.

Given, as indicated above, that none of the metrics developed so far can function independently as a reliable guide for locating evidence of fossilization, it seems necessary that a combination of several metrics be used to jointly identify fossilization. Moreover, it is important that any empirical research be preceded by a careful consideration of a variety of factors, some of which have been discussed or touched upon above, and others of which have yet to be explored. Furthermore, longitudinal studies are necessary to establishing long-term stabilization (cf. Selinker & Han, 2001; for recent attempts, see Han, 1998; Lardiere, 1998a,b, 2000; Long, 2003). As Larsen-Freeman (1997: 159) aptly puts it, 'we need a camcorder, not a camera to do our research'. In addition, following Long's (2003) suggestion, analyses of longitudinal data should be conducted at the level of types as well as of tokens so as not to 'miss changes in form-function relationships over time, zig-zag developmental curves, and U-shaped behavior' (p. 499).

Two recent longitudinal studies

Several ongoing studies along the above line of thinking are underway. Here I will mention two: Han (1998) and Long (2003). Han (1998) performed a two-year longitudinal study of two adult Chinese advanced users of L2 English. The informants were selected on the basis of a consideration of their length of residence in the target language environment, level of proficiency, motivation and the contexts in which they used the L2. Data comprised their written output from three contexts: (1) the writing of academic papers; (2) the writing of formal letters; and (3) the writing of informal letters. The study set off with two main premises: first, long-term stabilization is potentially a prelude to fossilization; and second, stabilized interlanguage features may display one of the three types of behaviors, namely, *invariant appearance, backsliding,* and *stabilized variation*. The following research questions were addressed: (1) Is L1 influence a primary factor leading to long-term stabilization? (2) Can long-term stabilization arise independently of L1 influence?

To investigate these, Han targeted three interlanguage structures, all of which may arguably come under the interlanguage subsystem of passivization: (1) pseudo-passives, a well-documented, typical structure in Chinese-English interlanguage (e.g., *The letter has received*); (2) passivization of unaccusative (e.g., *The cough was disappeared.*), which has been alluded to by L2 research to be a universal interlanguage tendency (see, e.g., Balcom, 1997; Hirakawa, 1995, 2001; Montrul, 2001; Oshita, 1997, 2001; Yip, 1995); and (3) a subset of target-like passives (e.g., *Your email message was received*), which occurred frequently in the interlanguage in question.

Qualitative as well as quantitative analyses of the longitudinal data – importantly focusing both on types and tokens– yielded the finding that L1 influence is a prime factor leading to long-term stabilization, but that independently of such influence, long-term stabilization may also arise from the complexity of the target language. More specifically, the stabilization of the pseudo-passives was ascribable to the informants' NL influence; the pseudo-passives were found to be a direct reflex of the NL topic-comment structure and discourse function. The subset of target-like passives, which proved to embody a more syntacticized form of the pseudo-passive, were driven by a similar influence from the NL (for a detailed analysis, see Han, 2000). The passivized unaccusatives, however, resulted from the informants' over-application – misled by the overt similarities between passives and unaccusatives (Zobl, 1989) – of the English passive rules and at the same time lack of acquisition of some narrow-range rules governing unaccusatives (Balcom, 1997). In the latter case, the stabilization was underlain by the complexity of the target language feature. In all three cases, it is important to note, the interlanguage forms appeared to have been impermeable to continuous exposure to relevant TL positive evidence.

In addition, the three types of interlanguage structures showed, over a period of two years, different kinds of behaviors that, in Selinker and Han's (2001) conjecture, can be associated with fossilization:

> Over a period of two years, in the interlanguage of both G & F, the pseudo-passive underwent *backsliding*, though not frequently, contingent on circumstances favoring the production of L1-motivated discourse. The subset of target-like passives, on the other hand . . . *appeared consistently*, as was to be expected. In contrast, passivized unaccusatives (+T) *appeared in variation with* non-passivized ones. (Han, 1998: 169; emphasis added)

Moreover, with data coming from different contexts, evidence was made available of the contextual influence (or lack thereof) on the stabilization of the three interlanguage features: the pseudo-passives appeared mostly in the informal writing context; the subset of target-like passives appeared across all three contexts; and the passivized unaccusatives also appeared across the contexts.

Findings from this study, however, can only be considered tentative if any conclusion concerning fossilization is to be drawn. A major vulnerability exists in the informant selection: both informants had resided in the target language environment for only two years when the study began. This could be a problem since one may argue that not enough time was allowed for them to acquire the target structures. In tandem with it, it is also worth mentioning, is the length of time the informants were followed; two years, in the eyes of many researchers, may not be long enough to establish stabilization. Indeed, one thorny issue always confronting research on fossilization is: What counts as sufficient duration of a longitudinal study? This issue will be the focus of discussion later in the chapter.

Of note, the two flaws identified with Han's study were both overcome in Long's (2003) study. Long undertook a by now 16-year-long case study of a Japanese woman named Ayako who immigrated to Hawaii at the age of 22 and had lived there for 37 years by the time of the first data collection. Ayako was reported to be highly acculturated, both socially and psychologically. Data comprising Ayako's oral output on six tasks[11] were collected at two points in time approximately 10 years apart. Transcripts of the data, according to Long (2003: 509–510), showed 'pervasive and persistent errors despite ample opportunity to acquire the target language and 'extensive amounts of variation, both synchronic and diachronic'. Data analyses by types and tokens, focusing on plural *s*-marking and past tense marking, offered the following findings: 'i) relatively stable suppliance of appropriate marking on certain nouns and verbs, ii) relatively stable omission of the same marking on others, and iii) highly variable, unpredictable performance, i.e., free variation, on still others' (2003: 511). Long termed this combination of stability and instablity 'volatility', and, interestingly, saw it as evidence against fossilization. His conviction was that stabilization and variation should be mutually exclusive and that only stabilization could be associated with fossilization. Thus, despite the 16-year longitudinal data and despite the fact that Ayako had lived in the target language environment for more than 52 years, Long nevertheless concluded:

> It's too early to say, on the one hand, whether parts of Ayako's IL have fossilized. The evidence so far suggests that they have not, and that the two small grammatical domains reported above, at least, may not even have stabilized, in spite of the fact that Ayako's speech is far from native-like after plenty of motivation and opportunity to have advanced further. (2003: 27)

Long's study, undoubtedly making a significant contribution to the accumulation of the SLA longitudinal database, leaves a number of questions open to discussion. First and foremost is the question of whether or not stabilization can be equated with fossilization. Another question is whether or not variation should be excluded from consideration as fossilization. Can there be 'fossilized variation' (Schachter, 1996a), in other words? To these questions we now turn.

Is stabilization synonymous with fossilization?

A recurrent issue in discussions of fossilization over the years has been: How closely should stabilization be tied with fossilization? Specific questions raised are: Are they different or synonymous? If they are synonymous, why do we need the term fossilization when we already have a term called stabilization? Han (1998), and later Selinker and Han (2001), provide a detailed discussion of this issue. In essence, they assert that stabilization and fossilization can form a continuum, but that the former should not simply be equated with the latter, given that there are at least three possible cases of stabilization:

1. A temporary stage of 'getting stuck'.
2. Interlanguage restructuring.
3. Long-term cessation of interlanguage development.

Case 1 is a natural phase in all learning. Case 2 is superficial; that is, restructuring of interlanguage knowledge produces a surface appearance of stabilization of certain interlanguage features. In both cases, learning may exhibit a plateau, which could, according to VanPatten (1988), persist for as long as four or five years. In the third case, stabilization becomes the harbinger of fossilization. Thus, only in the third case 'does the issue of fossilization indistinguishable from stabilization arise' (Selinker & Han, 2001: 282), in which stabilization becomes part of the fossilization process, with fossilization being the ultimate outcome.

When stabilization constitutes a prelude to fossilization, according to Han (1998; see also Selinker & Han, 2001), it is likely to display one of the following four behaviors: (1) non-variant appearance (i.e., stabilized interlanguage forms manifesting themselves invariantly over time), (2) backsliding (i.e., variational reappearance over time of interlanguage features that appear to have been eradicated), (3) stabilized inter-contextual variation (i.e., context-based variational appearance over time of interlanguage target-like and non-target-like features), and (4) stabilized intra-contextual variation (i.e., variational appearance over time of interlanguage target-like and non-target-like features in the same context). Importantly, all of these manifestations are predicated upon the conditions of ample exposure to input, adequate motivation to learn, readiness to learn, and sufficient opportunity for practice.

Given the intricate relationship held between stabilization and fossilization as described for Case 3 above, and that stabilization is directly observable while fossilization is not, but rather inferential, it only stands to reason to conceptualize fossilization as a process rather than a product, and, further, to operationalize it in terms of long-term stabilization which is impermeable to any external influences and irrespective of learning motivation and readiness.[12]

The view that stabilization, rather than fossilization, should constitute a most relevant domain of inquiry for empirical studies of fossilization is shared by many researchers. Long (2003), for example, believes that stabilization is the first sign of fossilization, that the difference between stabilization and fossilization is permanence, and that stabilization and fluctuation are mutually exclusive, as earlier mentioned. This understanding has led him to the conclusion that 'understanding the causes of *stabilization* (and destabilization) would seem to promise as much for SLA theory as work on fossilization' (p. 490; emphasis in original).

Long's position, however, raises both conceptual and empirical concerns. First, conceptually, identifying stabilization with fossilization potentially conflates learning plateau – a natural learning process – with permanent cessation of learning. As Long himself has speculated, 'the two (stabilization and fossilization) processes might share the same surface characteristics, but may differ in their underlying causes' (2003: 490). Second, empirically, equating the two may appear to be helpful in operationalizing fossilization. But then, lack of differentiation between the two may complicate the empirical research by suggesting the need to study every incidence of stabilization, for by implication, every incidence of stabilization is potentially a case of fossilization. This view may have underestimated the complexity of learning and fossilization. As argued above, stabilization and fossilization are not synonymous. Also debatable is Long's conception that stabilization and fluctuation are mutually exclusive. For one thing, it appears to be at odds with a by now well-established fact about IL development, namely that IL varies and that IL variations may stabilize at both competence and performance levels (see, e.g., Sorace [1996] on 'permanent optionality'; Johnson *et al.* [1996] on permanent indeterminate knowledge; and R. Ellis [1999] on 'long-lasting free variation').

In view of the complexity surrounding stabilization and fossilization, it would seem to make sense to conceptually keep stabilization and fossilization apart as, broadly, two different theoretical and empirical entities, while *selectively* investigating stabilization as part of the fossilization process. If Han (1998) and Selinker and Han (2001) were right about distinguishing between different cases of stabilization, it would follow that only Case 3 (i.e., long-term stabilization being a prelude to fossilization) would be an appropriate target for fossilization research.

Should a longitudinal study last five years or longer?

As already indicated, in fossilization research, an issue of persistent concern is the time span of a longitudinal study. Specifically, how long would be sufficient for determining that stabilization is functioning as a prelude to fossilization? As mentioned, a number of researchers have advocated a non-differentiated, arbitrary criterion of five years of LOR. This, as has been argued, is rather vacuous. The issue of time is perhaps far more complex than has been generally understood.

A useful point of departure for discussing this issue can be found in a statement made by Larsen-Freeman (1997: 152):

> While interlanguages of speakers of various first languages learning English as a foreign language have much in common, they also are distinctive, each constrained by the strange attractors of their L1s, which may be greater than the force of the strange attractor of English. Thus, the English pronunciation of a native speaker of Spanish will differ from that of a native speaker of Chinese. Many other fundamental differences mark the challenges present for learners from one native language background as compared with another. Besides the obvious linguistically-based differences are the learners' cultural backgrounds and reasons for learning (not learning) a second or foreign language in the first place.

What is captured more than anything else in this quote is a two-fold fact that has been continuously receiving attention from SLA researchers (see, e.g., Andersen, 1983; Bialystok & Miller, 1999; DeKeyser, 2000; Gass & Selinker, 2001; Hawkins, 2000; Henkes, 1974; Kellerman, 1984; Schachter, 1974, 1988, 1996a; Schumann, 1979; Sharwood Smith, 1991, 1994b; Sorace, 1996; Zobl, 1982), namely (1) that the same L2 may present differential challenges to individual learners from different L1 backgrounds, and (2) that features within the same target language may present differential challenges to an individual learner. As Hulstijn (2002b) notes, 'not all language phenomena are equal in terms of how they are processed and acquired'. Given this, the time it takes to acquire the same target language may vary from individual to individual,[13] and, by the same token, the time needed by an individual may vary for his or her acquisition of different features of the target language (for an early review of some empirical evidence, see Kellerman [1984]).

A question naturally arises: What determines how much time is needed for an individual to acquire a particular feature of the target language? As Larsen-Freeman has suggested, the 'linguistically-based differences' between an L1 and an L2 is a primary factor. Additional factors are 'learners' cultural backgrounds' and 'reasons for learning (or not learning)'. To this list one could easily add a few more; quality and quantity of exposure to the target language, mode of learning, opportunity to use the target language, learners' readiness, learners' processing strategies, input characteristics, and last but not least, the inherent complexity, formal and functional, of a given feature of the target language. These factors, along with a multitude of others (many of which are perhaps not yet known), may interact to co-determine the time needed for the acquisition of a given linguistic feature to be complete.[14] How then would this consideration tie into the issue of duration of a longitudinal study of fossilization?

If the above reasoning were on the right track, it would imply that positing an overarching time span for longitudinal studies of fossilization would be false and misleading, but that the time span should vary depending on which TL feature is under investigation. In principle, all other things being equal, the time required for determining if an interlanguage feature has stabilized (leading to potential fossilization) should, at the very least, be comparable to the time that an average learner under optimal learning conditions[15] would take to acquire the relevant TL feature. To illustrate, let us hypothetically assume that an average learner, X, took three years to acquire the English passive construction. To ascertain the 'stabilization → fossilization' status of this construction in the interlanguage of another learner, Y, at least three years of observation, *ceteris paribus*, would be necessary. By the same token, if an average learner, X, took 20 years to acquire English verbs of causative alternation (e.g., *break[vt]/break [vi]*), a longitudinal study of comparable length is warranted to establish the 'stabilization → fossilization' status in the interlanguage of Learner Y. The bottom line is that sufficient time should be allowed for the learners to learn and display learning.

A concrete example should suffice to clarify the point: R. Ellis (1992c) undertook a two-year longitudinal study of two child L2 learners' use of requests in an ESL classroom setting, the aim being to understand 'how and to what extent interaction in the classroom shapes the process of L2 acquisition' (p. 1). The two informants, J and R, aged 10 and 11 years, were almost complete beginners in English. Data collected primarily comprised paper-and-pencil records of their utterances while J and R were engaged in various types of interaction in the classroom. A multi-level analysis (e.g., formal complexity, level of directness, perspective, etc.) indicates, *inter alia*, that J and R progressed noticeably on a number of fronts, including producing fewer instances of verbless requests (e.g., *big circle*, when requesting a cutout of a big circle), having systematically extended the range of request types, and so forth. Yet they appeared to have failed to progress on others. For instance, during the two-year period, the preponderance of their requests was characterized by direct and simple directives, and the range of formal devices employed remained highly limited. In brief, a number of deficiencies seemed to have stabilized. Now, can we consider them fossilized? Certainly not. For both informants were beginners, and as R. Ellis pointed out, the features noted above are 'late-acquired,' and hence 'the developmental process was not complete' (p. 20). Thus in this case, although two years of longitudinal data have produced instances of stabilization, they are insufficient to establish any fossilization due to the fact that the target features would yet require a longer time to assimilate.

Clearly, the implementation of the sort of case-by-case suggestion given above would hinge on the availability of reliable temporal indexes for L2 acquisition, which, hopefully, future research will directly provide. Until then, such information can only be extrapolated from the existing literature. Moreover, the case-by-case suggestion implies that research efforts should concentrate on identifying local, as opposed to global, fossilization.

The Modular Nature of Fossilization

One unifying feature that emerged from the above review of empirical research is that none of the studies provided any evidence on the fossilization of an entire interlanguage system. Rather, they each identified one or more features of the interlanguage that appeared to have fossilized. Table 6.1 summarizes the studies discussed above, including their linguistic focuses.

The fact that only a subset of linguistic features have caught the attention of researchers suggests that when fossilization occurs, it more likely than not happens to certain linguistic features within an interlanguage system, rather than permeating the entire system. This, in turn, speaks to the modular nature of fossilization, which appears to have at least four facets of manifestation: (1) fossilization selectively affects linguistic features within a linguistic domain; (2) it selectively affects L2 comprehension and production; (3) it selectively affects L2 competence and performance, and (4) it selectively affects some domains of an interlanguage. This modular nature may in part explain the earlier noted intra-learner as well as inter-learner differential failure and success.

Evidence for the first facet of the modular nature is pervasive, and among the studies reviewed above, is most clearly seen in Lardiere (1998a) and Lennon (1991), both showing that while some linguistic features seemed to have fossilized, others successfully reached the target, importantly within the same linguistic domain, i.e., morphosyntax.

Table 6.1 Sample empirical studies of fossilization

Researcher	*Informants' L1*	*Informants' TL*	*Linguistic focus*	*Type of study*	*Fossilization assumed or established*
Schumann (1978a)	Spanish	English	Negation	One-year longitudinal case study	Established
Lardiere (1998a)	Chinese	English	Pronominal marking and past tense marking	Eight-year longitudinal case study	Established
Kellerman (1989)	Dutch	English	Hypothetical conditionals	Non-longitudinal, cross-sectional study	Assumed
Schouten (1996)	Dutch	English	Hypothetical conditionals	Non-longitudinal, cross-sectional study	Assumed
Hyltenstam (1988)	Finnish, Spanish	Swedish	Swedish lexical density, variation and sophistication	Non-longitudinal, group study	Assumed
Lennon (1991)	German	English	English adverb order; 'there is/there are'; 'have got'; 'always'; future time forms	Six-month longitudinal case study	Established
Thep-Ackrapong (1990)	Chinese	English	English infinitival complements and related structures	A-year-and-a-half longitudinal case study	Assumed

Table 6.1 *(contd.)*

Researcher	*Informants' L1*	*Informants' TL*	*Linguistic focus*	*Type of study*	*Fossilization assumed or established*
Mukattash (1986)	Arabic	English	Conflation of simple past tense with simple present; conflation of non-perfective phrases with the perfective; be-deletion; using the active voice instead of the passive	Sixteen-week longitudinal, group study	Established
Washburn (1991)	Miscellaneous	English	Characteristics of linguistic behavior	Non-longitudinal, group study	Assumed
Han (1998)	Chinese	English	Passives; unaccusatives	Two-year longitudinal case study (2 subjects)	Established
Long (2002)	Japanese	English	Plural -s marking; past time marking	Sixteen-year longitudinal case study	Established

Of the second facet of the modular nature, evidence also exists, albeit to a lesser extent. MacWhinney (2001; see also Bates & MacWhinney, 1981), for example, provided evidence for L2 learners' long-term preservation of syntactic 'accent' in comprehension. The case of which he made a particular mention concerns a native speaker of German. The informant had lived in the United States for 30 years, was married to an American, and had published several important textbooks in experimental psychology written in English. Nonetheless, he continued to 'process simple English sentences using the cue strength hierarchy of German'; that is, 'he used agreement and animacy cues whenever possible, largely ignoring word order when it competed with agreement and animacy' (p. 84). In this case, the informant, notwithstanding 30 years of life in the target language environment, still transferred L1-based processing strategies into L2 sentence processing. Yet no such transfer was witnessed in his academic writing.

On the third facet of the modular nature, namely that fossilization differentially affects competence and performance, both Coppieters (1989) and Sorace (1996) have provided compelling evidence that while very near-native L2 speakers can show identity with native speakers of the target language in terms of performance, their grammatical intuitions can be significantly different than those possessed by native speakers (cf. Davies, 2003).

Support for the fourth facet of the modular nature of fossilization has been largely observational. As early as 1969, Scovel offered the insight that adult learners typically fossilize in IL phonology at a greater distance from TL norms than in IL syntax, though largely based on anecdotal evidence (see also Flege, 1981).[16] More recent research, however, has clearly documented that fossilization can occur in some linguistic domains but not in others. Schmidt (1983) provides a case in point.

In a three-year longitudinal case study, Schmidt followed the progression (or lack thereof) of Wes – an adult Japanese immigrant to Hawaii – in each of the four areas of 'communicative competence' (Canale & Swain, 1980): grammatical competence, sociolinguistic competence, discourse competence, and strategic competence. Judged by the degree to which he acculturated into the TL society, Wes was a good learner; he had a positive attitude towards the TL and culture, and a strong drive to learn and communicate in English. He was outgoing and enjoyed mingling with native speakers of English, and so forth. A global evaluation indicated that Wes, indeed, appeared to have learned a lot during the three years of residence in Hawaii.[17] As reported, 'his ability to communicate in English has increased at steady and impressive rate' (Schmidt, 1983: 144). However, a detailed analysis of his output in each of the four areas of communicative competence afforded an interestingly different picture. In the area of grammatical competence, Wes showed a general lack of progress in, e.g., acquiring nine commonly studied grammatical morphemes (*copula BE, progressive ING, auxiliary BE, past irregular, plural, third singular, article, possessive,* and *past regular*). Schmidt writes: 'Over a 3-year period characterized by extensive and intensive interaction with native speakers, Wes's development in terms of what is generally considered to be the heart of SLA, the acquisition of productive grammatical rules, has been minimal and almost insignificant' (1983: 150).

Quite in contrast with his grammatical competence, Wes showed more development in his sociolinguistic competence, which became manifest, most visibly, in the disappearance over time of some of his early errors and the expansion of his repertoire of expressions. For example, in terms of his use of directives, 'progressive forms were no longer used for directive function with any frequency, while the use of imperatives increased (e.g., *Please next month send orders more quick*)' (1983: 154).

In terms of discourse competence, Wes was reported to exhibit greatest progress in this area. Particularly striking was his increased ability to achieve coherence, comprehensibility, and expressiveness in his oral narration. Moreover, he was said to be an active conversationlist who frequently nominated topics, a good listener as well as a good talker. Given these abilities, it is not surprising to learn subsequently that Wes was also good at using communicative strategies (i.e., strategic competence – the fourth component of 'communicative competence') to repair communication breakdowns – caused oftentimes by his limited command of the grammatical aspects of English. Of note, his repertoire of strategies underwent a significant expansion, from his earlier transfer of Japanese grammatical features when feeling short of elements of English to his later paraphrasing in English what he could not convey directly.

Thus, as far as this particular learner is concerned, differential success was attested in his interlanguage development, with fossilization seen occurring within but one linguistic domain. The explanation Schmidt offered for this case invoked a number of variables, such as age, lack of instruction, and absence of learning strategies that would aid grammar acquisition.

Evidence of the modular nature of fossilization may potentially challenge some of the empirical studies that claim to have provided counter evidence to the CPH-L2A. Birdsong (1999) cites a number of such studies (e.g., Birdsong, 1992; Cranshaw, 1997; Mayberry, 1993; Van Wuijtswinkel, 1994; White & Genesee, 1996) and shows that the rates of success by far range from 5% to 25% – occupying approximately 15% of a normal distribution curve. This rate, he agues, 'cannot be dismissed as peripheral' (p. 15). Lying in the background of Birdsong's contention is, as many probably have recognized, Long's (1990) criterion for falsification of the CPH-L2A. Long writes:

> Once the linguistic domain(s) and approximate age(s) involved in the claimed sensitive period(s) for SL development are specified, a single learner who began learning after the period(s) closed and yet whose underlying linguistic knowledge (not just performance on a limited production task) was shown to be indistinguishable from that of a monolingual native speaker would serve to refute the [CPH]. (p. 255)

Given this suggestion, it would seem that the so far attested rate of success has met Long's criterion to an outstanding degree, and is therefore posing a significant threat to the CPH-L2A. Such a deduction, however, would be simplistic. Even a cursory reading of some of the studies that have reported on instances of native-like attainment by adult L2 learners would reveal their inadequacy. To begin with, they have focused on a narrow range of features, mostly within one linguistic domain (e.g., morphosyntax, or phonology). Then, they mostly have employed a limited number of production and / or comprehension tasks for data elicitation (e.g., having L2 learners read aloud a set of sentences and having this production compared with that of native-speaking controls and rated for native-likeness by a panel of judges). As such, they have only tapped, at most, into a subsystem or a sub-skill area of their informants' interlanguage, and any conclusions thereby drawn are potentially biased.

While the exact criteria for robust data have yet to be established, one thing that is clear from our discussion above of the modular nature of fossilization is that success and failure co-exist in a given interlanguage. This is to say that it is highly probable for a given learner to achieve native-like proficiency in one or more linguistic subsystems while still falling short of such attainment in others. By implication, success in one linguistic subsystem does not necessarily generalize across others. Viewed in this perspective, the alleged evidence of falsification may not be valid unless sustained by similar evidence, at least from a number of representative domains, of the informants' competence.[18]

To conclude this section, the preponderance of evidence is in favor of the first sense of the modular nature of fossilization (i.e., fossilization selectively occurs to features within a linguistic domain). As far as L2 acquisition of English morphosyntax is concerned, over the years, researchers appear to have identified a considerable range of linguistic features as vulnerable to fossilization. Aside from those explored by researchers in the aforementioned studies (see Table 6.1), elsewhere in the literature we can find a number of others, as will be commented on in the next section.

Linguistic Features Prone to Fossilization

Kellerman (1984) discussed several such features in the domains of syntax, lexis and semantics vis-à-vis specific L1 groups and different TLs, some of which are listed in Table 6.2 .

It is worth noting that each of those features is associated with learners from a specific L1 background. In a similar vein, Yip (1995) explored four what she called fossilizable structures in the English interlanguage created by native speakers of Chinese:

[6–6] Pseudo-passive (e.g., *New cars must keep inside.*)
[6–7] Ergative construction (e.g., *The World War III will be happened.*)
[6–8] Tough-movement (e.g., *I am difficult to learn English; The message is easy to be expressed.*)
[6–9] Existential pseudo-relative (e.g., *There's a lot of people find their husband or wife in parties.*)

Of the four types of IL constructions, according to Yip, [6–6] and [6–9] are directly attributable to the influence of the native language, i.e., Chinese, while [6–7] and [6–8] are due to the complexity of the TL features. The implication of the latter two is that these structures may prove challenging to learners from other L1 backgrounds as well.

Table 6.2 Structures vulnerable to fossilization

Linguistic feature	*Target language*	*L1 group*
Subject-verb-object word order	Dutch or German	English
'Easy/Eager to please'	English	French, Arabic, Hebrew
Pronominal reflex of the NP head in a relative clause (e.g., *The film was about a boy that he wanted to be free . . .*)	English	Farsi, Arabic
Case-marking (e.g., *Jeder Republikaner betrachtete er also sein persönlicher Feind.*)	German	Dutch, English
Pseudo-passive (e.g., *The books have received.*)	English	Chinese, Japanese
Using English progressive duratively (e.g., *Day after day he was swotting for his exam.*)	English	Dutch
Make + complement (e.g., *They might make their friends get very upset about this.*)	English	Chinese

Recent SLA literature has seen much discussion of L2 acquisition of unaccusatives (i.e., [6–7]), a linguistic feature considered to be difficult for L2 learners in general (see, e.g., Balcom, 1995, 1997; Han, 1998; Hirakawa, 1995, 1997, 2001; Hwang, 1997; Ju, 2000; Oshita, 1997, 2001; Sorace, 1993, 1995; Sorace & Shomura, 2001; Yip, 1995; Zobl, 1989). Guided by the Unaccusative Hypothesis (Perlmutter, 1978),[19] researchers have discovered remarkable differences in L2 acquisition of unergatives (e.g., *swim*, *laugh*, and *eat*) vs. unaccusatives (e.g., *happen*, *arrive*, and *disappear*).[20] While learners from various L1 backgrounds showed considerable homogeneity in terms of the ease in mastering L2 unergatives, irrespective of whichever L2 it was, significant difficulties and divergence were exhibited in their acquisition of unaccusatives. As Montrul (2001: 149) notes, 'errors are more frequent or persistent with unaccusatives than unergative verbs'. In regards to unaccusatives, L2 learners are generally found to accept/ produce, the following types of constructions:

[6–10] 'Passivized' unaccusatives, e.g.,
  a. The most memorable experience of my life was happened 15 years ago. (Zobl, 1989)
  b. For last 15 years computers have drastically affected our life and this *will be continued* in the future. (Yip, 1995)

[6–11] Postverbal NP structures on unaccusatives, e.g.,
One day happened a revolution. (Oshita, 1997)

[6–12] Causativization of unaccusatives, e.g.,
He *falls* a piece of note into dough by mistake. (Hirakawa, 1995)

Researchers have developed various accounts for the differential behaviors of L2 learners vis-à-vis their acquisition of the two kinds of intransitive verbs. The prevailing interpretation (e.g., Zobl, 1989; Balcom, 1997; Oshita, 1999) seems to be that L2 learners are aware of the distinction between the two classes of intransitive verbs, but have misanalyzed the semantic-syntactic properties of unaccusatives. Thus, in the case of passivized unaccusatives, one conjecture is that the L2 learners might have subsumed the verb class of unaccusatives under the passive rule (e.g. Zobl, 1989) and have used passivization as a morphosyntactic means to mark the underlying syntactic movement that they detected. In both cases of postverbal NP structures on unaccusatives (see [6–11] above) and causativizing/transitivizing unaccusatives (see [6–12] above), on the other hand, misanalysis is considered to have taken place due to L1 influence[21] (see, e.g., Hirakawa, 1995).

Of the three different types of constructions, the passivized unaccusatives (see [6–10a, b] above) are the most prevalent across L2 learners of different L1 backgrounds. They are, in the prediction of Balcom (1997), likely to fossilize in the learners' interlanguage. For Balcom, the passivized unaccusatives are an indication that the L2 learners have successfully acquired the broad-range rules for the unaccusatives yet failed to acquire the relevant narrow-range rules, which, after Pinker (1989) and Levin and Rappaport Hovav (1995), should involve the following, specifically:

> 1. Detransitivization is restricted to verbs whose action can occur without the intervention of a volitional Agent;
> 2. lexical causatives must be a result of direct causation; and
> 3. for the passive rule to apply, logical objects must be affected. (Balcom 1995: 9)

Importantly, Balcom asserts:

> If ESL learners do not receive evidence of these narrow-range rules to restrict the application of their broad-range rules, inappropriate 'be + en' would become fossilized. (1997:9)

Linguistic structures that are prone to fossilization are by no means restricted to those discussed above. Other morphosyntactic structures that have often been reported as particularly troublesome for L2 learners include grammatical gender[22] (see, e.g., Harley, 1998) and third person singular possessive determiners for Francophone learners of English (J. White, 1998; Zobl, 1985), verbal morphology for L2 learners in general (Lardiere, 1998a; Long, 2003; Montrul, 2002; L. White, 2001), grammatical morphemes such as articles, plurals, and prepositions for L2 learners of English (Bardovi-Harlig & Bofman, 1989; Larsen-Freeman, 1983), English relative clauses for native speakers of Chinese and Japanese (Schachter, 1974), adverb placement in English for Francophone speakers (L. White, 1991), English locative alternation for native speakers of Korean (Bley-Vroman & Joo, 2001), English prepositional pied-piping in relative clauses and questions for learners in general (E. Klein, 1993; see also Bardovi-Harlig, 1987), tense/aspect form-meaning associations in English for learners in general (Bardovi-Harlig, 1995), transitive and intransitive verb conjugations in Hungarian for learners in general (MacWhinney, 2001), and so forth. In addition, Schachter (1988: 24) has observed:

> Most proficient ESL speakers do not have fully formed determiner systems, aspectual systems, or tag question systems. Many are not aware of the semantic subtleties of the modal system, comprehending and producing only deontic readings of modals, not even being aware of their possible interpretation as epistemics.

> Even more striking is the non-occurrence in proficient second language speaker production of a number of the so-called movement transformations, particularly raising, clefts, pseudoclefts, topicalizing rules . . . in fact, movement rules in general.

Interestingly, yet not surprisingly, difficult structures not only manifest themselves through learners' production but through their metalinguistic judgments of the grammaticality of L2 utterances as well. In a partial replication of the Johnson and Newport (1989) study, DeKeyser (2000) found that his adult arrivals (i.e., informants who arrived in the U.S. after the age of 16), all of whom were Hungarian native speakers of English as L2 and who had lived in the U.S. for an average length of 34 years, still had trouble with judging the ungrammaticality of the following structures:

1. present progressive with auxiliary omitted (e.g., *Tom working in his office right now.*);
2. determiners omitted (e.g., *Tom is reading book in the bathtub.*);
3. determiners used with abstract nouns (e.g., *The beauty is something that lasts forever.*);
4. wh-question without do-support (e.g., *Who you meet at the park everyday?*)
5. wh-questions without subject-verb inversion (e.g., *What Marsha is bringing to the party?*)
6. irregular plurals regularized (e.g., *A shoe salesman sees many foots throughout the day.*)
7. wrong subcategorization of verb for gerund, infinitive, and to+infinitive (e.g., *George says much too softly.*)
8. adverb between the verb and the object (e.g., *The student eats quickly his meals.*)

A consistent high correlation was reported for these structures between the informants' scores on a grammaticality judgment test and their ages of arrival. On this population (i.e., late arrivals), DeKeyser (personal communication, 2002) comments:

> I think all structures are fossilizable, really, and given that most of the subjects in this study have been here [in the U.S.] for decades, I would say these elements of language have indeed fossilized for them.

What is worth noting , for the purpose of understanding the modular nature of fossilization, is that the same population did not appear to have problems with other structures such as word order in declarative sentences (with the exception of adverb placement), do-support in yes-no questions, and pronoun gender. In other words, they all seemed to have mastered these structures.

Thus, as shown above, over the years researchers have discovered an array of linguistic features that seem difficult to acquire either by L2 learners across the board or by learners from a particular L1 background. Importantly, from their findings it has become possible to extrapolate some abstract categories prone to fossilization. Green and Hecht (1992), for example, were able to identify, through their study of German learners of English as an L2, a range of easy as well as difficult rules. Among the easy ones were those that (1) refer to easily recognized categories, (2) can be applied mechanically and (3) are not dependent on large contexts. Among the difficult ones, on the other hand, were those that 'do not allow of simple exhaustive descriptions and ... are not always governed by features of the immediate context' (1992: 180).

Similarly, Todeva (1992, cited in Long, 2003) pointed out three so-called high-risk categories of linguistic features: (1) categories lacking a straightforward form-function relationship, such as articles; (2) semi-productive rules, whose exceptions do not constitute clearly defined sets, such as English negative prefixation, dative-alternation, and stress shift in verb-to-adjective formations (e.g., analyze/analyzable, present/presentable, but admire/admirable); and (3) units of a highly arbitrary nature, such as prepositions, collocations, and gender assignment. Further, from these categories, Long (2003) surmised that morphology would be more vulnerable than syntax, inflections more at risk than free morphemes, and exceptional cases within a language-specific paradigm more problematic than regular ones.

The question, then, becomes: What renders a linguistic feature difficult, and hence prone to fossilizable? The explanation sought by early SLA researchers, in the era of the Contrastive Analysis Hypothesis (Lado 1957), was that difficulty arises from differences between a learner's native language and his or her target language. Note Lado's hypothesis:

> Since even languages as closely related as German and English differ significantly in the form, meaning, and distribution of their grammatical structures, and since the learner tends to transfer the habits of his native language structure to the foreign language, we have here the major source of difficulty or ease in learning the structure of a foreign language. Those structures that are similar will be easy to learn because they will be transferred and may function satisfactorily in the foreign language. Those structures that are different will be difficult because when transferred they will not function satisfactorily in the foreign language and will therefore have to be changed. (Lado, 1957: 59)

This hypothesis was subsequently subject to attack by researchers for its lack of empirical validity. For one thing, 'not only did errors occur that had not been predicted by the theory, but there was evidence that predicted errors did not occur' (Gass & Selinker, 1994: 63). Yet another problem with the CAH lies in drawing an absolute equation between differences and difficulty. NL-TL differences are at best a source of difficulty (Schachter, 1996a), but to view both as isomorphic is unjustified. Moreover, as Gass and Selinker (1994: 64) have rightly pointed out, 'To equate difference with difficulty attributes a psycholinguistic explanation to a linguistic description. It is a confusion of the product (a linguist's description) with the process (a learner's struggle with the second language)'.

Thus, rather than equating a linguistic property (i.e., difference) with a psycholinguistic one (i.e., difficulty), as the early SLA researchers did, recent attempts at understanding the notion of difficulty give considerable weight to factors that make up psycholinguistic complexity. Long (2003), for example, suggests that the linguistic structures that tend to fossilize are due largely to their attendant psycholinguistic qualities such as frequency, regularity, semantic transparency, communicative redundancy, and perceptual saliency. The implication is thus that infrequent, irregular, semantically non-transparent, communicatively redundant, and perceptually non-salient forms are most susceptible to fossilization (cf. Doughty & Williams, 1998).

Following Long's suggestion, a processing dimension should be built into the consideration of which linguistic structures are fossilizable:

> It is not the case that all inflectional morphology is vulnerable to maturational constraints – or, in the present context, likely to stabilize, or if such a thing exists, fossilize – but perhaps non-salient, irregular inflections, for example, or ambiguous, optional pragmatic rules, are the items that even good learners are most likely to miss and which are especially problematic for learners with low input sensitivity. (2003: 518)

The relevance of psycholinguistic complexity granted, ultimately, it would seem that a balanced understanding of 'difficulty' must take into account both linguistic complexity (i.e., the inherent complexity of linguistic features) and psycholinguistic complexity (i.e., processing complexity engendered by psycholinguistic factors), and more important, the ways in which the two interact to jointly create difficulty for L2 acquisition.

Already, some headway is being made along this line. A number of researchers (e.g., DeKeyser, 2002; Robinson, 1996, 2002) have recently delved into the notion of 'difficulty', through exploring the interplay between the objective complexity of linguistic features and the subjective perceptual ability, including learners' sensitivity to input (Long, 2003).[23] They seem to concur that 'saliency', be it externally engineered or internally created (Sharwood Smith, 1993), may alleviate difficulty, and further, that where learner internally-created salience (i.e., learner perceptual salience of, say, morphological regularity, semantic transparency, and frequency) is absent, externally engineered salience (e.g., input enhancement) is necessary. Following from this insight, linguistic features which are complex and which are devoid of learner-perceived and/or externally engineered salience are susceptible to fossilization. From a learnability perspective, what this implies is that linguistic features for which there is neither sufficient positive evidence nor negative evidence will be prone to fossilization (cf. L. White, 1991).

The Multiple Effects Principle

Much of what we have gained from examining studies of stabilization in interlanguage domains and subsystems amounts to an understanding that it is multiple, as opposed to singular, factors that underpin resistance and persistence. Different factors often seem to 'cluster together' to generate stabilization, as we have seen in the earlier mentioned case of Wes's lack of linguistic development (Schmidt, 1986).

A long-noted phenomenon in the vein of 'clustering together' is that language transfer tends to be the axis of multiple factors (see, e.g., Andersen, 1983; Han & Selinker, 1999; Jain, 1974; Kellerman,1989; Selinker, 1992; Selinker & Lakshmanan, 1992; Sharwood Smith, 1994; Wode, 1981; Zobl, 1980). This phenomenon is best captured in Selinker and Lakshmanan's (1992) Multiple Effects Principle (MEP):

> The Multiple Effects Principle A (MEP):
> **When two or more** SLA factors work in tandem, there is a greater chance of stabilization of interlanguage forms leading to possible fossilization.

The Multiple Effects Principle, moreover, provides an explicit link between fossilization and language transfer:

> The Multiple Effects Principle Bi: Weak form:
> Language transfer is a **privileged** co-factor in setting multiple effects.
>
> The Multiple Effects Principle Bii: Strong form:
> Language transfer is a **necessary** co-factor in setting multiple effects.

A pedagogic corollary is also proposed:

> The Multiple Effects Principle C:
> Apparently fossilized structures will not become open to destabilization through consciousness-raising strategies when multiple effects apply. (1992: 198; emphasis added)

As stated in the MEP, transfer is a central factor in staging the coalescence of multiple factors. Moreover, multiple factors dominated by language transfer not only stabilize but may ultimately fossilize an interlanguage. In addition, interlanguage forms that stabilize as a result of transfer-dominated multiple effects may be impermeable to any external influences including pedagogic intervention.

Empirical evidence for the MEP abounds in the SLA literature (see, e.g., Gass & Selinker, 1994: 91–93; Selinker & Lakshmanan, 1992). A more recent validation study of the MEP can be found in Han and Selinker (1999; see also Han, 2001b). The study, spanning one academic year, involves a detailed examination of a persistent and resistant structure in the interlanguage of an adult native-speaker of Thai learning Norwegian as the L2. [6–13a] and [6–13b] below contrast the interlanguage structure with the target structure:

[6–13a] Interlanguage
*På Dragvoll har mange studenter.
at Dragvoll have many students.
*At Dragvoll have many students.
[6–13b] Norwegian
På Dragvoll er det mange studenter.
at Dragvoll are there many students
At Dragvoll there are many students.

The interlanguage structure [6–13a] has the word order of AV ($_{null}$S)O, while the target structure [6–13b] comprises AVS(O).[24]

The informant for the study, Siri, was a highly motivated learner, yet despite the teacher's repeated correction of her persistent error (i.e., [6–13a]), she was unable to shed it from her interlanguage. In their search for the causal factors for the persistence and resistance of the interlanguage construction, Han and Selinker examined Siri's written output following the teacher's correction over a period of seven months. In addition, they elicited Siri's performance on a number of metalinguistically-oriented tasks such as grammaticality judgment, translation, and interview whereby Siri was invited to offer her interpretation of the teacher's correction. Thus, with data from multiple sources, the researchers were able to arrive at an unambiguous understanding of the causal factors:

> Siri's persistent error arose from L1 typological influence, and yet such influence was concealed by transfer of training (term from Selinker, 1972), a process whereby the learner found in the pedagogic input justification for her interlanguage rule and output.

Thus, in Siri's case, there was an interplay between L1 transfer and transfer of training. Of importance to note is that the textbook input was found to be a significant contributing factor to the learner's misanalysis of the target language. What is also worth noting about this study is that Han and Selinker's validation attempt went beyond purely discovering which factors had given rise to the stabilization of the interlanguage structure; one of the researchers, Han, actually made a destabilization attempt by conducting a special pedagogic session for the informant. Built on the two factors identified, she developed a four-step corrective strategy to counteract the known causes, namely:

> Step 1: Contradicting Siri's interlanguage-particular rule by going back to the textbook input and explaining what was meant by placing the verb in the second position;
> Step 2: counteracting native language transfer by contrasting the related L1 constructions with the related L2 constructions and explaining the notion of subject (cf. Kupferberg & Olshtain 1996);
> Step 3: checking on her knowledge restructuring by giving her several metalinguistic exercises, including one that invited her to identify and correct her own errors; and
> Step 4: helping her integrate the newly-gained knowledge into her interlanguage system by providing a real-world context for her to use the existential construction (*det være*) in inversion.

These procedures were designed to (1) improve the learner's understanding of the verb second feature of the target language (i.e., Step 1), (2) raise her awareness of the differences between the L1 and the L2, particularly in terms of word order (i.e., Step 2), and (3) facilitate her assimilation (i.e., Step 3) and integration of new knowledge into her IL system (i.e., Step 4).

The pedagogic assistance provided to Siri proved to be extremely successful in that as soon as Steps 1 and 2 were undertaken, she was able to complete the metalinguistic tasks with ease, including being able to recognize and correct the once persistent and resistant error in her own writing, and she was subsequently seen able to use the target structure accurately within the contexts the researcher created for her.[25] The follow-up observation, which lasted three months, produced clear and convincing evidence that the special pedagogic session had brought about sustained change in Siri's knowledge and behavior.

The Han and Selinker study thus lends support to, and expands on, the MEP in that once the multiple factors are known, pedagogic intervention directly targeting the known factors can destabilize the persistent and resistant IL structure, thereby leading to restructuring.

Returning to the theme of this section (i.e., multiple factors working in tandem), in principle, any factors shown in the taxonomy in Chapter 2 may combine to create long-term stabilization. Further, different combinations are possible for different linguistic features, hence the existence of variations within and across learners. It is important to end this section by noting that language transfer, though a long-recognized axis of multiple factors, is not present in every incidence of premature stabilization, as shown in Han (1998); other factors alone, or in combination, may also fabricate long-term stabilization of interlanguage features.

Summary

In this chapter, we have examined several aspects of local, as opposed to global, fossilization. First of all, through a selected review of empirical studies, we gained a glimpse into the empirical phenomenon of local fossilization, and simultaneously, the methodological approaches that researchers had employed in identifying it. What seemed clear was that none of the metrics attempted (e.g., corrective feedback, typical error, LOR) could, independently, serve as a reliable means for gathering evidence of fossilization, and hence that researchers should employ multiple metrics in conjunction with longitudinal observations. Moreover, it is necessary that they precede their studies with a careful investigation of external and internal learning conditions. As has been repeatedly stated, any argumentation on fossilization needs to be predicated on continuous exposure, adequate motivation, and sufficient opportunity for practice. In this sense, any studies of fossilization that are carried out in, e.g., an input-poor environment, would be weak in credibility, since one may very well argue that once put in an input-rich environment, the informants would be able to show progress.

A second task we attempted in this chapter was that, building on the selected review of empirical research, we explored the modular nature of fossilization. Fossilization, as has been documented, appears to affect individuals differentially; it affects certain interlanguage features in some subsystems for some learners but other features in the same or other subsystems for other learners. To help the reader understand the modular nature, we cited as well as briefly discussed a number of putatively fossilizable linguistic features, with reference mainly to English as a second language. Of note is that in their attempt to determine which linguistic features would be difficult and hence prone to fossilization, researchers have not only explored the surface complexity of linguistic features *per se*, but also tried to understand how that complexity interacts with the learners' perceptual ability in rendering certain linguistic features particularly difficult. It is conceivable that this line of inquiry would promise high gains, theoretically and pedagogically.

Going beyond a pure description of the modular nature of fossilization, we also explored a possible underlying mechanism, namely, multiple factors conspiring to create long-term stabilization of interlanguage features. In light of the MEP (Selinker & Lakshmanan, 1992), language transfer is a prime factor in staging the coalescence of multiple effects, thereby leading to the long-term persistence and resistance of interlanguage features. Nevertheless, other factors, independent of the L1, may also combine to generate various, prematurely stabilized patterns. Importantly, for a given individual learner, factors may cluster within and across those categories outlined in the taxonomy in Table 3.1. Collectively, the modular nature and the MEP make a rather plausible explanation for the inter-learner and intra-learner differential failure.

Notes

1. Schumann's study, however, was recently challenged by Berdan (1996). By adopting a generalized model of logistic regression, Berdan showed that Alberto had made slow but steady change.
2. The first recording lasts 34 minutes, the second 75 minutes and the third 31 minutes.
3. The Weak Continuity Hypothesis (Clahsen *et al.*, 1994; Radford 1994) predicts that only lexical categories and their projections, constrained by X-bar theoretic principles, are initially available to the (native) language acquirer and that 'syntactic development proceeds in "stages" whereby new functional projections are successively added as extensions of the VP, ultimately resulting (if development proceeds 'far enough') in a CP stage' (Lardiere, 1998a: 9). Researchers applying the hypothesis to SLA, according to Lardiere, have generally assumed the methodological approach whereby L2 learners' syntactic knowledge is inferred through the criterial rates of verbal inflectional morphology in the learners' production.
4. This technique allows a comparison of performance in two languages by each informant on the same structures. One may examine, for instance, whether the same or different structures are chosen in both languages and in the case of different structures, what the direction of the change is (i.e., towards the L2 structure or the L1 structure).
5. '+' indicates the presence of the periphrastic conditional (would + infinitive) and '–' indicates the use of a past tense.
6. Kellerman (personal communication, 2002) comments, based on his years of broad band observation, that the rule underlying the typical error is endemic, and that even the best speakers will obey it at some time.
7. In the case of 1, there was insufficient evidence because of scanty data.
8. 'e' indicates an empty element.
9. In addition, she looked at their history of repetition in ESL course work.
10. Flege and Liu (2001; cf. Flege, 1998) drew our attention to the fact that there can be an inverse correlation between AOA and LOR; that is, 'the later participants arrived in a predominantly L2-speaking environment, the shorter period of time they tended to have lived there and the less they tended to use their L2' (p. 529). This suggests that AOA itself does not provide an adequate basis for explaining younger vs. adult learner differences in L2 attainment.

11. The six tasks were (1) a semi-structured interview, (2) a picture description task of a detailed street scene, (3) a 20-item repetition test reflecting six differing degrees of processing complexity, (4) a picture description task of a six-frame cartoon strip story, (5) a 60-item repetition test of a wide range of grammatical features, and (6) a brief open-ended discussion of the informant's reflection on her experience completing the above tasks.
12. It is worth noting in passing that in the context of SLA, 'readiness' has so far been investigated more as an external than an internal construct. That is, an L2 learner's readiness is judged by an outsider (i.e., teacher, researcher). The internal perspective on readiness, on the other hand, though crucial, is largely ignored.
13. Evidence abounds of L2 learners from different L1 backgrounds approaching the same TL feature at different rates and via different routes. Hammarberg (1979, cited in Kellerman, 1984), for example, notices that while learners from different L1 backgrounds go through the same stages in their acquisition of the placement of the negative particle in Swedish in both main and subordinate clauses, native speakers of English learning Swedish as their L2 skip the first stage of preverbal negation, owing to the fact that English does not permit it. Thus, compared with learners of other L1 backgrounds, it takes them a relatively shorter time to acquire this particular TL feature. (For more examples, see Kellerman, 1984.)
14. Acquisition can be complete, but it may also be incomplete (Schachter, 1990). Fossilization, for me, does not entail zero acquisition, but rather incomplete acquisition.
15. By 'opitmal learning conditions', I mean continuous exposure to the TL input, adequate motivation to learn, and sufficient opportunity for practice.
16. The oft-mentioned cases are Joseph Conrad (1857–1924), English novelist, born in Poland, and Henry Kissinger (1923–), U.S. Secretary of State (1973–1977), born in Germany.
17. Note that the three years were not non-interrupted. Rather, they were intervened with several short trips Wes made to Tokyo.
18. Long (1990) recommends using grammaticality and appropriacy judgment measures over production data, suggesting that the former are capable of eliciting the underlying competence, whereas the latter are likely product of avoidance. Long's confidence in the former, in light of more recent SLA research, is somewhat premature, as judgment tasks are also plagued with problems, such as bias, general limitations on information processing and chance (see, e.g., G. Brown, 1996; R. Ellis, 1994; Han & Selinker, 2002).
19. The Unaccusative Hypothesis identifies two distinct types of intransitive verbs: unergatives and unaccusatives, and based on the recognition that they differentiate in a cluster of syntactic properties, which may, depending on the language, pattern with their hypothesized semantic underpinnings, it posits that unaccusativity is syntactically represented but semantically determined.
20. Unaccusative verbs share the following syntactic properties: the selection of a direct internal argument, the lack of an external argument, and the inability to assign accusative case (Levin & Rappaport Hovav, 1995). Unergative verbs, on the other hand, take an external argument. The two types of intransitive verbs therefore display distinct syntactic behaviors, as illustrated below.

    Unaccusatives
    ________ $[_{VP}$ v NP$]$

Unergatives
NP [$_{vp}$ V]
(Burzio, 1986)

21. The judgment is based on the fact that case [2]-like sentences are seen to be typically produced by L1-Italian and L1-Spanish speakers while case [3]-like sentences are found to be produced mainly by L1 Japanese learners. Both types of interlanguage constructions have 1:1 correspondence with their counterparts in the related L1s.
22. For simplicity, I am using 'English-French interlanguage' to refer to the interlanguage created by native speakers of English learning French as an L2.
23. Recently there has been a revival of interest in language aptitude (see, e.g., DeKeyser, 2000; Sawyer & Ranta, 2001).
24. 'A' stands for 'adverbial', 'V' for 'verb', 'S' for 'subject', and 'O' for 'object'. A distinctive feature of Norwegian, a verb-second language, is that, whenever an adverbial initiates a sentence, the sentence order is inverted from the canonical SV(O)A into AVS(O), as illustrated below:

Non-inversion (SVA)	Han kjører til sentrum etter timen. *he drives into town after the class* He drives into town after the class.
Inversion: (AVS)	Etter timen kjører han til sentrum. *after the class drives he into town* After the class he drives into town. (Manne, 1990: 59)

25. The pedagogic session occurred outside normal class hours in the seventh month and lasted 40 minutes.

Chapter 7

Second Language Instruction and Fossilization

So far we have pursued, albeit rather sketchily, a macro (i.e., cross-learner) and a micro (i.e., within-learner) perspective on fossilization. We have thereby established the argument that maturational constraints and native language influence are the major determinants of the general lack of success in adult L2 learning, but that the degree of such lack of success may vary from individual to individual due to the functioning of other variables. In this chapter, we will delve into one such variable, second language instruction, and explore its relationship to fossilization.

The reader may, understandably, query whether or not such an attempt makes any sense, since, in the conviction of many, one capability of instruction is precisely that it can prevent fossilization. R. Ellis (1988), for example, has advanced two claims in favor of formal instruction:

> [a] Learners will fail to acquire the more difficult rules (e.g., inversion and verb-end) once they have achieved communicative adequacy. Learners may need form-focused instruction to make them aware of grammatical features that have little communicative importance and yet constitute target language norms. *In other words, formal instruction serves to prevent fossilization.* [b] . . . naturalistic acquisition is often a very slow process; instruction may not alter the way in which learning takes place, but it may help to speed it up. (1988: 4; emphasis added)

Both claims are intuitively appealing. Nevertheless, it is important to point out that while R. Ellis's second claim has by far been quite well supported by empirical evidence, his first assertion regarding instruction and fossilization has as yet received little direct investigation, theoretical or empirical. As such, it essentially remains a speculation rather than a statement of an observed fact. Lack of validation notwithstanding, the influence of the assumption has in fact been so strong, not only among some second language researchers but among second language teachers in general, that it created an if-then type of conception; that is, if there is no grammar instruction (including error correction), fossilization will result (see, e.g., Higgs & Clifford, 1982). This conception has also been a major driving force behind the revival of general interest in grammar teaching since the early 1980s (VanPatten, 1988).

The questions I would, therefore, like to pose for this chapter are: Can instruction serve to prevent fossilization? If so, to what extent? Furthermore, I ask: Can instruction actually promote fossilization? To address these questions, it would only seem necessary to first develop an understanding of the extent to which instruction may aid adult L2 acquisition, and then explore aspects of instruction that may promote fossilization. This chapter is, accordingly, organized into two sections that separately address these questions.

To What Extent Does Instruction Aid Acquisition?

Unlike many other issues (e.g., CPH, UG) that have been subject to a long-term (at times, fierce) debate in the SLA research, the role of instruction in adult SLA as a whole has gone largely undisputed. Regardless of their theoretical orientations, researchers seem to concur, overtly or tacitly, that instruction does matter in adult SLA. This may in part be due to the reality that the second language teaching industry has survived all kinds of economic pressures (Bley-Vroman, 1989). But, of course, there is yet a more plausible explanation; that is, that the SLA research comparing classroom learners with the so-called 'street learners' has provided compelling evidence that instruction does aid acquisition (Krashen & Seliger, 1975; Long, 1983). Furthermore, research focusing on the effects of instruction has shown, both macro- and micro-scopically, that instruction in general is facilitative (for recent reviews, see Lightbown, 2000; Norris & Ortega, 2000; Spada, 1997). Indeed, few have questioned, or rather would ever question, that instruction is a defining characteristic of adult SLA (Bley-Vroman, 1989).

Such a general endorsement of instruction, however, is not bereft of the awareness that instruction is not always successful. Bley-Vroman (1989: 47–48), in recognition of the fact that 'a whole industry is built on the consensus that instruction matters in foreign language learning', cautions that 'not all instruction is expected to be equally successful, and some actually impede success' (see also Pica, 1994). Indeed, close inspection of the SLA literature dealing with the role of instruction reveals that researchers are on the whole rather prudent in pronouncing the positive effects of instruction. Long, a well-known, strong advocate of instruction, has, on many occasions, stressed the need to pinpoint instructional practices that may affect and effect the acquisition process, thus disfavoring an either-or or all-or-none approach to assessing the contribution of instruction to acquisition.

To what extent, then, does instruction facilitate acquisition? Long (1983: 359), after reviewing 13 early studies of instructional effects in terms of (1) the relative utility of instruction as well as (2) the absolute effect of instruction, concludes that 'there is considerable (albeit not overwhelming) evidence that instruction is beneficial (1) for children as well as adults, (2) for beginning, intermediate, and advanced students, (3) on integrative as well as discrete-point tests, and (4) in acquisition-rich as well as acquisition-poor environments'. Moreover, the benefits of instruction appear to be the strongest at beginning levels and in acquisition-poor environments.[1] However, Long's review provides little insight into how instruction has aided acquisition, for it gives no description of the types of instruction (e.g., explicit or implicit) for each of the studies reviewed (for more critique, see Pienemann, 1985; VanPatten, 1988). This gap is notably filled by a later study.

Eighteen years later,[2] in a much larger-scale synthesis and meta-analysis – this time of 49 experimental and quasi-experimental studies of the effectiveness of L2 types of instruction,[3] Norris and Ortega (2000) not only confirmed Long's (1983) finding – i.e., instruction does make a positive difference for classroom L2 acquisition– but also made significant headway in terms of identifying differential effectiveness vis-à-vis different types of instruction. Their main findings are summarized below:

a) focused L2 instruction results in large target-oriented gains;
b) explicit types of instruction are more effective than implicit types;
c) focus on Form and Focus on Forms[4] interventions result in equivalent and large effects;[5] and
d) the effectiveness of L2 instruction is durable. (2000: 417)

In the meantime, it was pointed out that 'generalizability of findings is limited because the L2 type-of-instruction domain has yet to engage in rigorous and empirical operationalization and replication of its central research constructs' (2000: 418), thus hinting that the experimental procedures, statistical measures included, are in themselves a potential variable that can affect the magnitude and strength of the effectiveness so far reported.

Compared with Long's (1983) review, Norris and Ortega's synthesis and meta-analysis is arguably a more rigorous way of gauging the overall effectiveness of instruction. It certainly has allowed a more detailed understanding of the differential effectiveness associated with different types of instruction. However, the study is not completely rid of bias, due in part to the procedures adopted for performing the meta-analysis. In conducting the meta-analysis,[6] Norris and Ortega initially sampled 250 what they referred to as 'study reports' that were published in journals and books between 1980 and 1998, from which 77 were then extracted based on the researchers' own established criteria, two of which, for example, read as follows:

> The study had a quasi-experimental or experimental design. Only those studies experimentally investigating the effectiveness of particular L2 instructional treatments could contribute data for the calculation of effect sizes.
>
> The independent variable(s): (a) constituted an adequately defined and reported instructional treatment (which could be treated as an independent variable and compared with other studies), and (b) targeted specific forms and functions, either morphological, syntactic, or pragmatic (as the theoretical underpinnings of type-of-instruction research focus on the acquisition of rule-governed aspects of the L2, with special attention to morphology, syntax, and, more recently, pragmatics). (2000: 432–433)

The 77 studies were then coded for the extent to which each addressed the following questions: '(a) Were instructional treatments best characterized as focus-on-form or focus-on-forms? (b) Were instructional treatments explicit or implicit? (c) Were outcome measures based on metalinguistic judgments, selected responses, constrained constructed responses, or free constructed responses? (d) Which findings were available for quantitative meta-analysis?'(2000: 435). As a consequence, 49 studies were filtered through for inclusion in the quantitative meta-analysis.

The meta-analysis and synthesis was therefore built on a rather stringent screening procedure, which, though understandably necessary for performing a quantitative analysis, can lead at best to an accurate portrait of a subset of research on L2 instructional effects. Given that only 49 studies form the basis for the data analysis, which is only one-fifth of the 'relevant studies' (i.e., 49/250) originally identified and which all have a relatively homogeneous research design (i.e., experimental or quasi-experimental), one cannot help but wonder: (1) How representative are these studies of the range of research that has been conducted to date on the effectiveness of L2 instruction? (2) What have the other four-fifths of the studies shown? (3) Do they (e.g., longitudinal studies in particular) contribute equally, if not more, to our understanding of the instructional effects, notwithstanding the fact that they have adopted a disparate methodological approach?

Of further concern is that within the pool of the eligible studies, there exist considerable variations – even among those allegedly belonging to the same category (e.g., focus on form) – due in large part to the fact that 'individual studies operationalize instructional treatments via widely differing independent variables and that variables in general are not consistently replicated from study to study' (Norris & Ortega, 2001: 196). These variations undoubtedly could jeopardize both the validity and reliability of the reported findings.

Still another source of threat to the validity of the cumulative research findings from the meta-analysis is the so-called 'file-drawer' problem. Norris and Ortega (2000: 43) note:

> Studies reporting statistically significant findings tend to be accepted for publication over studies reporting no statistically significant findings . . . As a result of such publication bias, it is assumed that a large number of studies exist in the file drawers of researchers who, having failed to reach statistical significance with a particular study, have filed the results away and tried again with a new study.

This problem, though completely beyond the control of the researchers, nevertheless speaks to the limited scope of sampling of the meta-analysis. Given these constraints, it is imperative to interpret the findings from the Norris and Ortega (2000) study as suggestive rather than definitive.

Explicit or implicit instruction?

To date, although positive effects have been consistently reported for instruction as a whole, as shown above, within the research community there has persisted a considerable lack of consensus concerning how instruction should be carried out. The focal point of controversy has been the mode of instruction (i.e., explicit or implicit). The reader is perhaps familiar with Krashen's (1982) position on this issue. Krashen's Monitor Theory essentially minimizes the value of explicit instruction (i.e., deductive through rule explanation and application) in favor of implicit instruction (i.e., inductive through provision of i+1 comprehensible input). He makes a distinction between learning and acquisition, each intended to represent a unique pathway to attaining knowledge of the target language such that learning leads to explicit knowledge (i.e., the conscious awareness of the formal properties of the target language which can be verbalized on demand), and acquisition to implicit knowledge (i.e., intuitions about the target language which can not be introspected or reported). At the heart of such a dichotomy are a number of assumptions, such as (1) that 'the [target language] system is too complex to be consciously learned' (Krashen, 1994: 48), and (2) that explicit knowledge and implicit knowledge are unrelated, and (3) that acquisition, but not learning, is what counts. Krashen's position is known as the non-interface position.[7] Not every SLA researcher subscribes to this view, however. Contra and alongside the non-interface position, there is a strong interface as well as a weak interface position.

The former holds that explicit knowledge can convert into implicit knowledge, and vice versa (see, e.g., Gregg, 1984; Sharwood Smith, 1981, 1994a,b). The latter, on the other hand, maintains that explicit knowledge is a source of implicit knowledge, but not in toto (R. Ellis, 1994a). Much of the subject of this theoretical controversy has therefore been: To what extent does explicit rule-based knowledge shape learners' underlying L2 linguistic competence and/or influence L2 spontaneous performance in genuinely communicative situations (Lightbown, 2000)? Translated into simple pedagogic terms, the question becomes: How useful is grammar-based instruction for second language development?

On this issue, the past two decades have seen the prevalence of the weak interface position; that is, there has been a rather widespread conviction that grammar-based instruction, though not sufficient in itself, has a significant contribution to make to at least the acquisition of certain features of an L2. Several influences, theoretical and empirical, have converged to shape this trend of thinking. On the theoretical front, the major influence comes from Schmidt's (1990, 1993, 1994b, 1995) Noticing Hypothesis which underscores the subjective experience of noticing as a necessary and sufficient condition for converting input to intake.[8] For Schmidt, noticing is the 'registration of the occurrence of a stimulus event in conscious awareness and subsequent storage in long term memory' (Schmidt, 1994b: 179). Of particular relevance to our discussion here is his claim that '[i]ntentional learning (explicit learning), including the attempt to form and test conscious hypotheses, is important . . . probably for learning some features of natural languages and not others' (1994b: 198). From this claim, it follows, then, that grammar-based instruction is necessary for at least the acquisition of some features of the target language.[9]

Echoing and furthering this position, in his construction of a theory of instructed SLA R. Ellis (1994a: 88–89) argues among other things:

> Explicit knowledge derived from formal instruction may convert into implicit knowledge, but only if the learner has reached a level of development that enables her to accommodate the new linguistic material. In such cases, the learner's existing knowledge constitutes a kind of filter that sifts explicit knowledge and lets through only that which the learner is ready to incorporate into the interlanguage system. In other cases, however – when the focus of the instruction is a grammatical property that is not subject to developmental constraints – the filter does not operate, permitting the learner to integrate the feature directly into implicit knowledge.

It is clear that, while conceptualizing explicit knowledge as a source of implicit knowledge, R. Ellis sees learners' developmental readiness as a threshold condition for explicit knowledge of developmental features becoming implicit. Also of note, under the conviction that 'acquisition constitutes a process of automatizing new knowledge' (p. 86), he associates knowledge conversion with automatization, suggesting that automatized explicit knowledge is part of implicit knowledge. But perhaps most insightful is his assertion that 'the test of whether explicit knowledge can become implicit is whether formal instruction directed at a specific linguistic feature results in the use of that feature in spontaneous communication' (p. 88), thereby suggesting that (1) explicit knowledge can turn into implicit knowledge through communicative practice (cf. De Bot, 1996), and (2) the goal of explicit instruction should be to facilitate the conversion of explicit knowledge into implicit knowledge.

Corroborating evidence that explicit knowledge can become automatized through focused production practice – i.e., becoming implicit according to R. Ellis's criterion – can be found in DeKeyser's (1997) report of an experiment with a miniature linguistic system called 'Autopractan'. Informants (N = 61 adult volunteers) in this study were explicitly taught four morphosyntactic rules and thirty-two vocabulary items in an artificial language. They were then tested on their metalinguistic understanding of the rules, and received corrective feedback on every error to establish correct understanding. The explicit teaching was then followed by 15 comprehension-based as well as production-based practice (i.e., automatization) and testing sessions, in which the informants, divided into three groups, were alternately assigned to different practice conditions (e.g., single-task vs. dual-task; comprehension vs. production). This design, as DeKeyser notes, 'allows for testing the specificity of procedural skills (comprehension vs. production) acquired as a result of systematic practice of that skill after all informants had achieved the same quantity and quality of explicit knowledge' (1997: 204). Finally, an overall testing session was administered to measure the automaticity that the informants had achieved vis-à-vis their use of the rules, as a function of practice. In this study, as in many others, automaticity was operationalized in terms of three observable variables: reaction times, error rates, and interference from and with simultaneous tasks. The study offers two major findings. The first is that language learning is analogous to other cognitive skills acquisition in that 'the learning curves observed . . . follow the same power law as for those other skills,' meaning that 'during initial practice declarative knowledge is turned into qualitatively different procedural knowledge and subsequently a much slower process of gradual automatization takes place, which requires little or no change in task components, only a quantitative change within the same components' (1997: 214). The second finding is that practice leads to automatization of highly specific skills. In other words, the degree of automaticity of one skill positively correlates with the amount of practice in that skill. DeKeyser nevertheless cautions against an over-generalization of these findings by drawing attention to two important caveats, namely that 'proceduralization and automatization may not be equally successful for all learners and all rules' (1997: 215), and that due to the nature of the study – using an artificial language as the linguistic target – the automatized knowledge documented in this study may not be comparable to the implicit knowledge typically acquired in the native language.

While R. Ellis and DeKeyser both view explicit knowledge as a potential source of implicit knowledge, others, who also hold a weak interface position, assign a different role for explicit instruction in L2 learning. N. Ellis (2002b), for example, believes that language learning – L2 learning included – is largely implicit. From a connectionist perspective, he views L2 learning as a process of 'gradual strengthening of associations between co-occurring elements of the language and that fluent language performance is the exploitation of this probabilistic knowledge' (p. 173). Yet, he recognizes that implicit learning may not always be sufficient, in which case attention and explicit instruction would be necessary. Note that for him, attention is needed for 'initial registration of a language representation' (p. 173) – which is in synch with Schmidt's (1990) Noticing Hypothesis – and for acquiring complex form-function mappings, and further, the role of explicit instruction is circumscribed to speeding up learning and improving formal accuracy. Neither, however, can substitute for implicit learning.

Is grammar instruction necessary?

Perhaps a better way of knowing whether grammar instruction is necessary in SLA would be through examining learners who have been immersed in an 'input-rich' environment, for if learning in this environment still proves inadequate, then, there is a justifiable need for externally engineered explicit assistance (i.e., grammar instruction). Naturally, our attention turns to the Canadian French immersion programs.

For the past three decades, these programs have been a fertile ground for SLA research, due, at least in part, to the fact that they provide an authentic exemplification of what Krashen has conceived of as an ideal environment for acquisition, where learners are exposed to abundant comprehensible input.[10] Of interest to our discussion here is the finding that the immersion students' performance outdistances their competence. Specifically, researchers have noticed that after 6 to 10 years in the program, early immersion students develop a native-like receptive ability yet their 'productive use of the second language still differs considerably in grammatical and lexical ways from that of native speakers' (Harley & Swain, 1984: 291; see also Kowal & Swain, 1997).

Swain (1991) offers a rather detailed picture of the French skills as well as academic achievement of students attending respectively a late immersion and sheltered course – what Swain refers to as 'two immersion offshoots'[11] – through a number of comparisons. In respect of language skills, when early and late immersion students were compared, no significant difference was observed. However, when immersion students were compared with similar-aged native speakers of French, both groups showed similar scores on listening comprehension and reading tests, but one group (i.e., native-speaking peers) outperformed the other (i.e., immersion students) on speaking and writing tests. With regard to academic achievement, the late immersion students seemed to be doing just as well as the regular English-instructed students. Similar results extend to students taking a sheltered course. The sheltered group appeared to have well-developed receptive skills, and they learned 'the subject matter as well as students taking the course in their first language' (1991: 97).

Overall, then, the results reveal that while immersion programs seem to enable learners to develop a functional level of proficiency, learning (in the sense of language development) in this environment has proven inadequate. Two specific gaps are identified. First, there is lack of opportunity for learner production. Second, there is lack of grammar and vocabulary learning. On the latter, the immersion students specifically reported 'not being able to get things like verb tenses and prepositions right' and 'not having the right words to write what [they] want to communicate' (1991: 94). Both problems, in Swain's view, are resolvable through the provision of 'more focused L2 input which provides the learners with ample opportunity to observe the formal and semantic contrasts involved in the relevant target subsystem', and the provision of 'increased opportunity for students to be involved in activities requiring the productive use of such forms in meaningful situations' (1991: 98). Learner production (output), in Swain's (1985, 1995) conceptualization (the 'Output Hypothesis'), is crucial inasmuch as it creates opportunity for learners to enhance fluency, test hypotheses, and notice gaps in the interlanguage. In addition, it provides a point of learner metalinguistic reflection. In essence, Swain advocates output production as a means to push learners beyond semantic processing to perform syntactic processing, a process essential for acquisition to occur (Gass & Selinker, 2001). It is important to point out, however, that learner output does not automatically fulfill these functions. It needs to be augmented consistently by teacher feedback (Han, 2002b; Swain & Lapkin, 1998). As Swain (1991: 98) rightfully recognizes, 'if students are given insufficient feedback or no feedback regarding the extent to which their messages have successfully (accurately, appropriately, and coherently) been conveyed, output may not serve these roles'.

Findings such as the above from the immersion programs indicate that the provision of comprehensible input, while necessary, is not adequate to promote target-like proficiency. Clearly, there is room for some *selective* grammar instruction, 'which is attuned to the maturity level and metalinguistic ability of the students' (Harley & Swain, 1984: 310; see also Sharwood Smith, 1981). It is noteworthy that researchers (e.g., Faerch & Kasper, 1986; R. Ellis, 1994a; Gass, 1988; Long, 1996; Pienemann, 1985; Sharwood Smith, 1986; L. White, 1987) who share this view hold that comprehension and acquisition are not necessarily correlative (let alone causative); that is, comprehension does not necessarily entail acquisition. This is so because meaning-based comprehension (i.e., semantic processing) may occur independently of acquisition (i.e., syntactic processing) through sole use of top-down processing strategies that draw on learners' existent linguistic knowledge and contextual information. As Long (1996: 425) notes:

> Environmental support in the form of comprehensible input is necessary for language learning, but insufficient for learning certain specifiable aspects of an L2. Paradoxically, comprehensible input may actually inhibit learning on occasion, because it is often possible to understand a message without understanding all the structures and lexical items in the language encoding it, without being aware of not understanding them all.

Researchers seem to concur that for acquisition to happen, some kind of structural analysis of input has to occur. However, the reality appears to be that learners do not perform much of structural analysis (i.e., syntactic processing) when left to their own devices. There is clear evidence from recent SLA research showing not only that when classroom learners engage in meaning-based interaction among themselves, 'they do not spontaneously attend to formal aspects of language very frequently or consistently' (Williams, 2001: 340), but that even when they do, they are not always successful (Pica *et al.*, 1996; Foster, 1998). It would therefore seem that where there is inadequate syntactic processing on the part of the learners, some external intervention would be desirable. A relevant question, then, is: How should the external intervention be best conducted?

As of yet, there is no uniform answer to the question. Views vary considerably on what I see as three sets of binary options: (1) intentional vs. incidental; (2) preemptive vs. reactive; and (3) proactive vs. reactive. First, on the intentional vs. incidental option, opinions are divided over whether form-related instruction should constitute a focus in its own right in the classroom (DeKeyser, 1994, 1995), or be integrated into the meaning-based tasks (Long, 1991; Long & Robinson, 1998). Second, on the preemptive vs. reactive divide, some researchers (e.g., DeKeyser, 1998; Lightbown, 1998, 2000; Spada, 1997) see a need for explicit form-related explanation to preempt errors. Others (e.g., Long & Robinson, 1998), however, think it unnecessary, but rather, that errors can be addressed 'on-line' as they arise in meaning-based communication. Third, on the proactive vs. reactive option, some researchers (e.g., Doughty & Williams, 1998) think it beneficial to make some prediction, prior to, say, a communicative task, on what kinds of forms learners will be likely to use, and 'pre-teach' them, but others disagree. Importantly, underlying these seemingly procedural differences are conceptual differences over such issues as (1) the explicitness (or 'obtrusiveness', to use Doughty & Williams's [1998] term), (2) the timing, and (3) the naturalness, of explicit instruction.

In spite of the conceptual differences, a general understanding has nevertheless been reached, namely that grammar instruction alone would be insufficient, and it needs to be supplemented by implicit learning through rich exposure to the target language input (see, e.g., N. Ellis & Laporte, 1994; MacWhinney, 1997). Simply put, a combination of explicit instruction and implicit learning would be most desirable. As MacWhinney (1997: 297) aptly expresses it:

> Students who receive explicit instruction, as well as implicit exposure to forms, would seem to have the best of both worlds. They can use explicit instruction to allocate attention to specific types of input . . . narrow their hypothesis space . . . tune the weights in their neural networks . . . or consolidate their memory traces. From the viewpoint of psycholinguistic theory, providing learners with explicit instruction along with standard implicit exposure would seem to be a no-lose proposition.

Viewed in this light, explicit instruction – which typically encompasses rule explication and / or corrective feedback –has, potentially, a useful contribution to make to learners' noticing of *specific* features in the input.

A corollary of this is that grammar instruction has a *selective* impact on learning (see, e.g., Lightbown & Spada, 1990; Pica, 1994). Crucially, it has now been generally recognized that the efficacy of explicit instruction depends on its interaction with other variables. Bialystok (1987), for example, notes that explicit teaching or learning can be beneficial when key relationships of the target structure are salient, but can be detrimental when they are not salient or obvious. Such insights are accumulating in the SLA literature. In the ensuing section we will examine some of them, in order to obtain an understanding of some of the variables underlying the selective capability of instruction.

The zone of capability

L2 research to date – laboratory experimental studies, quasi-experimental studies, and classroom descriptive studies – has produced some evidence as well as speculations on what I would call 'zone of capability' for explicit instruction, within which explicit instruction seems to be able to effect change in learners' mental representations and behavior. Operating and interacting with instruction in this zone are, *inter alia*, two related yet separable variables, linguistic complexity and cognitive complexity.

To begin, let us look at some empirical evidence. Pica (1994) specifically addresses the issue of selective impact of instruction by examining L2 acquisition of the English morphemes. Back in the early 1970s, both L1 and L2 researchers (see R. Brown, 1973, for evidence from L1A, and Dulay & Burt, 1975, for evidence of L2A) produced compelling evidence showing a fixed developmental sequence for acquisition of English morphemes, as shown in Table 7.1.

Pica's study targeted three of the morphemes in Table 7.1: simple plural -*s*, progressive -*ing*, and article *a*. They were assumed to be in ascending order of linguistic complexity, defined in terms of both formal (e.g., syntactic, phonological) complexity, and form-function transparency.[12] The study sought to verify (1) the intuitions of syllabus designers who organize instructional material around principles of linguistic complexity and (2) Krashen's claims that certain grammatical morphemes are more learnable than others because of their relatively low degree of linguistic complexity. Informants for the study were 18 native Spanish-speaking adult acquirers, equally divided into three groups that were subjected respectively to three input conditions: (1) formal classroom instruction, (2) everyday social interaction, and (3) a combination of instruction and everyday social

Table 7.1 Order of acquisition of English morphemes

present progressive -ing (*Mommy running*)
plural -s (*two books*)
irregular past forms (*Baby went*)
possessive 's (*daddy's hat*)
copula (*Annie is a nice girl*)
articles 'the' and 'a'
regular past -ed (*She walked*)
third person singular simple present -s (*She runs*)
auxiliary 'be' (*He is coming*)

Source: Lightbown and Spada (1999)

interaction. Data comprised informal conversations between individual informants and the researcher. Analyses of the informants' use of the three morphemes yielded interesting findings. First, in terms of article *a*, which was considered to be the most complex and hence the most difficult to learn, the three groups exhibited comparable production accuracy. Second, in terms of plural *-s*, which was assumed to be the simplest of the three and hence easy to learn, the group that were exposed only to classroom instruction showed greater production accuracy than the other two groups. Third, in terms of progressive *-ing*, which was assumed to be linguistically less complex than article *a* but more so than plural *-s*, the instruction only group were less accurate than the other two groups. Thus, as far as the acquisition of the three morphemes is concerned, classroom instruction showed a distinct yet non-uniform impact. As Pica (1994: 221) summarizes it:

> Classroom instruction appears to **assist** spontaneous production accuracy for the linguistic simple plural *-s*, but **inhibit** production accuracy for the less simple progressive *-ing*. For production of article *a*, a grammatical morpheme whose rules for form-function relationships are not readily transparent, formal instruction appears to have **no impact**, i.e., classroom learners followed the same production pattern as learners who had received no formal instruction. (p. 221; emphasis [bold] added)

Pica argues, from her findings, against the popular practice by syllabus designers whereby second language items are presented in order of increasing linguistic complexity. As an alternative, she recommends that more complex areas of the target grammar be excluded from direct presentation in the second-language syllabus so that attention can be focused on those items which appear to be responsive to explicit instruction. It could be argued, though, that in the alleged no-impact case, instruction did have some impact on classroom learners but that it was not any more effective than natural exposure, for without such impact, how was it possible that the instruction only group achieved a degree of accuracy comparable to the other two groups? What perhaps should have been claimed was that instruction was not at all superior to natural exposure in term of acquisition of article *a*.

Still, this study lends support to Krashen's (1981) insight that simple linguistic rules are more appropriate targets for explicit instruction than complex rules (cf. DeKeyser, 1994; Gass & Selinker, 2001; Robinson, 1996). It is worth noting that for Krashen as well as for Pica, linguistic complexity is not just correlative with cognitive complexity, but causative of it, a point to which we shall return shortly.

Complex rules are also known as 'fuzzy rules' (see, e.g., DeKeyser, 1994; N. Ellis & Laporte, 1997). There are at least two facets to the fuzziness that seem particularly apt to render these rules hard to teach and learn. First, certain linguistic items (e.g., English articles *the* and *a*) do not lend themselves to a formal analysis, and hence are difficult for teachers to describe and for learners to internalize. Typically, they have multiple form-function mappings (e.g., having one form perform multiple functions or having one function performed by multiple synonymous forms). An example would be the conjugations of transitive and intransitive verbs in Hungarian. The transitive conjugation is required for *John eats the apple* or *John eats Bill's apple,* but the intransitive conjugation is needed for *John eats an apple*. According to MacWhinney (2001: 82), 'there are some 13 conditions which . . . control the choice between the transitive and intransitive conjugations. There is no single principle that can be used to group these 13 conditions. Instead, transitivity, definiteness, and referential disambiguation all figure in as factors in making this choice . . . Here is an area where attempts at formal linguistic analysis on the learner's part only make matters worse'.

Second, certain linguistic structures have intricate semantic-syntactic mappings wherein the syntactic representation is semantically determined. Falling into this category are, *inter alia,* verbs of causative alternation and unaccusatives[13] (Levin & Rappaport Hovav, 1995). As an illustration of causative alternation, let us consider the English verb *break*. The verb *break* can be either transitive (e.g., *He broke the glass*) or intransitive (e.g., *The glass broke*). This overt-syntactic difference is underlain by a difference in the lexical process whereby a semantic structure is mapped onto an argument structure (i.e., the deep structure), as schematized below:

[7–1a] *Intransitive* break

LSR	[[*x* DO-SOMETHING] CAUSE [*y* BECOME *BROKEN*]]	
	↓	
Lexical binding	Ø	
Linking rules		↓
Argument structure		< *y* >

[7–1b] *Transitive* break

LSR	[[*x* DO SOMETHING] CAUSE [*y* BECOME *BROKEN*]]	
Linking rules	↓	↓
Argument structure	*x*	< *y* >

(Levin & Rappaport Hovav, 1995: 108)

Here LSR stands for lexical semantic structure. As shown, the two verb forms share a single LSR, but differ in the argument structure. This difference results from the fact that in the intransitive case, but not in the transitive case, binding of the external causer takes place in the mapping, through the linking rules, from the LSR onto the argument structure to indicate that, semantically, the action occurs without volitional control. As noted earlier, verbs of causative alternation and unaccusatives are candidates for fossilization due to their underlying complexities (see also Balcom, 1997; Montrul, 2001).

Complex rules, according to Krashen, can only be acquired over time through implicit exposure to comprehensible input, given a positive affective environment. Granting that implicit exposure is a better alternative than explicit instruction for learning complex rules (cf. N. Ellis & Laporte, 1997; Sharwood Smith, 1994b; see, however, Robinson, 1996, for counter evidence), some key questions still remain: Can complex rules ever be fully acquired? Can adult L2 learners be like child L1 acquirers who are able to acquire complex rules by generalizing from a rich database of, say, collocations and phrases?[14]

Related to, yet separable from, the notion of linguistic complexity is cognitive complexity – defined here as complexity imposed by the learner. It is clear from the above discussion that the two facets to linguistic complexity are both intrinsic to the linguistic features to be acquired. In other words, they are pertinent to the target language, and hence are external to the learner. As mentioned, for some researchers, linguistic complexity is causative of cognitive complexity. For others, there is perhaps a need to differentiate between linguistic complexity and cognitive complexity, with the latter pertaining to the learner's response to external stimuli. Such a distinction seems necessary, for there are times when linguistic features that are not complex (in the sense assumed above) nevertheless appear to be difficult for learners to acquire. A prime source of these features might be L1-L2 specifiable contrasts. Such contrasts, as Long (1996: 125) notes, 'provide fertile ground for premature IL stabilization'. An oft-cited example in this connection is the contrast in adverb placement between English and French. In English, an adverb may not interrupt a verb and its direct object, but it may in French. In the terms of Chomsky's (1986) Adjacency Parameter,[15] English assumes the parametric value of [+ strict adjacency] and hence does not permit **Mary does <u>slowly</u> her homework*, whereas French has the [– strict adjacency] value and hence permits *Marie fait <u>lentement</u> ses devoirs*. What is remarkable about this case is that English speakers learning French do not seem to have trouble acquiring the French verb-adverb-object structure, but Francophone speakers learning English, as research (see, e.g., L. White, 1991) has shown, have persistent difficulty undoing it in their L2 English, even when they have reached the advanced proficiency level. Thus, although the linguistic structure in question is not complex, it nevertheless presents a learnability problem for Francophone speakers learning English. L. White (1991), from a learnability perspective, argues that in the case of English speakers learning French, there is plenty of positive evidence to inform learners that French allows an extra possibility for placing adverbs – hence the difficulty in resetting the parameter to the French value (i.e., [- strict adjacent]) – but that in the case of Francophone speakers learning English, there is no direct positive evidence to the learners that the French verb-adverb-direct object string is not permissible in English, hence the difficulty in resetting the parameter to the English value (i.e., [+ strict adjacent]). In other words, in the case of Francophone speakers, there is nothing in the L2 input to block negative transfer from the L1. L. White's study shows that the French-English interlanguage structure is ultimately incapable of alteration through instruction (i.e., explicit rule explanation and corrective feedback). She points out that failure to reset to the L2 parametric value is a case of fossilization.

While in the above example, it is (1) the L1-L2 difference and (2) the absence of relevant positive evidence in the L2 input that have jointly created cognitive complexity for a particular group of learners, research has also shown that other factors such as lack of developmental readiness, transfer of training, and so forth may also contribute to cognitive complexity and create resistance to instruction. Pienemann (1985), for instance, suggests, in the name of the Teachability Hypothesis, that developmental features[16] can only be learned when learners are ready (i.e., they have possessed the processing prerequisites). His own experiment with teaching Stage III structure of the developmental sequence for German word order[17] to young L2 learners who were at Stages I and II shows, among other things, that the learners from both stages mastered the formal learning tasks in the instruction, but only those from Stage II were able to transfer their learned knowledge to their actual speech production. This, therefore, indicates that the taught structure was truly acquired by Stage II learners, but not by Stage I learners. In this case, only Stage II learners had possessed the processing prerequisites for acquiring the Stage III structure; hence they were able to fully process and acquire the new structure. Findings of this nature have also been reported for other learners in other contexts. For example, Bardovi-Harlig (1995: 165), in her cross-sectional study of the effect of instruction on L2 acquisition of English tense/aspect (i.e., simple past tense and pluperfect), found that 'learners benefit from instruction only when they are at the stage at which they would have naturally acquired the rule in question'. However, she points out – based on her observation of the non-emergence of the taught structure in the learners who appeared to be developmentally ready – that 'meeting the acquisitional stages . . . is necessary but not sufficient for the emergence of the [taught structure]'(p. 168). She thereby hints that in addition to 'developmental readiness', teaching and learning could still be tampered with by other intervening variables. (One such variable could be learners' level of understanding of the taught structure.) It is worth noting in passing that in her study, Bardovi-Harlig operationalized 'readiness' not in terms of reaching the point preceding the to-be-learned feature in a fixed sequence, as Pienemann did, but in terms of meeting morphosyntactic and semantic prerequisites. Thus, for the case of learning English pluperfect, two such prerequisites were posited: (1) stable use (i.e., appropriate communicative use at 80%) of simple past tense, and (2) the expression of reverse-order reports, with (1) having precedence over (2).

To recapitulate, central to Pienemann's (1985, 1986, 1989, 1998, 2002) processability theory is the argument that the trajectory of L2 development is determined by constraints derived from the architecture of the emerging L2 grammar. By the same token, these constraints govern teachability. Hence, linguistic structures that are beyond learners' current processing capacity are bound to be inaccessible, and impervious to instruction. Drawing on this insight, one may therefore interpret cognitive complexity as a dynamic notion – it is something that is capable of change as the learner moves along a developmental continuum. In addition, one could even hypothesize that instruction will potentially have an effect on the learning of any developmental features insofar as it meets the processing constraints. It comes as no surprise that Pienemann has proposed developing 'learnable syllabuses' – syllabuses that aim at accommodating learner-internal processing constraints.

In summary, when determining what is or is not teachable, we need to factor in both the linguistic complexity and the cognitive complexity. There may or may not be a causal relationship between the two. After all, the two are not of the same nature: whereas one (i.e., linguistic complexity) is primarily a static notion, the other (i.e., cognitive complexity) can be dynamic, subject to change as learners' proficiency increases. Consequently, instruction – after Pica's suggestion – should sidestep the linguistically complex structures,[18] on the one hand, and on the other hand, seek to ease cognitive complexity– after Pienemann's suggestion – by accommodating processing constraints.

Aside from the linguistic complexity and the cognitive complexity, researchers have also noted that some linguistic items may be hard to acquire simply due to their lack of perceptual saliency. Here again, we may distinguish between two types of saliency, the physical and the semantical. Certain linguistic features are perceptually non-salient due, for example, to their physical attributes such as their position in a sentence (e.g., sentence-medial as opposed to sentence-initial or final) and their syllabicity (e.g., syllabic as opposed to non-syllabic), while others are, semantically, non-salient because they carry little semantic value.

Semantic saliency has recently drawn much attention from researchers. Of note is VanPatten. In expounding his input processing theory, VanPatten (1996) posits a number of processing principles. Of particular relevance to the present discussion is P1 that states:

> P1. Learners process input for meaning before they process it for form.
>
> P1(a). Learners process content words in the input before anything else.
>
> P1(b). Learners prefer processing lexical items to grammatical items (e.g., morphological markings) for semantic information.
>
> P1(c). Learners prefer processing 'more meaningful' morphology before 'less' or 'nonmeaningful' morphology.

This principle, along with its three corollaries, specifies L2 learners' natural inclination to process input for meaning rather than form (cf. Skehan, 1998), and their ordered preference for meaning-related linguistic items. Of particular interest to us here is that it pinpoints linguistic items that are the least attended to by L2 learners, namely, morphological features that have low communicative value.

In VanPatten (1996), communicative value is defined as 'the relative contribution a form makes to the referential meaning of an utterance and is based on the presence or absence of two features: inherent semantic value and redundancy within the sentence-utterance' (p. 24). Simply put, the two variables (i.e., semantic value and formal redundancy) may enter into different combinations to determine the communicative value of given linguistic forms. Table 7.2 displays the major permutations and their resultant communicative value.

As Table 7.2 shows, a form that has inherent semantic value (i.e., + semantic) and that is not redundant (i.e., – redundant) has high communicative value. Conversely, if a form has semantic value (i.e., + semantic) but is formally redundant (i.e., + redundant), it has low communicative value. An example of the latter would be the English third person singular – *s*. This form undoubtedly has semantic content in that it encodes the semantic notion of third person singular, as well as the temporal frame within which the action occurs. Yet it is made redundant by the co-occurrence of lexical items (e.g., he, everyday) that express the same meanings. Moreover, syntactically, the English canonical subject-verb word order renders the – *s* redundant, for the notion of 'third person singular' is already carried by the subject. Hence, the form is of low communicative value, and as such, it has low perceptual salience. Linguistic forms of this type are developmentally late. As VanPatten (1996: 30) notes:

Table 7.2 Semantic value, redundancy, and communicative value

Communicative value	*Semantic value*	*Redundancy*	*Examples*
High	+	–	English *-ing*
Medium	+	+/–[19]	Tense markers
Low	–	+	Inflections on adjectives in Italian, e.g., *a* in *blanca* in the phrase *la casa blanca*
Low	+	+	English 3rd person *-s*

> Grammatical form conveying semantic information that also is encoded lexically will tend to not be detected; the learner instead relies on the lexical items for the semantic information. The learners' internal mechanisms will detect grammatical form early on only if it is relatively high in communicative value. Otherwise, grammatical form is detected over time only as the learner's ability to get meaning from the input is increasingly automatized (becomes more effort-free). This increasing automatization of comprehension releases attentional resources for the processing of form that was previously skipped (undetected).

Assuming its validity, this view raises at least one question for us: How long would it take before the learner could detect grammatical forms that are low in communicative value? VanPatten himself notes, albeit incidentally, that in pidgin and fossilized speech, 'it is precisely [this kind of] features that tend to be absent' (1996: 27), thereby hinting that if learners were to be left to their own devices, they would never process the non-salient forms. Indeed, as study after study has demonstrated, learners either do not care, or are unable, to pay attention to these forms. The answer to the question, then, as has been proposed by many (see, e.g., Harley & Swain, 1984), lies in explicit instruction.

The ongoing debate on its role in adult SLA notwithstanding, explicit instruction has by now been generally recognized as being able to (1) raise learners' awareness of aspects of the target language, and (2) speed up learning (see, e.g., R. Ellis, 1994b; N. Ellis & Laporte, 1997; Long & Robinson, 1998). Although views still differ as to whether or not awareness is crucial to learning, few have denied that the majority of adult L2 learners depend on external assistance such as rule explanation and corrective feedback for improving accuracy (*passim* the SLA literature). Even Krashen, an ardent advocate of implicit learning in lieu of explicit learning, succumbs to the view that conscious learning of 'late-acquired' aspects of language can be used to supplement acquisition (i.e., implicit learning).

Explicit instruction raises learners' consciousness through (1) facilitating noticing (i.e., drawing learners' attention to specific linguistic features in the input); and (2) facilitating comparison (i.e., helping learners see the difference between what they noticed in the input and what they produced in output). Therefore, in principle, explicit instruction should be able to drive learning, where learners fail to notice, or notice wrong, features. N. Ellis (2002a) gives a list of such scenarios, some of which are reproduced below:

a. Learners fail to notice cues because they are not salient or essential for understanding the meaning of an utterance;
b. Learners fail to notice that a feature needs to be processed in a different new way;
c. Learners fail to notice TL-specific patterns of form-function mapping, due to competitive interference from L1;
d. Learners notice the wrong things, generating false hypotheses, and chasing hares.

Whether or not explicit instruction can indeed bring about restructuring in these cases, thereby stimulating learning, has yet to be resolved empirically. A paramount issue, of course, is whether or not explicit instruction – once restructuring has taken place– can effect change in L2 spontaneous performance in genuinely communicative situations. After all, comprehension[20] and production are different systems such that one does not always feed into the other. As Pienemann (1985: 47) notes:

> Findings from language processing (cf. Bever, 1981; Forster, 1979) show that very different procedures underlie these two aspects of speech processing. There is also evidence from language acquisition that comprehension and production develop as separate abilities.

The crux of the issue, then, is: Can explicit instruction trigger changes in both comprehension and production systems? More precisely, do changes in knowledge representation correlate with changes in spontaneous production? Again, these questions seem to be taking us back to the earlier-mentioned theoretical interface vs. non-interface controversy. But, as Hulstijn and de Graaff (1994: 101) have pointed out, 'a discipline cannot exist of theories alone, it must advance through empirical work as well', For them, the question of whether or not grammar instruction aids L2 acquisition can hardly be answered with an unqualified 'yes' or 'no'. Rather, empirical research should be carried out to explore the conditions under which grammar instruction facilitates or otherwise impedes acquisition. To aid this effort, Hulstijn and DeGraaff have laid out a rich research program that contains nine concrete hypotheses, as follows:

> H1: The advantage of the provision of explicit instruction, in comparison with the non-provision of explicit instruction, is greater in the case of aspects falling outside the scope of UG than in the case of aspects falling inside its scope.
> H2: The advantage of explicit instruction is greater when the L1 setting of a parameter forms a superset and the L2 setting a subset of a parameter, than in the reverse situation.
> H3: The advantage of explicit instruction is greater in the case of complex rules than in the case of simple rules.
> H4: The advantage of explicit instruction is greater when a rule applies to many cases (large scope) and when it has a high success rate (high reliability) than when it has a small scope and-/or a low reliability.
> H5: The advantage of explicit instruction is greater when language production can only be based on rule application than when it can be based not only on rule application but also on the retrieval of individually stored items ('items learning').
> H6: The advantage of explicit instruction is greater in the case of complex inflectional rules (which are also reliable and large in scope) than in the case of simple inflectional rules (also reliable and large in scope).
> H7: The advantage of explicit instruction is greater in the case of L2 comprehension than in the case of L2 production.
> H8: As for L2 comprehension, the advantage of explicit instruction is greater in the case of grammatical features with semantic implications than in the case of purely formal (semantically redundant) features.
> H9: As for L2 production, the advantage of explicit instruction is greater in the case of purely formal (semantically redundant) features than in the case of grammatical features with semantic implications.

These hypotheses, extensive in scope, highlight the interaction between instruction and constraining variables such as linguistic domain, complexity, scope and reliability, and semantic or formal redundancy of the target structures. They have yet to be tested on a variety of learner populations in various learning contexts. But prior to that, a correct understanding of the hypotheses is essential. An example would serve to illustrate the importance.

At first glance, H3 seems to have been refuted by Pica's (1994) study. (Recall that her study showed that instruction had more impact on the acquisition of simple rules than of complex ones.) A closer examination of Pica's study and of Hulstijn and De Graaff's, however, would discount this interpretation. For one thing, the researchers differed in the way they defined the notion of complexity. In Hulstijn and De Graaff (1994: 103), complexity was construed, in a declarative manner, in terms of 'the number (and/or the type) of criteria to be applied in order to arrive at the correct form'. A hypothetical example: Language X and language Y both have two suffixes, – *s* and – *os*, for marking plurality, but they differ in the way each applies the suffixes. In language X, the suffix –*s* is added to singular nouns ending on a vowel, and the suffix –*os* to nouns ending on a consonant. In language Y, in contrast, -*s* is added to nouns ending on a vowel as well as to nouns ending on a consonant and containing a front vowel in the penultimate syllable, and –*os* to nouns ending on a consonant and containing a back vowel in the penultimate syllable. Thus, in terms of the number of criteria used to derive a correct form, the rule governing plurality marking in language Y is more complex than in language X. Clearly, this view on complexity has focused more on the formal properties than anything else. In contrast, in Pica (1994) complexity was associated more with form-function transparency than with formal complications. Hence, Pica's definition of complexity had a wider scope than that pursued by Hulstijn and De Graaff. Another, yet related, aspect of difference is that while Hulstijn and De Graaff applied the notion of complexity to categorical rules (i.e., rules that have a high reliability), Pica applied it to fuzzy rules (i.e., prototypes or rules that have a low reliability).[21] Owing to these differences, findings from Pica's study do not constitute falsifying evidence for H3. Clearly, H3 can also be recast as follows: the advantage of explicit instruction is greater in the case of complex categorical rules than in the case of simple categorical rules. The rationale behind this hypothesis was that 'simple formal phenomena may be salient enough in the input to be discovered by L2 learners spontaneously, without the help of explicit instruction', and that 'in the case of complex phenomena . . . explicit instruction may save learners considerable time in discovering their intricacies' (Hulstijn & De Graaff, 1994:103; for a recent discussion of the notion of complexity, see DeKeyser, 1998).

Summing up our discussion thus far of the question we posed at the outset, i.e., to what extent instruction aids acquisition, the answer appears to be 'to some extent'; that is, instruction 'is useful to some extent, for some forms, for some students, at some point in the learning process' (DeKeyser, 1998: 42; cf. Larsen-Freeman, 1995). As such, it can undoubtedly make a difference to adult L2 learning, yet its role in the process appears to be *supplemental* as opposed to *fundamental*. Implicit learning via exposure to naturalistic input, on the other hand, remains essential to developing L2 competence. Further, the supplemental role – in the view of many (e.g., R. Ellis, 1994a; Long & Robinson, 1998) – is compensatory in nature. Due to the fact that adult learners have a weakened capacity for implicit learning,[22] comprehensible input, though necessary, is not always sufficient. Specifically, adult learners are found to be particularly inapt at learning, from comprehensible input alone, linguistic items that 'are rare, and / or semantically lightweight, and / or perceptually nonsalient, and / or cause little or no communicative distress' (Long & Robinson, 1998: 23). Hence, for successful learning of these forms, and for destabilizing the 'hard-to-control fossilizable use of structures' (Mellow *et al.*, 1996), instruction has been assumed to be necessary. However, as Allwright (1984: 4) points out, 'learners do not learn everything they are taught'. Thus, even on the acquisition of those linguistic features, the effect of instruction, it is recognized, may be constrained by a host of linguistic and psychological variables including linguistic domain, complexity, semantic and functional saliency, learner readiness, and, perhaps, learners' personal agenda.[23] An insight we have gained from the L2 research to date is that not all linguistic features are equally amenable to explicit instruction; whereas some linguistic features are teachable, others may never be. Hence, from the fact that a vast number of L2 learners around the globe learn L2 through instruction, it does *not* follow that explicit instruction (alone) is capable of turning out competent L2 users. If this conclusion is correct, then it does follow that subjecting L2 learners solely to explicit instruction can impede learning – an issue to which we now turn.

To What Extent Does Instruction Promote Fossilization?

Among second language teachers, there appears to be a rather widespread fear of fossilization – which VanPatten (1988) has called *fossilophobia* – and a parallel conviction that corrective feedback – an essential part of explicit instruction – prevents fossilization. The two excerpts below may attest to this sentiment.

> **Teacher 1:**
> Hi everyone!
> I am a teacher trainee who has just started his teaching practicum. I have chosen the Communicative Approach as a theoretical framework for my classroom activities and practices. Nevertheless, the CA tends to keep a blind eye on errors because communication is its ultimate aim. I wonder whether I should focus on correction of erroneous productions of my students particularly at the levels of pronunciation and grammar because, I think, neglecting errors coupled with the limited exposure to authentic language will simply result in fossilization.
> *Source*: TESL-L@CUNYVM.CUNY.EDU.
> **Teacher 2:**
> A teacher has authority to correct student errors but too much negative

> cognitive feedback would cause students to quit talking. However, if we let their errors slide, we get fossilization of errors. Are some methods of corrective feedback more effective than others in your experience?
> *Source*: SLART-L@LISTSERV.CUNY.EDU.

Over the last several years, I have witnessed numerous messages of similar nature, on TES-L and SLRT-L.[24] They all seem to entertain the notion that errors have to be dealt with or otherwise can fossilize, and that teacher correction is *the* way to save learners from fossilization.

Teachers are by no means alone in this conception. Sharing the view are also some L2 researchers (e.g., Higgs & Clifford, 1982; Lightbown & Spada, 1999; Montrul, 2001; Tomasello & Herron, 1988; Vigil & Oller, 1976; Valette, 1991). For example, Vigil and Oller (1976: 284–295) assert:[25]

> Unless learners receive appropriate sorts of cognitive feedback concerning errors, those errors can be expected to fossilize.
>
> . . .
>
> As long as some non-excessive corrective feedback is available to prod the learner to continue to modify attempts to express himself in the target language, it is predictable that the learner's grammatical system will continue to develop. If the corrective feedback (whether self-generated or provided by the learner's interlocutors) drops below some minimal level or disappears altogether, the grammar, or the rules no longer attended by corrective feedback, will tend to fossilize.

Echoing this, Higgs and Clifford 1982: 78) add:

> When students are regularly rewarded for linguistically inaccurate but otherwise successful communication of meaning or intent that the threat of proactive interference in the form of fossilization looms large.

It has thus been conceived that the absence of corrective feedback gives way to fossilization (for a rebuttal of Vigil & Oller's view and of Higgs & Clifford's view, see, respectively, Selinker & Lamendella [1979] and VanPatten [1988]). Quite clearly, this either/or kind of conception confers upon corrective feedback an absolute capability to eradicate errors and thereby to prevent fossilization. However, this does not seem to fit reality; 'there has been and continues to be empirical evidence that a mastery-oriented emphasis on identifying and correcting learner errors may not be as effective as teacher would like to be' (Cohen, 1997: 133; see also Chaudron, 1988).

Two specific findings out of many can be brought to bear on the issue at hand. The first is that corrective feedback is capable of effecting positive change in some interlanguage features, but not in others (see, e.g., Han & Selinker, 1999; Long *et al.*, 1998; see also the discussion above on the role of explicit instruction). As Doughty and Williams (1998: 205) aptly state it, 'some forms do not need or may not benefit from [corrective feedback]'. Given the modular nature of language, the finding is not at all surprising (Sharwood Smith, 1999), and it alone could discount the view of corrective feedback as a (or worse, the) device for counteracting fossilization. The second finding is that the efficacy of corrective feedback is contingent on a variety of moderator variables, including, but not limited to, the manner of delivery, timing, developmental readiness, learner attention, and perhaps most importantly, whether or not the provision of corrective feedback is based on an understanding of the true causal factors for the learning problem (see, e.g., Han, 2001b; Han & Selinker, 1999). Both findings, therefore, imply that a blind conviction in the power of corrective feedback to combat fossilization is unjustified. This said, it is important to recognize that although much investigation, theoretical and empirical, has been carried out to date, the general understanding of when, what, and who(m) to correct is still limited; conflicting findings are as yet the norm rather than the exception (see Chaudron, 1988; Muranoi, 2000; Nicholas *et al.*, 2001, for reviews). As a consequence, we have not yet reached a categorical understanding on (1) which linguistic structures for (2) which learners at (3) which point in the developmental process under (4) which conditions are amenable to (5) which corrective strategies (cf. Han, 2002c). Until such understanding is available to us, we can only remain speculative, rather than certain, about the extent to which corrective feedback can, positively or negatively, impact on adult SLA.

What research to date has made crystal clear, however, is that corrective feedback is a far more complex process than has been previously conceived. In this process, (1) there is a two-way relationship between the feedback giver and the receiver (Vigil & Oller, 1976), importantly, both being in the role of information provider; and (2) for feedback to stimulate restructuring and change in behavior, there needs to be harmony in attention between the two parties. Consider that a teacher is the feedback giver and a student the feedback receiver (Han, 2001b), in which case, it is necessary that both parties tune in to each other's output to ensure mutual understanding of each other's intent. If this fails to happen, the teacher's corrective feedback, as attested in Han (2001b), will be, at best, useless, but at worst, it can promote fossilization inasmuch as it reinforces interlanguage deviance.

Of note, recent SLA research has seen an increasing sense of the need to understand learners' responses to corrective feedback and their perceptions thereof. The empirical studies conducted over the last several years have largely attested to the validity of this line of inquiry; the results are revealing. Roberts (1995), for instance, showed that his informants were unaware of the teacher feedback most of the time, thus rendering a considerable amount of the teacher feedback useless. In their investigation of L2 learners' perception of corrective feedback, Mackey *et al.*, (2000: 492) found that 'there was evidence of uptake of a little over half (52%) of all the feedback provided.' Findings such as these seem to point up a paradox with corrective feedback. That is, in theory, corrective feedback is meant to draw learners' attention to gaps between the TL input and their interlanguage output but in reality, learners oftentimes fail to notice or misinterpret the corrective intent of the feedback provided. Gass (1988) alerts us that if the learner fails to discern the real difference between the information available in the correction and his or her error, fossilization is likely to result. Thus, it is not so much the corrective feedback *per se* but the learner's understanding thereof which may potentially determine whether or not fossilization will occur.

The importance of the learner perspective on corrective feedback has even led Long and Robinson (1998) to forsake *error correction* – a term typically reserved for a pedagogic strategy employed by teachers – in favor of *corrective feedback*. This is quite understandable, given that it is the learner, not the teacher (i.e., an outsider), who has control over what errors will be corrected. Error, after all, is an externally norm-referenced notion.[26] As Gass and Selinker (1994: 67) aptly put it:

> Errors are only errors from a teacher's or researcher's perspective, not from the learner's. Taken from the perspective of a learner who has created a systematic entity called an interlanguage (IL), everything that forms part of that interlanguage system by definition belongs there. Hence, there can be no errors in that system. *Errors are only errors with reference to some external norm* (in this case the TL). (emphasis in original)

Following from this line of reasoning, for corrective feedback to be potentially useful, it is necessary that some sort of attention-getting mechanism be built in the feedback process to enable the learner to perceive it for what it is, and further, to recognize the gap between the feedback and his or her own output. Unfortunately, these crucial, procedural details are, more often than not, absent from the real-world feedback process.

Moving from the if/then type of conception of corrective feedback and fossilization to teachers' fossilophobia: Does teachers' fear of fossilization have any validity? The answer seems to be in the affirmative. One of the understandings that L2 research has generated is that classroom learning provides learners with a unique experience that, on the one hand, has notable advantages (e.g., resulting in faster learning rate, as mentioned earlier) but that, on the other hand, has conspicuous limitations. Some of the limitations arise from the constraints intrinsic to the learning setting (e.g., impoverished input, the restrictive opportunity for use of language), but others are contrived (e.g., the way instruction is practiced in the classroom). All these constraints, as will be argued and shown shortly, may, in turn, be conducive to fossilization.

Pursuing a systematic understanding of these constraints is of great importance to the construction of any proper theory of instructed second language acquisition, though over the past several decades, it has almost become a standard practice for L2 researchers to explore and report the positive effects of instruction rather than both the positive and the negative ones. The as yet lack of systematic research on the latter notwithstanding, insights and evidence (direct and indirect) are already accumulating that suggest that instruction does have an inhibiting impact on learning. Some of these insights are presented and discussed below. In the interest of space, I will center the discussion around three possible sources of hindrance to learning: (1) classroom input; (2) pedagogic strategies, and (3) opportunities for practice.

Classroom input

That classroom input – comprised primarily of (1) teacher talk, (2) textbooks, and (3) peer speech – is constraining in many ways has been recognized by SLA researchers. Gass and Selinker (2001: 326), for instance, claim that 'instructed learning may . . . result in inappropriate conclusions drawn by the learners precisely because the input is often impoverished and because emphasis on certain forms is selective'. Similarly, R. Ellis (1994a: 84) points out that 'the input that learners derive in the classroom, whether from the teacher or other learners, may not always be the best kind for acquisition'. Entertaining this view are also Lightbown and Spada (1999: 17) who maintain that 'instructional input contributes further to the complexity of the [learning process]'. These claims seem well justified by empirical evidence (see, e.g., Kasper, 1982; Lightbown, 1983; Swain, 1988, 1991; Tarone & Liu, 1996; L. White, 1991). Swain (1991: 99), for example, has provided the following picture of teachers' use of language in the early immersion classes:

> Teachers created few opportunities for systematically using contrasting forms and functions in their content teaching. Rather, teacher talk was spontaneously used in service of the content being taught. Consequently, for example, the use of different verb forms was extraordinarily

> skewed. Over 75% of the verbs used were in the present or imperative. Only about 15% of verbs used by the teachers were in the past tense, 6% in the future tense and 3% in the conditional. Of the 15% used in the past tense, about two-thirds were in the past indefinite and one-third in the imperfect. The use of the imperfect was almost completely limited to the verbs *avoir, être, faire,* and *vouloir*. Its use with action verbs was virtually nonexistent (Swain, 1989). Sorting out form and function on this basis would be difficult, and indeed, it is an enduring problem of the immersion students.

In a similar context, Lyster (1998: 51) examined the provision of corrective feedback by teachers in four French immersion classrooms at the elementary level. He found that 'teachers frequently use positive feedback to express approval of the content of learners' messages, irrespective of well-formedness, to accompany, also in equal proportions, recasts, non-corrective repetition, and even topic continuation moves following errors'. The following examples serve to illustrate how repetition was used by the same teacher to perform the corrective and non-corrective functions.

[7–2] Non-corrective repetition
(T3, Language Arts, Jan. 16)
St: *Il faut qu'ils fassent plein de travail.*
'They have to do a lot of work'
T: *Il faut qu'ils fassent plein de travail?*
'They have to do a lot of work?'

[7–3] Corrective repetition
(T3. Language Arts, Mar. 29)
St: *J'ai réussi ma lettre.*
'I succeeded my letter'.
T3: *Je comprends pas, **t'as** réussi **ta** lettre.*
'I don't understand, you succeeded your letter.'

(Lyster, 1998: 63–69)

In [7–2], by repetition with rising intonation, the teacher sought confirmation of the student's message, and in [7–3], repetition was used in conjunction with, and preceded by, a clarification request to draw the student's attention to the problematic utterance, hence performing a corrective function. The dual functions of repetition, corrective and non-corrective vis-à-vis form and content, may not always be easily distinguishable, and could in fact create obscurity and ambiguity for students. Ambiguity of the above sort in the classroom discourse is further compounded by the fact that the teacher sometimes misused positive feedback, as illustrated by [7–4]:

[7–4] Positive feedback
(T3, Math, Jan. 16)
St: *Moi j'ai arrivée au fin.* [Error]
'I am got to end.'
T3: *OK. Très bien.* [Approval] *Bon, on est supposé d'avoir presque le numéro un de fait. Je vais aller voir.* [Topic continuation]
'OK. Very good. Alright, we should have number one almost done. I'm going to see.'

(Lyster, 1998: 69)

It is evident from [7–4] that in a desire for topic continuation, the teacher inadvertently reinforced the student's error (i.e., *Moi j'ai arrivée au fin*) with positive feedback (i.e., *OK. Très bien*). The teacher's approval may have sent a confusing message not only to the student but also to other participants in the class who may have noticed the problematic nature of the student's utterance. This kind of input, in light of insights from Allwright (1984), inhibits rather than promotes learning. Allwright conceptualizes classroom interaction as a process whereby learning opportunities are created independently by teachers and by learners. The corollary is that learning can be limited by the opportunities teachers create for learners, and that it can be determined by the degree to which teacher-created learning opportunities match learner-sought opportunities. From this, it further follows (1) that teachers' failure to provide corrective feedback where and when it is expected may reduce learners' opportunity to learn, and (2) that teachers' provision of wrong feedback, as is the case above, may guide learning in the wrong direction. An equally relevant point has made by Vigil and Oller (1996: 285), namely that '. . . any forms that elicit favorable feedback will tend to fossilize'. Needless to say, teaching as manifested in [7–4] is not accelerating, but rather slowing down, the learning process.

A major drive for grammar development, as many have argued, lies in whether or not learners are able to recognize discrepancies between the target language grammar and their own, and further, whether or not they are able to restructure their own grammar (see, e.g., Gass, 2000; Mackey *et al.*, 2000; Mackey & Philp, 1998). Teacher corrective feedback is meant precisely to aid this process, though, in practice, it is not always successful, as earlier mentioned. Failure to induce learner noticing is often attributable to the existence of a mismatch in attention between the teacher and the learner, due largely to the lack of understanding on the teacher's part of the factors underlying the learning problem. Han (2001b) provides clear evidence showing that teacher corrective feedback, when delivered on the basis of hunch as opposed to a sound understanding of the causal factors, can prolong the existence of interlanguage deviance, thereby promoting fossilization.

The impoverished input does not derive solely from teachers, however. An equally potent source thereof is textbooks. Limited in scope and complexity, textbooks usually take on a rather artificial format, with input organized and sequenced according largely to the textbook writers' own interpretation of how languages should be learned. Typically, target language forms are presented in discrete (if not isolated) units, and accompanied by exercises created to practice them almost exclusively.[27] Moreover, due to various constraints, only a subset of forms may be represented there. As a consequence, learners are provided with a rather skewed picture of the target language, and are led into overusing or inappropriately using the linguistic forms. Overuse or inappropriate use, as Lightbown (1983: 219) aptly points out, indicates that 'the learner has an incorrect or incomplete understanding of the functions of the form and the limits of its use'.

In her analysis of the use of grammatical morphemes by young French-speakers receiving formal ESL instruction and of aspects of the target language to which they were exposed in the classroom, Lightbown (1983) identified that the frequency with which given forms appeared in the classroom input was a leading cause of the learners' overuse of linguistic forms, and further, that it had a delayed effect on their learning. An example follows:

> The grade 6 students had practiced *–ing* and copula and auxiliary *–s* to the point of overlearning. Even though the *–ing* was relatively infrequent in grade 6 classroom language, their overlearning of the form may have caused it to remain in their speech throughout that year. Subsequently, the decline in frequency of *–ing* and the corresponding rise in frequency of uninflected verbs may have led to their later preference for uninflected verbs in their speech. (1983: 239)

This kind of sudden rise and recession in the use of linguistic forms by the classroom learners is in marked contrast with how learning unfolds in a naturalistic environment, where learners would gradually build up their system, starting with using uninflected verbs and gradually adding grammatical markers. Lightbown cautions that 'by forcing learners to repeat and overlearn forms which have no associated meaning to contrast them with any other form(s), we may be setting up barriers which have to be broken down before the learners can begin to build up their own interlanguage systems' (1983: 239).

Another notable fact from this study is that the learners' production manifested a different order of acquisition of the morphemes under investigation than that reported for naturalistic learners in other studies (see, e.g., Krashen, 1977; Dulay & Burt, 1978).[28] For Lightbown (1983: 240), this difference was directly attributable to the nature of the classroom input that the learners had received:

> The fact that our learners' accuracy orders differ from those observed in previous studies may be due to the exposure they had to a distorted version of the English language and to the fact that they were required to repeat and practice sentences whose grammatical complexities were far beyond what they would have included in their speech if they had been acquiring English through communicative interaction involving more varied natural language.

As far as textbooks are concerned, the distorted version of the target language may, as is the case above, arise from the artificial sequence of input, but it may also be induced by the way in which a textbook presents grammatical rules. Through a longitudinal case study (see Chapter 6), Han and Selinker (1999; see also Han, 2001b) documented how a textbook explanation of a rule governing an inverted structure in the target language, Norwegian, had misled a learner to formulate incorrect knowledge about the word order, and that such incorrect understanding coalesced with the influence of the learner's native language, resulting in an interlanguage construction that was both persistent and resistant to the teacher feedback.

Still another source of distorted input is peer speech. A case in point is the classrooms where communicative language teaching dominates. As K. Johnson (1996: 129) notes:

> Many communicative techniques placed the emphasis on 'getting the message across', and sometimes this inevitably occurs at the expense of grammatical correctness. Often the result is that learners develop sophisticated strategies across in almost any situation, but in so doing they develop a form of pidgin.

These classrooms typically provide large quantities of comprehensible but flawed input in the form of highly motivating but highly inaccurate peer speech (Valette, 1991; cf. R. Ellis, 1994; Lightbown, 1991).[29] The extensive student–student interaction – usually devoid of any linguistic assistance from the teacher – generates abundant output, which then turns into input for the students themselves. This kind of input is not an authentic sample of the target language, but rather of other students' interlanguages. In many cases, it is not qualitatively superior to that possessed by the student himself or herself. The errors and inaccuracies students hear can reinforce their own misanalysis of the target language, thus creating a vicious circle (Chaudron, 1988; R. Ellis, 1994b; Flege & Liu, 2001; Lightbown, 1985, 1991, 2000; L. White, 1990; Wong Fillmore, 1992). Lightbown and Spada (1990) note that the students trained in an exclusively meaning-focused L2 classroom setting are able to speak fluently and confidently, but that their oral production is marked by numerous errors, errors common to virtually all students. Aside from hearing each other's faulty speech, another contribution to the common errors is likely to be the fact that the students share the same native language. Usually, communication conducted by L2 learners with a homogeneous L1 background is less likely to break down, and hence negotiation of form between learners rarely occurs (cf. Foster, 1998; Williams, 2001). This is partly because accompanying the same L1 is also the fact that these learners share the same conceptual framework; they have highly homogeneous ways of conceptualizing and verbalizing their life experiences. Thus, even when a student gets stuck in conveying a particular message because of lack of linguistic resources, his peers are able to figure out what he or she is trying to say. Moreover, research (e.g. Kowal & Swain, 1997) has shown that when communication difficulties do arise during student–student interaction, students do not always have adequate resources to overcome them. My speculation is that when this scenario occurs, learners will in all likelihood be pushed so far that they produce additional interlanguage forms. Hammerly (1991, cited in Johnson & Johnson, 1998) asserts that in the immersion classroom context, fossilization could occur as early as Grade 2 or 3 due to the fact that students are under pressure to communicate, and are encouraged to do so regardless of grammar, and he recommends greater emphasis on accuracy in the beginning and intermediate stages of L2 learning, and fluency at the more advanced level (see, however, VanPatten [1988] for an opposite view).

Some of the evidence presented above (e.g., Lightbown, 1983; Han & Selinker, 1999) alludes to a phenomenon known as 'transfer of training' (Selinker, 1972):

> Here some special feature in the input intentionally or unintentionally created by the teacher or textbook leads to acquisition with a non-native result. Overemphasis of a structure thought to be difficult for the learner (such as the English passive forms) might lead to a non-native degree of frequency or occurrence in the learner's IL and this would be the consequence of an artificial bias in the input. (Sharwood Smith, 1994: 37)

Clearly, the transfer of training effect can come about as a result of biased input, but it may also follow from teachers' use of pedagogic strategies, a point to which we now turn.

Pedagogic strategies

As early as 1975, Stenson showed that teachers' pedagogic strategies might in themselves be a source of student errors. Among the many examples she cited is the following:

> [The students] were given the definition of *point out* through example sentences with appropriate gestures, and then asked to use it in sentences. Those students who did not merely paraphrase the teacher's examples were all clearly treating the construction as two separate lexical items, *point*, which they already knew, and the preposition *out*. Thus, the new lexical item came out sounding to them like just another way to say *point to* or *point at*. One student with a little more imagination offered 'When I see a ship in the sea, I point out', which the teacher corrected to '... I point it out to my friends'. This is probably not what the student meant at all ... Immediately after *point out*, and without fully understanding it, the students were given *notice* and asked to use it in sentences. This led to the sentence 'The barometer noticed that it wouldn't be fine'. This student appears to have confused the two new vocabulary items and, since one word bears a causative relation to the other, this reinforces the confusion. The student might not make a mistake like this in a normal conversation – he would be more inclined to use a word he's sure of, like *show*, if he ever needed to talk about barometer reading ...

In this case, it could be argued that it was the teacher's decontextualized explanation of the lexical items, coupled with her request for immediate, decontextualized production, that had 'forced' the students into producing the interlanguage utterances.

There is little doubt that teachers' use of pedagogic strategies is very often driven by their assumptions about how languages should be taught. Cohen (2000; see also Cohen, 1997) reports on a case study of himself learning Japanese by attending a four-month, 'accelerated' Japanese course at a university in the United States. His teacher, a female native speaker of Japanese, had the following as part of the rationale for her pedagogic procedures in the classroom: (1) having cues for tasks (i.e., the instructions and the prompts) entirely in Japanese would be too difficult for the students and would take them too much time; (2) having learners provide native-language responses to reading passages helps to determine if the learners accurately understood the sentence structure, and such understanding is essential in successful incremental learning; and (3) since in this way the learners can not simply lift material directly from the prompt or from the text in composing their response, translation is used to see if they really understand the meaning of the material. Thus, this teacher saw translation as a crucial medium of second language learning. Taught through an instructional method with such a heavy emphasis on translation, Cohen reports:

> When spoken to in Japanese, the learner needed to translate what the interlocutor was saying into English in order to understand it, and when he spoke he needed to think it out in English first and then translate it into Japanese. This was also his experience in reading and writing, where he came to rely on translation almost exclusively. (Cohen, 1997: 144)

Using translation to aid comprehension and production requires that the initial processing be conducted in English. This, while seemingly creating a source of security for the learner, 'slows down his receptive and productive processing, took him out of the Japanese context into the world of English'. As a consequence, 'his Japanese was being "laundered" by English and by American culture' (1997: 144). Such a translation schemata may become automatic, according to Sajavaara (1986), and may result in fossilization of L1 features in the learner's second language. Indeed, a goal of second language learning, as Kroll *et al.* (2002: 137) put it, is 'to enable learners to understand and speak L2 . . . without mediation through the first language'.

Evidence of transfer of training seems pervasive. The introspective report below, provided by a student pseudo-named Cathy, who attended my Interlanguage Analysis class at Teachers College, Columbia University in Spring, 2001, further illustrates the transfer-of-training effect.

Training

> In order to succeed in my Japanese classes here, my teacher tries to get me to notice particles daily by saying the particle in a sentence more loudly or by pausing in his sentence before the use of a particle, asking me to 'fill in' the missing particle. At other times, we also do a drill where he gives a noun or noun phrase followed by a particle and we must complete the sentence. My teacher will often say a word or topic and then follow it by the particle 'wa'. This 'wa' he calls 'topic marker wa'. So if he wants to ask for information about a Mr. Smith he might say: 'Smith san wa' meaning 'As for Smith . . . ' I will reply with some kind of sentence following 'Smith san wa' that has to do with Smith as a topic.

Transfer of training

> In this [grab bag] game with a native speaker of Japanese, I found myself so hyper about proper particle use that I did not notice when the 'wa' sound was not a particle, but the end of a word I was seeking. Let me explain. I wanted to ask my friend: 'How do you say "ring" in English'? I thought my friend was using a technique my Japanese teacher had used with me when trying to elicit definitions. In my friend and my guessing game, the following dialog occurred with each of us pointing at a ring on my finger.
>
> **Me:** Yubi-wa? (As for fingers ... what can we say about fingers?)
> **Friend:** Yubiwa? (Ring? . . . Do you mean 'ring'?)
>
> I got frustrated because I thought my friend was repeating my question (What can we say about rings?) rather than answering the question. So I tried to rephrase my question:
>
> **Me:** Yubi no mono desu ka? (Is it a finger thing?)
> **Friend:** Yubi no mono wa yubiwa to iimasu (As for this finger thing, we call it a 'yubiwa').
>
> In this situation, I couldn't recognize that my friend was giving me the word for 'ring': 'yubiwa', I only heard 'yubiwa' as a question or the start of a sentence that I was supposed to complete. My friend never imagined that I heard the 'wa' as a particle . . .

It thus appears that too much forced noticing led to an over-sensitivity on Cathy's part to the particle 'wa' to the point that, regardless of context, she would process incoming signal 'wa' exclusively as a particle. In this case, instruction clearly had a debilitative effect on learning. Quite similarly, another student, pseudo-named Yoko, reports:

> I have one instance that I do not seem to be able to get rid of, in speaking English.
>
> I think I overuse 'I think' (just like I just did) as the beginning of a main clause followed by a subordinate clause. In Japanese, this beginning of a main clause comes at the end of an entire clause, so this structure is very different between English and Japanese. And learning this structure is also very important – in Japanese, the main verb of an entire sentence comes at the end so you can hold the main idea (the main verb) till the last when you speak, but in English, you cannot hold it till the end but have to say it right away, as a main verb in the main

> clause. So we needed a lot of practice . . .
>
> Therefore, when we learned the structure of an English main clause which is accompanied with a subordinate clause, we practiced using 'I think' a lot. 'I think I'll go,' 'I think that he is at school now,' 'I think it's good,' etc.
>
> Now I think I learned the structure, and I sometimes notice I use 'I think' where I do not really need to use it, especially when I am nervous and I am expected to say something ... For instance, when I go to my advisor's office to talk about my paper, I think I start off saying 'I think' a lot, like, 'I think I made a reference list' though I DID make the list, or 'I think I'll go and check' although I know I am going to go and check, and so forth.

Similar to the preceding case, here the salience artificially engineered by the teacher-led emphatic practice of 'I think' to combat native language influence had impinged on the learner production system to such an extent that the student seemed to have lost control over her use of the expression. While the student thought she had learned it, she in fact had overlearned it to the detriment of her performance.

Not only can transfer of training result from teachers' 'overdoing', as shown above (see also Takahashi, 1996), but it may also seem able to arise from the discourse patterns of the classroom. Wilkinson (1998) provides a case in point. The researcher reports on an eight-month longitudinal study of the overseas sojourn of seven English-speaking participants in a summer-abroad program in Valcourt, France. Her qualitative analysis of the recordings of the participants' conversations held during their stay in France shows that 'the indirect messages of the classroom (e.g., discourse patterns and nonnative speaker identity) were assimilated by the students far more accurately than the information directly taught (e.g., correct verb conjugations)'(1998: 34). Specifically, the students were carrying over classroom discourse patterns and learner identity to real life contexts, thereby creating an 'omnipresent classroom' for themselves. Such classroom transfer had a series of negative repercussions:

> Through conversations with her guest, Amelia's host mother seemed to question Amelia's intelligence; Ashley viewed Gilbert (a ten-year-old child in the host family) as uncooperative, and he appeared to be similarly disinterested in continuing the conversation with his demanding interlocutor. Such clashes over discourse and role expectations extended to a variety of settings, often leading to more unfavorable social repercussions and additional cross-cultural misunderstandings. (1998: 28)

Wilkinson's study has pointed, among other things, towards the need to consider the underlying messages transmitted by current instructional practices, and to examine questions such as: regardless of the content of a lesson, does the discursive structure of the classroom suggest that only one pattern exists for organizing interaction? One avenue of investigation may be to examine the nature of the opportunity for practice in the classroom.

Opportunity for use of language

The classroom setting affords limited opportunities for learners to use language for real-life purposes (cf. Seliger, 1977; Lightbown, 2000). Evidently this deficiency restricts, rather than promotes, learning, especially the learning of appropriate pragmatic and sociolinguistic features of the target language (Bardovi-Harlig & Dörnyei, 1998; R. Ellis, 1992; Kasper, 1982; Kasper & Schmidt, 1996; Lyster, 1994; Tarone & Swain, 1995). R. Ellis (1992) found that the classroom environment not only made it impossible for the two learners, J and R, to produce a wide range of requests in accordance with situational factors, but also promoted their production of linguistically incomplete requests. R. Ellis notes that 'the classroom environment is insufficient to guarantee the development of full target like norms, possibly because the kind of "communicative need" that the learners experienced was insufficient to ensure development of full range of request types and strategies' (1992: 20). This explanation is plausible, and may, at least in part, explain Wilkinson's (1998) findings.

In some classroom settings such as French immersion classes discussed earlier, the opportunity for production is simply rare. This, according to Swain (1985, 1993), is the root cause of the observed early cessation of learning among young learners, and has prompted her to propose the Output Hypothesis which argues for a role of production in second language development. (For her recent conceptualization of the role of output, see Swain, 1995; for a recent review of research on the Output Hypothesis, see Shehadeh, 2002.)

That the classroom provides limited and restrictive practice opportunities has led Seliger (1977) to suggest that learners who are able to derive the maximum benefit from classroom learning are those who are able to extend practice opportunities beyond the classroom, and not those who are dependent on what is available in the classroom. He refers to the former type of learners as *high input generators*, and the latter type *low input generators*.

Summary

In considering the role of instruction in adult SLA, we examined its potential positive as well as negative impact on learning. On the positive side, apart from its widely recognized capability to accelerate learning and increase learners' sensitivity to formal properties of the target language, instruction appears to be necessary and helpful for the acquisition of some linguistic features by some learners at some point in the developmental process (cf. DeKeyser, 1998; Larsen-Freeman, 1995). In this sense, instruction, occurring at the right time, may serve to prevent fossilization. Nevertheless, it is also important to keep in mind that the influence of instruction is mitigated by a variety of linguistic and psycholinguistic variables such as linguistic domain, complexity, semantic and functional saliency, learner readiness, and, perhaps, learners' personal agenda (Allwright, 1984). As Long (1991: 43) aptly notes, 'language learning is . . . partly governed by forces beyond a teacher's or textbook writer's control'.

On the negative side, instruction can impede learning. Due largely to the existence of setting-internal constraints, instruction provides a restrictive learning experience. Within the limited space we identified three potential sources of such experience – classroom input, pedagogic strategies, and opportunity for practice – in relation to a particular learning phenomenon known as 'transfer of training' (Selinker, 1972). Thus, inasmuch as it stifles or impedes development, instruction promotes fossilization.

Notes

1. Pienemann (1985) points out three major problems with the studies reviewed by Long, one of which is that all informants in these studies had some degree of exposure to the natural acquisition context, thereby rendering the results ambiguous. To attribute the differences in results exclusively to differences in learning contexts would, therefore, seem presumptuous.
2. The intervening years witnessed the publication of several review studies, including R. Ellis (1990, 1994), Spada (1997) and Lightbown (2000). I, however, must skip them here due to space constraints.
3. The studies were published in second language teaching and learning related journals between 1980 and 1998.
4. Long (1991) makes a distinction between Focus on Form and Focus on Forms: 'Whereas the content of lessons with a focus on forms is the forms themselves, a syllabus with a focus on form teaches something else – biology, mathematics, workshop practice, automobile repair, the geography of a country where the foreign language is spoken, the cultures of its speakers, and so on – and overtly draws students' attention to linguistic elements as they arise incidentally in lessons whose overriding focus is on meaning, or communication'. On this conception, the metalinguistic focus under the Structural Approach is classified as focus on forms, while that under the Communicative Approach, which is primarily meaning-based, as focus on form, the latter being incidental in nature as opposed to being dominant and overriding.
5. Specifically, the following pattern was observed for the FonF and FonFS types of instruction, exhibiting some superiority of FonF to FonFS: FonF explicit > FonFS explicit > FonF implicit > FonFS implicit.
6. On a meta-analysis, primary data are treated according to a common scale, and

findings from individual studies converted to comparable values, in order to enable an estimate of the magnitude of an observed relationship or effect, typically referred to as the effect size.

7. Krashen was the first in the SLA field to differentiate between explicit and implicit knowledge. Such a distinction is supported by some neurophysiological evidence showing that the two types of knowledge are subserved by neurofunctionally different systems (Paradis, 1994). It has been suggested that implicit knowledge is stored in various areas of the left hemisphere (represented in distributed neural networks) and explicit knowledge in the medial temporal lobe, including the hippocampus (Hulstijn, 2002b).
8. Prior to Schmidt's explicit articulation of the Noticing Hypothesis, SLA researchers (see, e.g., Sharwood Smith, 1981; Rutherford, 1988) had discussed, and suggested the importance of a similar notion, 'consciousness-raising'.
9. Here no implication is intended that explicit learning and grammar-based instruction are isomorphic. As Schmidt (1994b: 20) has pointed out, 'it is possible for learners to form conscious hypotheses about the target language without being told the rules or forming hypotheses that are different from the teacher's version of a rule, as well as for learners to be taught a rule but not to understand it or be able to make any use of it in the process of learning'.
10. In the French immersion programs, French as a second language constitutes the primary medium of instruction. In other words, different subjects are taught in 'comprehensible' French.
11. Compared to the immersion program, the shelter program starts at a later age and is less intensive.
12. Hulstijn (personal communication, 2002) points out that this conceptualization of linguistic complexity is over-simplistic in that it carries the assumption that we are dealing with 'rules' that present learners across the board with 'graded' difficulty. Further, he suggests, after Pinker (1999), a more qualitative view of linguistic forms to be differentiated vis-à-vis 'stored' and 'computed'. Under this view, it is possible that for one learner, a certain linguistic form is 'stored', but for another it is 'computed', and the concept of 'rule' is applicable only in the case of computation, and not in the case of storage.
13. Unaccusatives are of two kinds: unaccusatives without transitive counterparts (e.g., *happen, disappear*) and unaccusatives that are part of causative alternation; the latter have transitive counterparts (e.g., *break*).
14. To the latter question, Long and Robinson's (1998: 20) answer appears to be negative, for they are convinced that 'older learners no longer have the same capacity as young children to attain native norms in a new language simply from exposure to its use'.
15. This parameter is later reformulated into the 'verb-raising parameter' that incorporates a whole cluster of properties other than adverb placement, such as negation, question formation, quantifier placement and differences between finite and non-finite clauses (see Pollock, 1989; Chomsky, 1989).
16. Maintaining a distinction between developmental features that are constrained by developing speech-processing mechanisms (e.g., word order) and variational features that are not (e.g., vocabulary), Pienemann claims that developmental features develop according to a fixed sequence, while variational features can be taught and learnt at any time (cf. Meisel *et al.*, 1981).
17. This sequence has the following six stages:
    Stage x = Canonical Order

die kinder spielen mim ball (Concetta)
'the children play with the ball'
Stage x + 1 = Adverb Preposing (ADV)
da kinder spielen (Concetta)
'there children play'
Stage x + 2 = Verb Separation (SEP)
alle kinder muß die pause machen (Concetta)
'all children must the break have'
Stage x + 3 = Inversion (INV)
dann hat sie wieder die knoch gebringt (Eva)
'then has she again the bone bringed'
Stage x + 4 = Verb Final (V-END)
er sagt, daß er nach hause kommt
'he said that he home comes'

(Pienemann, 1998: 45)

18. Contrary views do exist. N. Ellis (2002b: 174), for example, notes that 'there do seem to be more complex associations that require more conscious explicit learning and hypothesis testing to acquire'.
19. Linguistic forms of this type are sometimes redundant and sometimes non-redundant, contingent on whether or not they co-occur with lexical indicators of times in a sentence (VanPatten, 1996).
20. 'Comprehension' here refers not only to comprehending the meaning of input but also understanding the linguistic rules.
21. Prototypical rules are deemed harder to learn than categorical rules. As Long and Robinson (1998: 28) put it, 'they are probabilistic, and impossible to reduce to economical rule statements that apply without exception to the morphological forms concerned'.
22. One could argue that this reduced capacity is an indication that adult learners no longer have access to an innate language-specific faculty, and they therefore resort to generative cognitive procedures in learning a second language. Schachter (1988) has pointed out three other indications, including (1) heavy reliance on input; (2) asymmetric behavior on grammatical intuitions tests, and (3) drawing on insights from a variety of sources (e.g., first language, input data, and other fully developed conceptual structures that are distinct from, but that interact with, the language module) in shaping L2 knowledge.
23. To help explain why learners learn less than is taught them, Allwright (1984; see also Schumann & Schumann, 1977) postulates the Personal Agenda Hypothesis, stating that 'at least part of any mismatch between what teachers teach and what learners learn could be due to the learners' ability to selectively take from a lesson only those things that they want, and only in the manner that they want to do it in' (p. 8).
24. Both are electronic listservs and are devoted to discussions of language learning and teaching issues.
25. According to Selinker and Lamendella (1978), these were the first explicit and testable claims regarding the source of fossilization.
26. Here we adhere to Corder's (1967) distinction between 'error' and 'mistake'. The term 'error' thus denotes an IL form that systematically deviates from the norm (i.e., TL) and that is beyond the learner's awareness, whereas 'mistake' refers to a slip of the tongue or a slip of the pen, which the learner is able to self-correct.

27. This is specially true of textbooks that adopt synthetic approaches to language learning.
28. The classroom learners in the study generally followed the sequence of copula – auxiliary – plural – -ing – 3rd singular – possessive, whereas Krashen's (1997) study revealed a different one: -ing, plural, copula – auxiliary – 3rd singular, possessive (Lightbown, 1983: 224).
29. This is true more of beginning and intermediate level classes than of advanced level classes.

Chapter 8

Summary and Conclusion

SLA researchers have long been baffled why native-like attainment, if existent, is rare among adult L2 learners. In this book we have approached the conundrum through the lens of fossilization (Selinker, 1972). Lying under the constellation of insights, facts, and arguments discussed throughout is the view that the observed general lack of success in adult L2 learning is made up of inter-learner and intra-learner variational success/failure. I have argued that maturational constraints and native language interference – both being constants (as opposed to variables) – jointly set a limit to adult learners' ability to learn a second language such that full attainment of L2 competence is virtually impossible, but that linguistic, cognitive, psychological and social variables may interact to yield differential success/failure across and within learners.

In this concluding chapter, I will first recapitulate the main points that emerged from the discussion in the foregoing chapters, and, then, discuss their implications for research and practice. Finally, by way of conclusion, I will pose questions and offer directions for future research on fossilization.

A Synopsis

Our inquiry in fossilization began, in Chapter 1, with an analysis of L2 ultimate attainment, which led to the recognition of three facets thereof: (1) general lack of success, (2) differential success and failure across learners, and (3) differential success and failure within learners. This conception challenges a prevailing, monolithic view that, in essence, equates L2 adult learners' ultimate attainment solely with permanent deviation from the target language (*passim* the SLA literature). Following our conception, it is possible that among second language learners, there be different ultimate attainments, some being closer to the target than are others. It is also possible that, for the interlanguage system created by every individual learner, there be multiple ultimate attainments corresponding to its various linguistic domains and subsystems, some of which have successfully reached the target and others of which have remained short of it.

Crucially, this conceptualization, modular in nature, has set the stage for the ensuing theorizing about fossilization in this book. In accordance with the three facets of ultimate attainment, it is suggested that fossilization be viewed at a macroscopic and a microscopic level. The former enables a cross-learner perspective, where fossilization – manifested as general lack of full attainment – can be understood in terms of generic causal factors. The latter, on the other hand, offers a within-learner perspective, where fossilization – manifested as differential failure – can be examined in terms of the operation of specific variables.

Such a conceptual framework is, apparently, at odds with the many ways in which fossilization has been construed over the last three decades. As a review in Chapter 2 of a selection of the existing definitions showed, there have existed a broad spectrum of conceptions of fossilization, ranging from viewing fossilization as a product or a process, to viewing fossilization as happening locally or globally, to viewing fossilization as pertinent to target-like forms or non-target-like forms, and to viewing fossilization as synonymous (or not) with stabilization. I have argued in favor of the view that for operational purposes, fossilization be looked at more as a process than as a product, and that fossilization happens locally rather than globally.

Chapter 3 further explored conceptual differences by presenting a range of common variables with which the term 'fossilization' has come to be associated, and miscellaneous explanations that have been launched from a variety of perspectives. Two factors, maturational constraints and NL transfer, were underscored as primary determinants of the general lack of success observed across the L2 learning community; they predispose adult L2 learners to fossilization. Other variables such as lack of instruction, lack of attention, satisfaction of communicative needs, and so forth were considered moderating variables such that, acting in concert with the primary determinants, they can affect the scope as well as the timing of fossilization.

Guided by this conception, Chapter 4 examined one of the two hypothesized primary determinants of fossilization, critical period effects. It began by reviewing the notion of 'critical period', and its application to second language acquisition. Research evidence was, then, mustered to show that adult L2 acquisition is indeed subject to maturational constraints, but that the influence of the latter shows a number of characteristics. First, there is not an absolute critical period in SLA but rather a period of heightened sensitivity to environmental stimuli, within which learning is successful and beyond which learning is *still possible but highly variable and less successful*. This period is biologically founded, hence endogenous in nature, but its function hinges on the interaction between innate neural processes and exogenous stimulation. Second, the critical period applies differentially to certain language domains and subsystems, and hence is modular in nature. Third, CP effects are intricately tied up with cognitive, affective and social factors, not the least of which is L1 transfer.

Chapter 5 took up transfer, the other one of the two hypothesized primary determinants of fossilization. Issues included for discussion were (1) transfer-inspired delay in L2 learning, (2) the *transfer to somewhere* principle (Andersen, 1983) and the *transfer to nowhere* principle (Kellerman, 1995a), (3) transfer of L1-based thinking for speaking, and (4) L1 preprogramming, each of which taps into a different aspect of the transfer process, but all of which point to L1 as a source of fossilization in L2 learning. In regard to (1), L1 transfer errors, on the whole, tend to persist in the interlanguage, particularly when they coincide with IL developmental features. Restructuring of their underlying rules is often difficult, thereby creating delays in L2 learning. With respect to (2) and (3), the insight we gained was that not only can transfer occur due to (perceived) surface similarities between an L1 and an L2, but it can also occur in spite of differences. Moreover, transfer is not merely a conscious, selective, and idiosyncratic process, but an unconscious process, driven by the L1-based *thinking for speaking* system, whereby the L1-specific way of verbalizing one's conceptualization of experience finds its expression in the interlanguage production and comprehension. Finally, in regard to (4), L1 can preprogram L2 learning such that it permanently biases learners' sensitivity to L2 input. As such, L1 transfer imposes cognitive constraints on L2 learning that, pervasively and profoundly, curtail the ability to fully attain native-like competence.

Following a macroscopic analysis of fossilization in Chapters 4 and 5, Chapter 6 provided a microscopic view on fossilization. A selection of empirical studies were reviewed. The purpose of the review was not only to present evidence of fossilization, but, more importantly, to closely examine a range of methodologies that L2 researchers had adopted for investigating fossilization. In the latter connection, five major methodological approaches were discussed: (1) the longitudinal approach, (2) the typical-error approach, (3) the advanced-learner approach, (4) the corrective-feedback approach, and (5) the length-of-residence approach. None of these approaches, however, were found to be reliable enough as a means to gather evidence of fossilization; what was deemed desirable was to use a combination of approaches. Also discussed in this chapter were the relationship between stabilization and fossilization, the duration of longitudinal studies, and the modular nature of fossilization. Further substantiating the modular view, a number of linguistic features that had generally been found prone to fossilization were then discussed, and the Multiple Effects Principle (Selinker & Lakshmanan, 1992) explored as an explanation for local cessation of learning, and, further, for inter-learner and intra-learner differential failure.

In attempting to exemplify how the causal variables, as identified and described in Chapter 3, contribute to fossilization, Chapter 7 looked into one such variable, L2 instruction, and explored its relationship to fossilization. The reason that this particular variable was chosen as the target of an in-depth inquiry came from a dual fact: first, that there exists a rather widespread conviction among second language teachers and some L2 researchers that instruction (corrective feedback, in particular) prevents fossilization; and second, that L2 research on instruction to date has primarily focused on revealing its positive effects on L2 learning, and little is yet known as to whether instruction can also have any negative impact on learning. This chapter, therefore, raised the following questions: Can instruction serve to prevent fossilization? If so, to what extent? Also, can instruction promote fossilization? A review of the literature on L2 instruction – importantly, including not only studies that have offered positive findings but also those yielding insights into its negative impact – pointed to the following understanding: On the positive side, instruction can (1) accelerate learning, (2) can increase learners' overall sensitivity to formal properties of the target language, and (3) is necessary and helpful for the acquisition of some linguistic features by some learners at some point in the developmental process (cf. DeKeyser, 1998; Larsen-Freeman, 1995). On the negative side, instruction can inhibit learning due to the existence of three major sources of constraints on classroom learning: input (from textbooks, teachers, and peers), pedagogic strategies, and opportunity for practice.

Implications for Research and Practice

Now what implications does the foregoing lengthy discussion of fossilization hold for research and practice?

First, for research: Over the past 30 years of SLA research, fossilization has evolved from a monolithic concept (originally tied to 'backsliding') to a much more complex one, linked to multiple manifestations of failure in learning. As a consequence, fossilization has become a major window on to the issue of why adult L2 learning is not as successful as child FLA, or more pertinently, why the majority of adult L2 learners are unable to reach the level of competence they have aspired to. In accordance with the expanded conceptual scope of fossilization, research attempts have also significantly broadened to encompass those that study individual learners by examining the local cessation of learning taking place in various interlanguage domains such as phonology, morphology, syntax, lexicon and pragmatics, as well as those that look at general failure as manifested in the ultimate attainment across adult L2 learners. Given this complex scenario, it is essential that researchers make it clear what they understand by fossilization.

It has now become a necessity that when defining fossilization, in whichever terms of one's liking, two properties be adhered to: it is a process whereby (1) learning stabilizes prematurely (i.e., short of the target) (2) despite continuous exposure to input, adequate motivation to learn, and sufficient opportunity for practice.[1] Incorporating them in any definition of fossilization could have some immediate yet profound benefits. First of all, it would enforce a more rigorous use of the term on both the macroscopic and microscopic levels, thereby uniting, rather than dividing, research efforts launched from different perspectives. Second, it would help channel research attention, which is, currently, thinly spread over a wide range of variables, onto those that are most revealing about the mechanisms of L2 acquisition. And third, it would significantly facilitate the interpretation of research findings across the board.

Closely associated with the need for a clear definition of fossilization is also the need for identifying and defining the target language. SLA studies to date have, in general, ignored the latter. In fossilization research, which is essentially target-language-referenced, this is of prime importance, given the existence of multiple varieties of English. Concerted effort should be made at the outset of research to determine the nature of the social and linguistic environment within which learners have developed their L2. Care should be taken to ensure that the target language against which the interlanguage is examined is indeed what the learners have been exposed to. In addition, external and internal perspectives might both be necessary to ensuring that what researchers determine to be the norm is indeed the norm pursued by the learners.[2]

At this juncture, it is pertinent to mention that the notion of 'target language', while pivotal in second language research, seems to be no longer of universal acceptance. Larsen-Freeman (1997: 151), for example, has recently challenged it by noting:

> The very phrase 'target language' is misleading because there is no endpoint to which the acquisition can be directed. The target is always moving.

Citing Lewis (1993: 160), she adds that 'the notion of a definable target is an idealization anyway as there is no such thing as a homogeneous speech community'. Though both claims bear much truth in them, they are, in my view, as yet insufficient to constitute a basis for repudiating the existence of any target language. With respect to the first claim, though the target language is indeed developing as interlanguages are, the rate of change, as

Larsen-Freeman concedes, differs.[3] The second claim about the absence of a homogeneous speech community, on the other hand, bypasses a crucial fact, namely that within a speech community, speakers have a common linguistic system to follow. Clearly, if this were not the case, the phrase 'speech community' would not have existed in the first place. The issue of whether or not 'target language' is a valid construct in SLA research is too complicated to deal with in a few lines here, but suffices it to say at this point that it deserves further investigation.

Perhaps an equally, if not more, questionable notion is 'native-speaker competence'.[4] What does *that* entail? Though researchers (myself included) have oftentimes resorted to the construct in order to argue for lack of success in L2 ultimate attainment, no one has ever dissected the construct to reveal its nature and scope. If it is yet another idealization – as I suspect it is – based on abstraction from idiosyncratic competences possessed by individual native speakers, and if it encompasses all linguistic domains including morphology, syntax, phonology, semantics, lexicon, and pragmatics, is it rational to set it as a benchmark against which to compare individual L2 learners' ultimate attainment? (For recent discussions of the concept of 'native speaker', see Davies 2003; Han, in press.)

Continuing on this train of thought, what also appears to be in need of a more rigorous understanding in fossilization research is 'success'. As mentioned in Chapter 1, there is a lack of consensus, within the L2 research community, about what 'success' should mean. One question worth asking in this concern is whether success should be researcher-determined or learner-determined. If it is researcher-determined, it will be desirable to achieve, among researchers, some uniformity in determining the degree and scope of success. If, however, it is learner-determined, then it should be incumbent on researchers to find out what the learner's definition of success is before advancing any claims about success or failure.

Aside from the conceptual issues, methodological issues are equally outstanding and therefore merit some serious attention. For example, most of the empirical studies to date are non-longitudinal. Fossilization is therefore largely assumed rather than established through longitudinal observation. What is even more problematic is that the assumption is often made on the basis of criteria that lack principled motivation. As mentioned, there is a suggestion that five years of residence in the TL environment be used as an index of ultimate attainment. Such criterion flatly fails on logical grounds. First, it is highly unlikely that learning will not continue after five years, given continuous exposure to input and adequate motivation to learn. Second, five years of residence is not necessarily positively correlated with the quantity of exposure to the TL (cf. Flege & Liu, 2001). As many have noted, even in the TL environment, there are communities or individuals whose contact with the target language is minimal. Oyama (1975: 264), for example, comments:

> That circumstance can prohibit or inhibit learning of a language by normally capable people is obvious; many large cities are full of households, for example, in which the mother, who has been in the United States for decades, still speaks particularly no English. These are women whom custom and economics have conspired to keep monolingual. Such social and cultural factors, which, of course, can affect men as well as women, are pervasive and powerful.

In this opinion Selinker and Lamendella (1978: 154) both concur:

> As the U.S. immigrant experience has shown, it is possible to exist for even 50 years on the fringes of a target society, with resulting minimal occasion to use the TL, and a concomitant lack of opportunity to continue learning in one's IL.

In essence, time can *not* be counted on as a reliable source of information on the environmental condition for L2 learning. What needs documenting is both the types of interaction that learners have in the L2 environment and their intensity, as Klein (1986) has suggested. (See also Krashen, 1976.)

In the light of the various problems identified so far, a more logical methodological procedure to follow, it would seem, is to establish a longitudinal perspective of some length, depending, *inter alia*, on the characteristics of the targeted linguistic feature, learners' learning history and conditions, within which to then study stabilization. This would entail, at least, four phases of research: (1) determining whether or not the informants are in both an externally and internally favorable position to make progress; (2) establishing stabilization; (3) identifying its underlying processes; and (4) analyzing the processes and making *well-grounded* judgments about whether or not the stabilized linguistic feature will result in fossilization. Such would be a more systematic approach to studying fossilization than any that has so far been attempted, and would have some positive consequences. First of all, it would require researchers to precede their investigation with a *careful examination* of learning conditions, external and internal, not a forthright assumption of an equation between LOR and exogenous circumstances favoring or disfavoring language acquisition. Second, it would take researchers beyond their current scope of concern, i.e., identifying stabilization, into exploring the underlying processes or factors, hence shifting the focus of attention away from product to process. Finally, it would tie fossilization research in with SLA research of other issues such as transfer, UG, input, critical period, just to name a few, as researchers strive for a sound interpretation of the processes that cause the attested stabilization. Indeed, as Kellerman (personal communication, 2002) rightly points out, 'the question is not *just* why one person "fossilizes" and another doesn't – it's what *causes* the "fossilization" in the first place'. Research to date suggests that there is no one ontological account of fossilization. Future research should therefore concentrate on exploring the interaction of multiple factors (e.g., linguistic, psycholinguistic, neurolinguistic, and sociolinguistic).

Turning now to implications for practice: Some second language educators see researching fossilization as accentuating the negative at the expense of the positive. Contrary to this view, however, the analysis of fossilization in this book has shown that fossilization is an *inevitable* process in adult second language acquisition, and as such, it deserves due attention from both researchers and educators. Disregarding it could carry the consequence of engendering more failure in learning. Rather, equipped with a sound understanding of fossilization, educators can be more realistic in setting expectations for teaching and more effective in facilitating learning. Such an understanding entails, among other things, (1) an awareness of major causal factors, (2) an awareness of the complexity of the learning process, and (3) an awareness of the difficulties confronting learners from different L1 backgrounds.

The discussion of the relationship between instruction and fossilization in Chapter 7 dispels the myth that 'formal instruction serves to prevent fossilization' (R. Ellis, 1988: 4), and it, at the same time, reveals that instruction can facilitate as well as debilitate learning. That is, instruction, occurring at the right time, *may* prevent fossilization. Yet due largely to the existence of setting-internal constraints – classroom input, pedagogic strategies, and opportunity for practice – instruction may also restrict and bias learning. In the latter sense, instruction is also a source of fossilization.

This said, the modular view on fossilization as presented in Chapter 6 (pp. 00–00) calls for an immediate abandonment of such faulty notions as 'fossilized learner' and 'fossilized competence'. Under the modular view, fossilization does not permeate the entire interlanguage nor does it debilitate any learner completely from learning. As has been argued repeatedly, success and failure co-exist in each and every individual learner's interlanguage. On this account, any bias on the second language educators' part against any learners because of their slow learning or even persistent low proficiency would be unjustified. Labeling learners as fossilized or something of that kind does nothing but creates stress and anxiety in learners that further inhibits their learning. Instead, a careful examination, in this case, would be beneficial to both teachers and learners, that seeks to understand, and subsequently combat, factors underlying the lack of progress.

Further, viewing fossilization more as a process than a product encourages educators to 'look further at [apparently] fossilized errors and see what can be done about them' (Larsen-Freeman, 1995: 145) or to seek ways to prevent fossilization from materializing. Already in the L2 literature, insights can be found on how to combat fossilization. Harley (1993), for example, claims that crosslingual analyses can help to undo fossilized errors. Tarone (2003) recommends use of communication strategies and language play as creative forces to destabilize an interlanguage, thereby preventing it from fossilization. H. Johnson (1992) proposes a specific pedagogic strategy called the 'tennis clinic strategy' to propel the 'fluent-but-fossilized' learners to move forward linguistically.[5]

General Directions for Future Research

Based on the current research, we can anticipate that future empirical research on failure in L2 learning will continue to proceed from two major perspectives, cross-learner vs. within learner, which focus respectively on the general lack of success and the inter-learner and intra-learner differential failure.

Fossilization research, which is largely oriented towards understanding local failure, i.e., failure that occurs in certain domains and subsystems of individual learners' interlanguages, is likely to develop in two directions in the years to come. The first would be the continuation of the current tradition of performing longitudinal descriptive and exploratory studies to document cases of fossilization. An important mission of these studies, as Birdsong (2003) has aptly suggested, should be to distinguish 'between what [learners] *inevitably* can't do and what [they] *typically* don't do' (emphasis original). The second direction, which has yet to be taken, would be to conduct cross-sectional (or otherwise) studies to validate the alleged causal factors (see Table 3.1). As pointed out in Chapter 3, L2 researchers have by now generated a wide spectrum of explanations, yet most of which have limited empirical basis. Thus, focused investigation of each is necessary not only to validating it as an explanation for fossilization, but also to assessing the extent and scope of its influence on learning. Take the causal variable of 'absence of instruction' as an example. Schmidt's (1983) study has suggested it as one of the possible causes of persistent lack of progress in Wes's interlanguage. In this case, what has yet to be discovered through validation studies is the direct connection (or lack thereof) between absence of instruction and fossilization. Questions of high relevance to this concern include: Do classroom learners suffer less fossilization than do naturalistic learners?

All things being equal, does the absence of grammar instruction cause cessation of learning?

In pointing out the need to conduct univariate cause–effect studies to empirically validate the hypothesized causal variables, we should be mindful of the fact that second language learning is a complex nonlinear process whereby variables tend to overlap, and interact, with others to affect the course of development (Larsen-Freeman, 1997). Efforts should therefore also be made towards understanding how variables combine to generate fossilization (cf. Selinker & Lakshmanan, 1992).

In a nutshell, both descriptive studies and experimental studies are warranted to enhance the general understanding of fossilization; they should be complementary to each other in that the former directly contributes to the ongoing empirical database, and the latter investigates the etiology.

Research on fossilization, however, should not be confined to empirical inquiries; rather, it should also develop theoretically. So far little attempt has been made to construct theories of fossilization or to integrate insights from fossilization studies into general theories of SLA. As noted in Chapter 1, the existing SLA theories (with few exceptions) are biased towards explaining learning – with lack of learning largely ignored. Such theories are partial, and hence short of validity. Clearly, any robust SLA theory should account for both learning and non-learning. As Gass (1988) has stated:

> The ultimate goal of second language acquisition research is to come to an understanding of what is acquired (*and what is not acquired*), and the mechanisms that bring second language knowledge about. (emphasis added)

In conclusion, the issues of why L2 learners are unable to reach the level of competence they have aspired to in spite of rich exposure to input, adequate motivation to learn and sufficient opportunity to use the target language, and why L2 learners fail in some respects but not in others are not trivial. They are comparable, in magnitude, to the issues of how second language acquisition is possible, and how it actually happens – the two putatively fundamental issues in SLA research. Both sets of issues, though having received unequal attention thus far, should be at the base of the general understanding of adult SLA. It is therefore my hope that the discussion of fossilization in this book will provide an impetus for researchers to develop principled approaches to investigating the phenomenon of lack of learning in adult SLA. One ultimate goal of this line of inquiry, needless to say, is to be able to offset forces that inhibit learning through maximizing the usability of the available resources to individual learners.

Notes

1. This suggestion is a total departure from a number of early conceptions of fossilization (see, e.g., Schumann, 1978a; Klein & Dittmar, 1979; Clahsen *et al.*, 1983; Hyltenstam, 1985) that actually viewed socio-psychological factors, including motivation, to be determinants of whether fossilization would occur or not.
2. Researching fossilization in the context of bilingualism calls for greater prudence, for it is compounded by the fact that there learners are pursuing two targets (i.e., an L1 and an L2), as opposed to one target, as in the case of adult SLA. Moreover, the two targets can be non-parallel, say, basic interpersonal communicative skills (BICS) for the L1 and cognitive academic language proficiency (CALP) for the L2. A clear understanding of the norm pursued by the bilinguals for each language is therefore essential to the validity of the research in this context.
3. Out of the context, however, this could be given a different reading. From a psycholinguistic point of view, there is perhaps indeed not a static target for a learner in the developmental process. That is, as the learner's proficiency grows, the target changes, both being in a dynamic process. For example, for a given L2 learner of Chinese, at point X, the SVO word order is the target., but at point Y, the topic-comment construction becomes the target.
4. I thank the audience for my presentation at SLRF 2002 for raising this issue.
5. This strategy has the following four stages: (1) The communicative goal is set; (2) Students plan what they will want to say, including things they need to learn; (3) Students learn (through communication individually with the teacher); and (4) Students communicate (H. Johnson, 1992: 186).

References

Achebe, C. (1966) *Things Fall Apart*. London: Heinemann.

Allwright, D. (1984) Why don't learners learn what teachers teach? The Interaction Hypothesis. In D. Singleton and D. Little (eds) *Language Learning in Formal and Informal Contexts* (pp. 3–18). IRAAL.

Allwight, D. & Bailey, K. (1991) *Focus on the Language Classroom*. Cambridge: Cambridge University Press.

Andersen, R. (1983) Transfer to somewhere. In S. Gass and L. Selinker (eds) *Language Transfer in Language Learning* (pp. 177–201). Rowley, MA: Newbury House.

Balcom, P. (1995) Argument structure and multi-competence. *Linguistica Atlantica* 17, 1–17.

Balcom, P. (1997) Why is this happened? Passive morphology and unaccusativity. *Second Language Research* 1, 1–9.

Bardovi-Harlig, K. (1987) Markedness and salience in second language acquisition. *Language Learning* 37, 385–407.

Bardovi-Harlig, K. & Bofman, T. (1989) Attainment of syntactic and morphological accuracy by advanced language learners. *Studies in Second Language Acquisition* 11, 17–34.

Bardovi-Harlig, K. (1995) The interaction of pedagogy and natural sequences in the acquisition of tense and aspect. In F. Eckman, D. Highland, P. Lee, J. Mileham and R. Weber (eds) *Second Language Acquisition Theory and Pedagogy* (pp. 151–68). Mahwah, NJ: Lawrence Erlbaum.

Bardovi-Harlig, K. and Dörnyei, Z. (1998) Do language learners recognize pragmatic violations? Pragmatic vs. grammatical awareness in instructed L2 learning. *TESOL Quarterly* 32, 233–59.

Bates, E. and MacWhinney, B. (1981) Second language acquisition from a functionalist perspective: Pragmatics, semantics and perceptual strategies. In H. Winitz (ed.) *Annals of the New York Academy of Sciences Conference on Native Language and Foreign Language Acquisition* (pp. 190–214). New York: New York Academy of Sciences.

Berdan, R. (1996) Disentangling language acquisition from language variation. In R. Bryley and D. Preston (eds) *Second Language Acquisition and Linguistic Variation*. Amsterdam: John Benjamins.

Bever, T. (1981) Normal acquisition processes explain the critical period for language learning. In K.C. Diller (ed.) *Individual Differences and Universals in Language Learning Aptitude* (pp. 176–98). Rowley, MA: Newbury House.

Bialystok, E. (1978) A theoretical model of second language learning. *Language Learning* 28 (1), 69–83.

Bialystok, E. (1987) A psycholinguistic framework for exploring the basis of second language proficiency. In W. Rutherford and M. Sharwood Smith (eds) *Grammar and Language Teaching* (pp. 31–40). Rowley, MA: Newbury House.

Bialystok, E. (1994) Analysis and control in the development of second language proficiency. *Studies in Second Language Acquisition* 17 (1), 157–68.

Bialystok, E. and Hakuta, K. (1994) *In Other Words: The Science and Psychology of Second-language Acquisition*. New York: Basic Books.

Bialystok, E. and Miller, B. (1999) The problem of age in second language acquisition: Influences from language, structure, and task. *Bilingualism: Language and Cognition* 2 (2), 127–45.

Birdsong, D. (1992) Ultimate attainment in second language acquisition. *Language* 68, 706–55.

Birdsong, D. (1999) Whys and whynots of the Critical Period Hypothesis for second language acquisition. In D. Birdsong (ed.) *Second Language Acquisition and the Critical Period Hypothesis* (pp. 1–22). Mahwah, NJ: Lawrence Erlbaum.

Birdsong, D. (2003) Why not fossilization. Panelist presentation at the 2003 AAAL Annual Conference, Arlington, Virginia.

Birdsong, D. and Molis, M. (2001) On the evidence for maturational constraints in second-language acquisition. *Journal of Memory and Language* 44, 235–49.

Bley-Vroman, R. (1989) What is the logical problem of foreign language learning? In S. Gass and J. Schachter (eds) *Linguistic Perspectives on Second Language Acquisition* (pp. 41–68). Cambridge, UK: Cambridge University Press.

Bley-Vroman, R. and Joo, H-R. (2001) The acquisition and interpretation of English locative constructions. *Studies in Second Language Acquisition* 23 (2), 207–20.

Bongaerts, T. (1999) Ultimate attainment in L2 pronunciation: The case of very advanced late L2 learners. In D. Birdsong (ed.) *Second Language Acquisition and the Critical Period Hypothesis* (pp. 133–60). Mahwah, NJ: Lawrence Erlbaum.

Brown, G. (1996) *Performance and Competence in SLA*. Cambridge, UK: Cambridge University Press.

Brown, R. (1973) *A First Language*. Cambridge, MA: Harvard University Press.

Burzio, L. (1986) *Italian Syntax*. Dordrecht: Reidel.

Bussman, H. (ed.) (1996) *Routledge Dictionary of Language and Linguistics*. London: Routledge.

Canale, M. and Swain, M. (1980) Theoretical bases of communicative approaches to second language teaching and testing. *Applied Linguistics* 1 (1), 1–47.

Carroll, S. (2001) *Input and Evidence: The Raw Material of Second Language Acquisition*. Amsterdam: John Benjamins.

Carroll, S. (2002) Induction in a modular learner. *Second Language Research* 18 (3), 224–49.

Chaudron, C. (1988) *Second Language Classrooms*. Cambridge, UK: Cambridge University Press.

Chomsky, N. (1965) *Aspects of the Theory of Syntax*. Cambridge, MA: MIT Press.

Chomsky, N. (1986) *Knowledge of Language: Its Nature, Origin, and Use*. New York: Praeger.

Chomsky, N. (1989) Some notes on economy of derivation and representation. *MIT Working Papers in Linguistics* 10, 43–74.

Clahsen, H., Meisel, J. and Pienemann, M. (1983) *Deutsch als Zweitsprache. Der Spracherwerb ausländischer Arbeiter*. Tübingen: Gunter Narr.

Clahsen, H., Eisenbeiss, S. and Vainikka, A. (1994) The seeds of structure: A syntactic analysis of the acquisition of case marking. In T. Hoekstra and B.D. Schwartz (eds) *Language Acquisition Studies in Generative Grammar: Papers in Honor of Kenneth Wexler from the 1991 GLOW Workshops* (pp. 85–118). Philadelphia, PA: John Benjamins.

Cohen, A. (1997) Developing pragmatic ability: Insights from the accelerated study of Japanese. In H. Cook, K. Hijrida and M. Tahara (eds) *New Trends and Issues in Teaching Japanese Language and Culture* (Technical Report no. 15, pp. 133–59). Honolulu, HI: University of Hawai'I, Second Language Teaching and Curriculum Center.

Cohen, A. (2000) Developing language ability: Can old dogs learn new tricks? APPLE lecture, Teachers College, Columbia University.

Colombo, J. (1982) The Critical Period concept: Research, methodology, and theoretical issues. *Psychological Bulletin* 91 (2), 260–75.

Cook, V.J. (1991) The poverty-of-the-stimulus argument and multi-competence. *Second Language Research* 7 (2), 103–17.

Cook, V.J. (1992) Evidence for multi-competence. *Language Learning* 42 (4), 557–91

Cook, V.J. (1995) Multi-competence and the learning of many languages. *Language, Culture and Curriculum* 8 (2), 93–8.

Cook, V.J. (1999) Going beyond the native speaker in language teaching. *TESOL Quarterly* 33 (2), 185–209.

Coppieters, R. (1989) Competence differences between native and near-native speakers. *Language* 63, 544–73.

Corder, S.P. (1967) The significance of learners' errors. *International Review of Applied Linguistics* 5, 161–70.

Corder, S.P. (1978) Language-learner language. In J.C. Richards (ed.) *Understanding Second and Foreign Language Learning* (pp. 71–93). Rowley, MA: Newbury House.

Corder, S P. (1981) *Error Analysis and Interlanguage*. Oxford: Oxford University Press.

Corder, S.P. (1983) A role for the mother tongue. In S. Gass and L. Selinker (eds) *Language Transfer in Language Learning* (2nd edn) (pp. 85–97). Amsterdam: John Benjamins.

Cranshaw, A. (1997) A study of Anglophone native and near-native linguistic and metalinguistic performance. Unpublished PhD dissertation, Montréal University.

Curtiss, S. (1977) *Genie: A Linguistic Study of a Modern Day 'Wild Child'*. New York: Academic Press.

Curtiss, S. (1988) Abnormal language acquisition and the modularity of language. In F.J. Newmeyer (ed.) *Linguistics: The Cambridge Survey, Volume II* (pp. 96–116). Cambridge, UK: Cambridge University Press.

Curtiss, S. (1989) The Case of Chelsea: A new test case of the Critical Period for language acquisition. Unpublished manuscript, University of California, Los Angeles.

Davies, A. (2003) *The Native Speaker: Myth and Reality*. Clevedon: Multilingual Matters.

De Bot, K. (1996) The psycholinguistics of the output hypothesis. *Language Learning* 46, 529–55.

DeKeyser, R. (1993) The effect of error correction on grammar knowledge and oral proficiency. *Modern Language Journal* 77 (4), 501–15.

DeKeyser, R. (1994) How implicit can adult second language learning be? *AILA Review* 11, 83–96.

DeKeyser, R. (1995) Learning second language grammar rules: An experiment with a miniature linguistic system. *Studies in Second Language Acquisition* 17, 379–410.

DeKeyser, R. (1997) Beyond explicit rule learning: Automatizing second language morphosyntax. *Studies in Second Language Acquisition* 19, 195–221.

DeKeyser, R. (1998) Beyond focus on form. In C. Doughty and J. Williams (eds) *Focus on From in Classroom Second Language Acquisition* (pp. 42–63). Cambridge, UK: Cambridge University Press.

DeKeyser, R. (2000). The robustness of critical period effects in second language acquisition. *Studies in Second Language Acquisition* 22, 499–533.

DeKeyser, R. (2002, March) What makes form-meaning connections difficult? Paper presented at FMSLA, Chicago.

Doughty, C. and Williams, J. (1998) Pedagogical choices in focus on form: In C. Doughty and J. Williams (eds) *Focus on Form in Classroom Second Language Acquisition* (pp. 197–261). Cambridge, UK: Cambridge University Press.

Dulay, H. and Burt, M. (1975) Creative construction in second language learning and teaching. In M. Burt and H. Dulay (eds) *On TESOL '75: New Directions in Second Language Learning, Teaching and Bilingual Education* (pp. 21–32). Washington, DC: Teachers of English to Speakers of Other Languages.

Dulay, H. and Burt, M. (1978) From research to method in bilingual education. In J. Alatis (ed.) *International Dimensions of Bilingual Education* (pp. 551–75). Washington, DC: Georgetown University Press.

Eisenstein, M. and Starbuck, R. (1989) The effect of emotional investment on L2 production. In S. Gass, C. Madden, D. Preston, and L. Selinker (eds) *Variations in Second Language Acquisition* (pp. 125–140). Clevedon: Multilingual Matters.

Ellis, N.C. (1994) Implicit and explicit processes in language acquisition: An introduction. In N. Ellis (ed.) *Implicit and Explicit Learning of Languages* (pp. 1–32). San Diego: Academic Press.

Ellis, N. (2002a, February) The processes of second language instruction. Plenary speech, FMSLA conference, Chicago.

Ellis, N. (2002b) Frequency effects in language processing: A review with implications for theories of implicit and explicit language acquisition. *Studies in Second Language Acquisition* 24 (2), 143–88.

Ellis, N. and Laporte, N. (1997) Contexts of acquisition: Effects of formal instruction and naturalistic exposure on second language acquisition. In A. de Groot and J. Kroll (eds) *Tutorials in Bilingualism* (pp. 53–83). Mahwah, NJ: Lawrence Erlbaum.

Ellis, R. (1985) *Understanding Second Language Acquisition*. Oxford: Oxford University Press.

Ellis, R. (1988) Are classroom and naturalistic acquisition the same? *Studies in Second Language Acquisition* 11, 305–28.

Ellis, R. (1990) *Instructed Second Language Acquisition*. Oxford: Basil Blackwell.

Ellis, R. (1991) Grammaticality judgments and second language acquisition. *Studies in Second Language Acquisition* 13, 161–186.

Ellis, R. (1992) Learning to communicate in the classroom: A study of two language learners' requests. *Studies in Second Language Acquisition* 14, 1–23.

Ellis, R. (1994a) A theory of instructed second language acquisition. In N. Ellis (ed.) *Implicit and Explicit Learning of Languages* (pp. 79–114). New York: Academic Press.

Ellis, R. (1994b) *The Study of Second Language Acquisition*. Oxford: Oxford University Press.

Ellis, R. (1999) Item vs. system learning: Explaining free variation. *Applied Linguistics* 20 (4), 460–80.

Elman, J., Bates, L., Johnson, E., Karmiloff-Smith, M., Parisi, A. and Plunkett, K. (1996) *Rethinking Innateness: A Connectionist Perspective on Development*. Cambridge, MA: MIT Press.

Epstein, S., Flynn, S. and Martohardjono, G. (1996) Second language acquisition: Theoretical and experimental issues in contemporary research. *Behavioral and Brain Sciences* 19, 677–714.

Eubank, L. (1995) Generative research on second language acquisition. *Annual Review of Applied Linguistics* 15, 93–107.

Eubank, L., Beck, M. and Aboutaj, H. (1997) OI effects and optionality in the interlanguage of a Morocan-Arabic speaking learner of French. Paper presented at the American Association of Applied Linguistics, Orlando, Florida.

Eubank, L. and Gregg, K. (1999) Critical periods and (second) language acquisition: Divide et impera. In D. Birdsong (ed.) *Second Language Acquisition and the Critical Period Hypothesis* (pp. 65–100). Mahwah, NJ: Lawrence Erlbaum.

Færch, C. and Kasper, G. (1986) The role of comprehension in second-language learning. *Applied Linguistics* 7, 257–74.

Flege, J. (1981) The phonological basis of foreign accent. *TESOL Quarterly* 15, 443–55.

Flege, J. (1988) Factors affecting degree of perceived foreign accent in English sentences. *Journal of the Acoustical Society of America* 84, 70–79.

Flege, J. (1998) The role of subject and phonetic variables in L2 speech acquisition. In M. Gruber, D. Higgins, K. Olsen and T. Wysoki (eds) *Papers from the 34th Annual Meeting of the Chicago Linguistic Society: Vol. 2. The Panels* (pp. 213–32). Chicago, IL: Chicago Linguistic Society.

Flege, J.E. and Liu, S. (2001) The effect of experience on adults' acquisition of a second language. *Studies in Second Language Acquisition* 23, 527–52.

Flege, J., Munro, M. and MacKay, I. (1995) Factors affecting strength of perceived foreign accent in second language. *Journal of the Acoustical Society of America* 97, 3125–34.

Flexner, S. (ed.) (1993) *Random House Unabridged Dictionary* (2nd edn). New York: Random House.

Flynn, S. and O'Neil, W. (1988) *Linguistic Theory in Second Language Acquisition*. Dordrecht: Kluwer Academic.

Forster, K. (1979) Levels of processing and the structure of the language processor. In Cooper and E. Walker (eds) *Sentence Processing: Psycholinguistic Studies Presented to Merrill Garrett* (pp. 27–85). New York: Halsted.

Foster, P. (1998) A classroom-perspective on the negotiation of meaning. *Applied Linguistics* 19, 1–23.

Gass, S. (1988) Integrating research areas: A framework for second language studies. *Applied Linguistics* 9, 198–217.

Gass, S. (1994). The reliability of second-language grammaticality judgments. In E. Tarone, S. Gass and A. Cohen (eds) *Research Methodology in Second-Language Acquisition* (pp. 302–22). Hillsdale, NJ: Lawrence Erlbaum.

Gass, S. and Lakshmanan, U. (1991) Accounting for interlanguage subject pronouns. *Second Language Research* 7 (3), 181–203.

Gass, S. and Selinker, L. (1994) *Second Language Acquisition: An Introductory Course.* Hillsdale, NJ: Lawrence Erlbaum.
Gass, S. and Selinker, L. (2001) *Second Language Acquisition: An Introductory Course* (2nd edn). Mahwah, NJ: Lawrence Erlbaum.
Gass, S., Sorace, A. and Selinker, L. (1999) *Second Language Learning Data Analysis.* Mahwah, NJ: Erlbaum.
Gleason, J. and Ratner, N. (1998) Language acquisition. In J. Gleason and N. Ratner (eds) *Psycholinguistics* (pp. 347–408). New York: Harcourt Brace College.
Gregg, K. (1984) Krashen's Monitor and Occam's Razor. *Applied Linguistics* 5, 79–100.
Gregg, K. (1996) The logical and developmental problems of second language acquisition. In W. Ritchie and T. Bhatia (eds) *Handbook of Second Language Acquisition* (pp. 50–81). New York: Academic Press.
Green, P. and Hecht, K. (1992) Implicit and explicit grammar: An empirical study. *Applied Linguistics* 13 (2), 168–84.
Hale, K. (1988) Linguistic theory. In S. Flynn and W. O'Neil (eds) *Linguistic Theory in Second Language Acquisition* (pp. 26–33). Dordrecht: Kluwer Academic.
Hammarberg, B. (1979) On intralingual, interlingual and developmental solutions in interlanguage. In K. Hyltenstam and M. Linnarud (eds) *Interlanguage* (pp. 7–24). Stockholm: Almqvist and Wiksell International.
Hammerly, H. (1983) *Synthesis in Second Language Teaching: An Introduction to Linguistics.* Blaine, Washington: Second Language Publications.
Hammerly, H. (1991) *Fluency and Accuracy: Toward Balance in Language Teaching and Learning.* Clevedon, UK: Multilingual Matters.
Han, Z-H. (1998) Fossilization: An investigation into advanced L2 learning of a typologically distant language. Unpublished PhD dissertation, University of London.
Han, Z-H. (2000) Persistence of the implicit influence of NL: The case of the pseudo-passive. *Applied Linguistics* 21 (1), 78–105.
Han, Z-H. (2001a) Review of Grenfell and Harris (1999) 'Modern Languages and Learning Strategies in Theory and Practice'. *Language Teaching Research* 5 (3), 270–73.
Han, Z-H. (2001b) Fine-tuning corrective feedback. *Foreign Language Annals* 34 (6), 582–99.
Han, Z-H. (2002a). Fossilization: Five Central Issues. Paper presented at the Second Language Research Forum (SLRF), Toronto, Canada. On WWW at http://www.tc.columbia.edu/Academic/TESOL/Faculty/Fossilization.pps.
Han, Z-H. (2002b) Rethinking the role of corrective feedback in communicative language teaching. *RELC Journal* 33 (1), 1–34.
Han, Z-H. (2002c) A study of the impact of recasts on tense consistency in L2 output. *TESOL Quarterly* 36 (4), 543–72.
Han, Z-H. (2003a) Fossilization: From simplicity to complexity. *International Journal of Bilingual Education and Bilingualism* 6 (2), 95–128.
Han, Z-H. (2003b, March) Fossilization: Facts, fancies, fallacies, and methodological problems. Panelist presentation at the 2003 AAAL Annual Conference. Arlington, Virginia.
Han, Z-H. (In press) 'To be a native speaker is not to be a non-native speaker'. *Second Language Research.*
Han, Z-H. and Selinker, L. (1999) Error resistance: Towards an empirical pedagogy. *Language Teaching Research* 3 (3), 248–75.

Han, Z-H. and Selinker, L. (2001) Second language instruction and fossilization. Presentation at the 35th International TESOL Annual Convention, St Louis.

Han, Z-H. and Selinker, L. (2002) 'Why is this happened?' SLA validation: Replication and beyond. Ms., Teachers College, Columbia University.

Harley, B. (1993) Instructional strategies and SLA in early French immersion. *Studies in Second Language Acquisition* 15, 245–59.

Harley, B. (1998) The role of focus-on-form tasks in promoting child L2 acquisition. In C. Doughty and J. Williams (eds) *Focus on Form in Classroom Second Language Acquisition* (pp. 156–74). Cambridge: Cambridge University Press.

Harley, B. and King, M. (1989) Verb lexis in the written compositions of young French L2 learners. *Studies in Second Language Acquisition* 11, 415–39.

Harley, B. and Swain, M. (1978) An analysis of the verb system by young learners of French. *Interlanguage Studies Bulletin* 3 (1), 35–79.

Harley, B. and Swain, M. (1984) The interlanguage of immersion students and its implications for second language teaching. In A. Davies, C. Criper and A.P.R. Howatt (eds) *Interlanguage* (pp. 291–311). Edinburgh: Edinburgh University Press.

Harley, B. and Wang (1997) The critical period hypothesis: Where are we now? In A. de Groot and J. Kroll (eds) *Tutorials in Bilingualism* (pp. 19–52). Mahwah, NJ: Lawrence Erlbaum.

Hartford, B. (1993) Tense and aspect in the news discourse of Nepali English. *World Englishes* 12, 1–13.

Hawkins, R. (2000) Persistent selective fossilization in second language acquisition and the optimal design of the language faculty. *Essex Research Reports in Linguistics* 34, 75–90.

Hawkins, R. and Chan, Y.C. (1997) The partial availability of Universal Grammar in second language acquisition: The 'failed features' hypothesis. *Second Language Research* 6, 187–226.

Henkes, T. (1974) Early stages in the non-native acquisition of English syntax: A study of three children from Zaire, Venezuela, and Saudi Arabia. Unpublished PhD dissertation, Indiana University, Bloomington.

Higgs, T. and Clifford, R. (1982) The push toward communication. In T. Higgs (ed.) *Curriculum, Competence, and the Foreign Language Teacher* (pp. 57–79). Lincolnwood, IL: National Textbook.

Hirakawa, M. (1995) L2 acquisition of English unaccusative constructions. *Proceedings of BUCLD* 19, 291–302.

Hirakawa, M. (1997) On the unaccusative/unergative distinction in SLA. *JACET Bulletin* 28, 17–27.

Hirakawa, M. (2001) L2 acquisition of Japanese unaccusative verbs. *Second Language Research* 23 (2), 221–46.

Hornstein, N. and D. Lightfoot (eds) (1981) *Explanation in Linguistics: The Logical Problem of Language Acquisition*. London: Longman.

Hulstijn, J.H. (1989) A cognitive view on interlanguage variability. In M. Eisenstein (ed.) *The Dynamic Interlanguage: Empirical Studies in Second Language Acquisition* (pp. 17–31). New York: Plenum.

Hulstijn, J. (2002a) Towards a unified account of the representation, processing, and acquisition of second language knowledge. In M. Pienemann (ed.) *Second Language Research: Issues in SLA and Language Processing* (special issue) (pp. 193–223).

Hulstijn, J. (2002b, February) The construct of input in an interactive approach to second language acquisition. Paper presented at the Form-Meaning Connections in Second Language Acquisition Conference, Chicago.

Hulstijn, J. and De Graaff, R. (1994) Under what conditions does explicit knowledge of a second language facilitate the acquisition of implicit knowledge? A research proposal. *AILA Review* 11, 97–112.

Hwang, J-B. (1997) Implicit and explicit instruction for the L2 acquisition of English unaccusative verbs. Manuscript, University of Oregon.

Hyltenstam, K. (1985) L2 learners' variable output and language teaching. In K. Hyltenstam and M. Pienemann (eds) *Modelling and Assessing Second Language Acquisition* (pp. 113–36). San Diego: College-Hill.

Hyltenstam, K. (1988) Lexical characteristics of near-native second language learners of Swedish. *Journal of Multilingual and Multicultural Development* 9, 67–84.

Hyltenstam, K. and Abrahamsson, N. (2001) Age and L2 learning: The hazards of matching practical 'implications' with theoretical 'facts'. *TESOL Quarterly* 35 (1), 151–70.

Ioup, G., Boustagui, E., Tigi, M. and Moselle, M. (1994) Reexamining the critical period hypothesis: A case study of successful adult SLA in a naturalistic environment. *Studies in Second Language Acquisition* 16, 73–98.

Jain, M. (1974) Error analysis: Source, cause and significance. In J.C. Richards (ed.) *Error Analysis: Perspectives on Second Language Acquisition* (pp. 189–215). New York: Longman.

Jarvis, S. (1998) *Conceptual Transfer in the Interlingual Lexicon*. Bloomington, IN: IULC.

Jarvis, S. and Pavlenko, A. (2000, September) Conceptual restructuring in language learning: Is there an end state? Paper presented at SLRF 2000, Madison, WI.

Johnson, H. (1992) Defossilizing. *ELT Journal* 46 (2), 180–89.

Johnson, K. (1996) *Language Teaching and Skill Learning*. Oxford: Blackwell.

Johnson, K. and Johnson, H. (1998) *Encyclopedic Dictionary of Applied Linguistics*. Oxford: Blackwell.

Johnson, J. and Newport, E. (1989) Critical period effects in second language learning: The influence of maturational state on the acquisition of English as a second language. *Cognitive Psychology* 21, 60–99.

Johnson, J., Shenkman, K., Newport, E. and Medin, D. (1996) Indeterminacy in the grammar of adult language learners. *Journal of Memory and Language* 35, 335–52.

Ju, M. (2000) Overpassivization errors by second language learners. *Studies in Second Language Acquisition* 22, 85–111.

Juffs, A. and Harrington, M. (1995) Parsing effects in L2 sentence processing: Subject and object asymmetries in Wh-extraction. *Studies in Second Language Acquisition* 17, 483–516.

Jung, J-Y. (2002) Issues in acquisitional pragmatics. *Teachers College-Columbia University Working Papers in TESOL and Applied Linguistics* 2 (2), 1–34. On WWW at http://www.tc.columbia.edu/tesolalwebjournal/JungFinal.doc.pdf.

Kachru, B.B. (1990) *The Alchemy of English: The Spread, Functions, and Models of Non-native Englishes*. Chicago: University of Illinois Press.

Kasper, G. (1982) Teaching-induced aspects of interlanguage discourse. *Studies in Second Language Acquisition* 4, 99–113.

Kasper, G. and Schmidt, R. (1996) Developmental issues in interlanguage pragmatics. *Studies in Second Language Acquisition* 18, 149–69.

Kellerman, E. (1977) Toward a characterization of the strategy of transfer in second language learning. *Interlanguage Studies Bulletin* 2, 58–145

Kellerman, E. (1978) Giving learners a break: Native speaker intuitions as a source of predictions about transferability. *Working Papers on Bilingualism* 15, 59–92

Kellerman, E. (1984) The empirical evidence for the influence of the L1 in Interlanguage. In A. Davies, C. Criper and A.P.R. Howatt (eds) *Interlanguage* (pp. 98–122). Edinburgh: Edinburgh University Press.

Kellerman, E. (1989) The imperfect conditional: Fossilization, cross-linguistic influence and natural tendencies in a foreign language setting. In K. Hyltenstam and L. Obler (eds) *Bilingualism across Life Span* (pp. 87–115). Cambridge, UK: Cambridge University Press.

Kellerman, E. (1995a) Crosslinguistic influence: Transfer to nowhere? *Annual Review of Applied Linguistics* 15, 125–50.

Kellerman, E. (1995b) Age before beauty. In L. Eubank, L. Selinker and M. Sharwood Smith (eds) *The Current State of Interlanguage* (pp. 219–32). Amsterdam: John Benjamins.

Klein, E. (1993) *Toward Second Language Acquisition: A Study of Null-prep*. Dordrecht: Kluwer Academic Press.

Klein, E. (2001) (Mis)construing null prepositions in L2 intergrammars: A commentary and proposal. *Second Language Research* 17 (1), 37–70.

Klein, W. (1986) *Second Language Acquisition.* Cambridge, UK: Cambridge University Press.

Klein, W. (1993) The acquisition of temporality. In C. Perdue (ed.) *Adult Language Acquisition: Cross-linguistic Perspectives, Volume II* (pp. 73–118). Cambridge, UK: Cambridge University Press.

Klein, W. and Dittmar, N. (1979) Developing grammars. *The Acquisition of German Syntax by Foreign Workers*. Berlin: Springer.

Klein, W. and Perdue, C. (1993) Utterance structure. In C. Perdue (ed.) *Adult Language Acquisition: Cross-linguistic Perspective, Volume II* (pp. 3–40). Cambridge, UK: Cambridge University Press.

Kowal, M. and Swain, M. (1997) From semantic to syntactic processing: How can we promote it in the immersion classroom? In R. Johnson and M. Swain (eds) *Immersion Education: International Perspectives* (pp. 284–309) Cambridge, UK: Cambridge University Press.

Krashen, S. (1977) Some issues relating to the monitor model. In H.D. Brown, C.A. Yorio and R.H. Crymes (eds) *On TESOL'77. Teaching and Learning English as a Second Language: Trends in Research and Practice* (pp. 144–58). Washington, DC: Teachers of English to Speakers of Other Languages.

Krashen, S. (1981) *Second Language Acquisition and Second Language Learning.* Oxford: Pergamon.

Krashen, S. (1982) *Principles and Practice in Second Language Acquisition.* Oxford: Pergamon.

Krashen, S. (1994) The input hypothesis and its rivals. In N. Ellis (ed.) *Implicit and Explicit Learning of Languages* (pp. 45–77). New York: Academic Press.

Krashen, S. and Seliger, H. (1975) The essential contributions of formal instruction in adult second language learning. *TESOL Quarterly* 9, 173–83.

Krashen, S. and Seliger, H. (1976) The role of formal and informal learning environments in second language learning. *International Journal of Psycholinguistics* 6, 15–21.

Krashen, S., Long, M. and Scarcella, R. (1982) Age, rate, and eventual attainment in second language acquisition. In S. Krashen, R. Scarcella and M. Long (eds) *Child–adult Differences in Second Language Acquisition*. Rowley, MA: Newbury House.

Kroll, J., Michael, E., Tokowicz, and Dufour, R. (2002) The development of lexical fluency in a second language. *Second Language Research* 18 (2), 137–71.

Lado, R. (1957) *Linguistics Across Cultures*. Ann Arbor, MI: University of Michigan Press.

Lamendella, J. (1977) General principles of neuro-functional organization and their manifestation in primary and non-primary language acquisition. *Language Learning* 27, 155–96.

Lantolf, J. and Ahmed, M. (1989) Psycholinguistic perspectives on interlanguage variation: A Vygotskyan analysis. In S. Gass, C. Madden, D. Preston and L. Selinker (eds) *Variation in Second Language Acquisition* (pp. 93–108). Clevedon: Multilingual Matters.

Lardiere, D. (1998a) Case and tense in the 'fossilized' steady state. *Second Language Research* 14, 1–26.

Lardiere, D. (1998b) Dissociating syntax from morphology in a divergent L2 end-state grammar. *Second Language Research* 14, 359–75.

Lardiere, D. (2000) Mapping features to forms in second language acquisition. In Archibald, J. (ed.) *Second Language Acquisition and Linguistic Theory* (pp. 102–29). Malden, MA: Blackwell.

Larsen-Freeman, D. (1983) Assessing global second language proficiency. In H.W. Seliger and M.H. Long (eds) *Classroom Oriented Research* (pp. 287–304). Rowley, MA: Newbury House.

Larsen-Freeman, D. (1995) On the teaching and learning of grammar: Challenging the myths. In F. Eckman, D. Highland, P. Lee, J. Mileham and R. Reber (eds) *Second Language Acquisition Theory and Pedagogy* (pp. 131–50). Mahwah, NJ: Lawrence Erlbaum.

Larsen-Freeman, D. (1997) Chaos/Complexity science and second language acquisition. *Applied Linguistics* 19 (2), 141–65.

Larsen-Freeman, D. and Long, M. (1991) *An Introduction to Second Language Acquisition Research*. New York: Longman.

Lenneberg, E. (1967) *Biological Foundations of Language*. New York: Wiley.

Lennon, P. (1991) Error elimination and error fossilization: A study of an advanced learner in the L2 community. *I.T.L. Review of Applied Linguistics* 93–4, 129–51.

Levin, B. and Rappaport Hovav, M. (1995) *Unaccusativity at the Syntax-lexical Semantics Interface*. Cambridge, MA: MIT Press.

Lewis, M. (1993) *The Lexical Approach*. Hove: Language Teaching.

Lightbown, P. (1983) Exploring relationships between developmental and instructional sequences in L2 acquisition. In H. Seliger and M. Long (eds) *Classroom Oriented Research in Second Language Acquisition* (pp. 217–45). Rowley, MA: Newbury House.

Lightbown, P. (1985) Input and acquisition for second language learners in and out of classrooms. *Applied Linguistics* 6, 263–73.

Lightbown, P. (1991) Getting quality input in the second/foreign language classroom. In C. Kramsch and S. McConnell-Ginet (eds) *Text and Context: Cross-disciplinary Perspectives on Language Study* (pp. 187–97). Lexington, MA: D.C. Heath.

Lightbown, P. (1998) The importance of timing in focus on form. In C. Doughty and J. Williams (eds) *Focus on Form in Classroom Second Language Acquisition* (pp. 177–96). Cambridge: Cambridge University Press.

Lightbown, P. (2000) Classroom SLA research and second language teaching. *Applied Linguistics* 21 (4), 431–62.

Lightbown, P. and Spada, N. (1990) Focus on form and corrective feedback in communicative language teaching: Effects on second language learning. *Studies in Second Language Acquisition* 12, 429–48.

Lightbown, P. and Spada, N. (1999) *How Languages are Learned?* Oxford: Oxford University Press.

Lin, Y-H. (1995) An empirical analysis of stabilization / fossilization: Incorporation and self-correction of Chinese learners. Unpublished PhD dissertation, Barcelona University.

Lin, Y-H. and Hedgcock, J. (1996) Negative feedback incorporation among high-proficiency and low-proficiency Chinese-speaking learners of Spanish. *Language Learning* 46 (4), 567–611.

Long, M. (1983) Does second language instruction make a difference? A review of the research. *TESOL Quarterly* 17, 357–82.

Long, M. (1985) A role for instruction in second language acquisition: Task-based language training. In K. Hyltenstam and M. Pienemann (eds) *Modelling and Assessing Second Language Acquisition* (pp. 77–100). Clevedon: Multilingual Matters.

Long, M. (1988) Instructed interlanguage development. In L. Beebe (ed.) *Issues in Second Language Acquisition: Multiple Perspectives* (pp. 115–41). Rowley, MA: Newbury House.

Long, M. (1990) Maturational constraints on language development. *Studies in Second Language Acquisition* 12, 251–85.

Long, M. (1991) Focus on form: A design feature in language teaching methodology. In K. de Bot, R. Ginsberg and C. Kramsch (eds) *Foreign Language Research in Cross-cultural Perspective* (pp. 39–52). Amsterdam: John Benjamins.

Long, M. (1996) The role of the linguistic environment in second language acquisition. In W. Ritchie and T. Bhatia (eds) *Handbook of Second Language Acquisition* (pp. 413–65). New York: Academic Press.

Long, M. (1997) Fossilization: Rigor mortis in living linguistic systems? Plenary speech at EUROSLA 7, Barcelona.

Long, M. (2003) Stabilization and fossilization in interlanguage development. In C. Doughty and M. Long (eds) *Handbook of Second Language Acquisition* (pp. 487–536). Oxford: Blackwell.

Long, M., Inagaki, S. and Ortega, L. (1998) The role of implicit negative feedback in SLA: Models and recast in Japanese and Spanish. *Modern Language Journal* 82 (3), 357–71.

Long, M. and Robinson, P. (1998) Focus on form: Theory, research, and practice. In C. Doughty and J. Williams (eds) *Focus on Form in Classroom Second Language Acquisition* (pp. 16–41). Cambridge, UK: Cambridge University Press.

Lowther, M. (1983) Fossilization, pidginization and the Monitor. In L. MacMathuna and D. Singleton (eds) *Language Across Cultures* (pp. 127–39). Dublin: Irish Association for Applied Linguistics.

Lyster, R. (1994) La négotiation de la forme: Stratégie analytique en classe d'immersion. *Canadian Modern Language Review* 50, 446–65.

Lyster, R. (1998) Recasts, repetition, and ambiguity in L2 classroom discourse. *Studies in Second Language Acquisition* 20, 51–81.

Mackey, A., Gass, S. and McDonough, K. (2000) How do learners perceive interactional feedback? *Studies in Second Language Acquisition* 22, 471–97.

Mackey, A. and Philp, J. (1998) Conversational interaction and second language development: Recasts, responses, and red herrings? *Modern Language Journal* 82 (3), 338–56.

MacWhinney, B. (1992) Transfer and competition in second language learning. In R.J. Harris (ed.) *Cognitive Processing in Bilinguals* (pp. 371–90). Amsterdam: Elsevier.

MacWhinney, B. (1997) Implicit and explicit processes: Commentary. *Studies in Second Language Acquisition* 19, 277–82.

MacWhinney, B. (2001) The competition model: The input, the context, and the brain. In P. Robinson (ed.) *Cognition and Second Language Instruction* (pp. 69–90). Cambridge, UK: Cambridge University Press.

Mandler, G. (1999) Emotion. In B. Bly and D. Rummelhart (eds) *Cognitive Science* (pp. 367–84). San Diego: Academic Press.

Manne, G. (1990) *Ny I Norge*. Oslo: Fag og Kultur.

Marinova-Todd, S., Bradford, M. and Snow, C. (2000) Three misconceptions about age and L2 learning. *TESOL Quarterly* 34 (1), 9–34.

Mayberry, R. (1993) First-language acquisition after childhood differs from second-language acquisition: The case of American Sign Language. *Journal of Speech and Hearing Research* 36, 1258–70.

McCabe, A. (1998) Discourse and text. In J. Gleason and N. Ratner (eds) *Psycholinguisics*. New York: Harcourt Brace College.

Meisel, J., Clahsen, H. and Pienemann, P. (1981) On determining developmental stages in natural second language acquisition. *Studies in Second Language Acquisition* 3 (2), 109–35.

Mellow, D., Reeder, K. and Forster, E. (1996) Using time-series research designs to investigate the effects of instruction. *Studies in Second Language Acquisition* 18 (3), 325–50.

Montrul, S. (2000) Transitivity alternations in L2 acquisition: Toward a modular view of transfer. *Studies in Second Language Acquisition* 22, 229–73.

Montrul, S. (2001) Introduction. *Studies in Second Language Acquisition* 23, 145–51.

Montrul, S. (2002) Incomplete form-meaning connections in the grammars of Spanish heritage speakers. Paper presented at FMSLA, Chicago.

Moyer, A. (1999) Ultimate attainment in L2 phonology. *Studies in Second Language Acquisition* 21, 81–108.

Mukattash, L. (1986) Persistence of fossilization. *IRAL* 24 (3), 187–203.

Muranoi, H. (2000) Focus on form through interaction enhancement: Integrating formal instruction into a communicative task in EFL classrooms. *Language Learning* 55 (4), 617–73.

Nakuma, C. (1998) A new theoretical account of 'fossilization': Implications for L2 attrition research. *IRAL* 36 (3), 247–56.

Nemser, W. (1971) Approximative systems of foreign language learners. *IRAL* 9, 115–23.

Nicholas, Lightbown, P. and Spada, N. (2001) Recasts as feedback to language learners. *Language Learning* 51 (4), 719–58

Nikolov, M. (2000) The Critical Period Hypothesis reconsidered: Successful adult learners of Hungarian and English. *IRAL* 38, 109–24.

Norris, J. and Ortega, L. (2000) Effectiveness of L2 instruction: A research synthesis and quantitative meta-analysis. *Language Learning* 50, 417–528.

Norris, J. and Ortega, L. (2001) Does type of instruction make a difference? Substantive findings from a meta-analytic review. In R. Ellis (ed.) *Form-focused Instruction and Second Language Learning* (pp. 157–213). Oxford: Blackwell.

Odlin, T. (1989) *Language Transfer*. Cambridge, UK: Cambridge University Press.

Odlin, T. (1993) Book review: 'Rediscovering Interlanguage' by Selinker (1992). *Language* 69 (2), 379–83.

Oshita, H. (1997) 'The unaccusative trap': L2 acquisition of English intransitive verbs. Unpublished PhD dissertation, University of Southern California, Los Angeles.

Oshita, H. (2001) The unaccusative trap in second language acquisition. *Studies in Second Language Acquisition* 23, 279–304.

Oyama, S. C. (1976) A sensitive period for the acquisition of a nonnative phonological system. *Journal of Psycholinguistic Research* 5 (3), 261–83.

Paradis, M. (1994) Neurolinguistic aspects of implicit and explicit memory: Implications for bilingualism and SLA. In N. Ellis (ed.) *Implicit and Explicit Learning of Languages* (pp. 393–419). New York: Academic Press.

Patkowski, M. (1980) The sensitive period for the acquisition of syntax in a second language. *Language Learning* 30, 449–72.

Patkowski, M. (1990) Age and accent in a second language: A reply to James Emil Flege. *Applied Linguistics* 11, 73–89.

Pavlenko, A. and Jarvis, S. (2001) Conceptual transfer: New perspectives on the study of cross-linguistic influence. In E. Németh (ed.) *Cognition in Language Use: Selected Papers from the 7th International Pragmatics Conference, Volume 1* (pp. 288–301). Antwerp: International Pragmatics Association.

Penfield, W. and Roberts, L. (1959) *Speech and Brain Mechanisms*. New York: Atheneum.

Perdue, C. (1984) *Second Language Acquisition by Adult Immigrants: A Field Manual*. Rowley, MA: Newbury House.

Perdue, C. (1993) *Adult Language Acquisition: Cross-linguistic Perspectives, Volume I: Field Methods*. Cambridge, UK: Cambridge University Press.

Perlmutter, D. (1978) Impersonal passives and the unaccusative hypothesis. *Proceedings of the Berkeley Linguistics Society* 4, 157–89.

Pica, T. (1994) The selective impact of classroom instruction on second-language acquisition. *Applied Linguistics* 6 (3), 214–22.

Pica, T., Lincoln-Porter, F., Paninos, D. and Linnell, J. (1996) Language learners' interaction: How does it address the input, output, and feedback needs of language learners? *TESOL Quarterly* 30, 59–84.

Pienemann, M. (1985) Learnability and syllabus construction. In K. Hyltenstam and M. Pienemann (eds) *Modeling and Assessing Second Language Acquisition* (pp. 23–75). Clevedon, UK: Multilingual Matters.

Pienemann, M. (1986) Psychological constraints on the teachability of language. In C.W. Pfaff (ed.) *First and Second Language Acquisition Processes* (pp. 143–68). Rowley, MA: Newbury House.

Pienemann, M. (1989) Is language teachable? Psycholinguistic experiments and hypotheses. *Applied Linguistics* 10 (1), 52–79.

Pienemann, M. (1998) *Language Processing and Second Language Development*. Amsterdam: John Benjamins.

Pienemann, M. (2002) Introduction. In M. Pienemann (ed.) Special issue: Issues in SLA and Language Processing. *Second Language Research* 18 (3), 189–92.

Pienemann, M., Johnston, M. and Brindley, G. (1988) Constructing an acquisition-based procedure for second language assessment. *Studies in Second Language Acquisition*, 217–43.

Pinker, S. (1989) *Learnability and Cognition: The Acquisition of Argument Structure*. Cambridge, MA: MIT Press.

Pinker, S. (1999) *Word and Rules*. London: Weidenfeld and Nicolson.

Pollock, J. (1989) Verb movement, Universal Grammar and the structure of IP. *Linguistic Inquiry* 20, 365–424.

Preston, D. (1989) *Sociolinguistics and Second Language Acquisition*. Oxford: Blackwell.

Pulvermüller, F. and Schumann, J. (1994) Neurobiological mechanisms of language acquisition. *Language Learning* 44, 681–734.

Radford, A. (1994) *Syntax: A Minimalist Program*. Cambridge, UK: Cambridge University Press.

Richards, J., Platt, J. and Platt, H. (eds) (1992) *Longman Dictionary of Language Teaching and Applied Linguistics* (2nd edn). Essex: Longman.

Rizzi, L. and Roberts, L. (1989) Complex inversion in French. *Probus* 1, 1–30.

Roberts, M. (1995) Awareness and the efficacy of error correction. In R. Schmidt (ed.) *Attention and Awareness in Foreign Language Learning* (pp. 163–82). Honolulu, HI: University of Hawai'i, Second Language Teaching & Curriculum Center.

Robinson, P. (1996) Learning simple and complex second language rules under implicit, incidental, rule-search and instructed conditions. *Studies in Second Language Acquisition* 18 (1), 27–68.

Robinson, P. (2002) Task complexity, cognitive resources, and syllabus design: A triadic framework for examining task influences on SLA. In P. Robinson (ed.) *Cognition and Second Language Instruction* (pp. 287–318). Cambridge: Cambridge University Press.

Rutherford, W. (1983) Language typology and language transfer. In S. Gass and L. Selinker (ed.) *Language Transfer in Language Learning* (pp. 358–70). Rowley, MA: Newbury House.

Rutherford, W. (1988) *Second Language Grammar: Learning and Teaching*. London: Longman.

Sajavaara, K. (1986) Transfer and second language speech processing. In E. Kellerman and M. Sharwood Smith (eds) *Crosslinguistic Influence in Second Language Acquisition* (pp. 66–79). Oxford: Pergamon.

Sawyer, M. and Ranta, L. (2001) Aptitude, individual differences, and instructional design. In P. Robinson (ed.) *Cognition and Second Language Instruction* (pp. 318–53). Cambridge, UK: Cambridge University Press.

Schachter, J. (1974) An error in error analysis. *Language Learning* 24, 205–14.

Schachter, J. (1988) Second language acquisition and Universal Grammar. *Applied Linguistics* 9 (3), 219–35.

Schachter, J. (1989) Testing a proposed universal. In S. Gass and J. Schachter (eds) *Linguistic Perspectives on Second Language Acquisition* (pp. 73–88). Cambridge: Cambridge University Press.

Schachter, J. (1990) On the issue of completeness in second language acquisition. *Second Language Research* 6, 93–124.

Schachter, J. (1996a) Maturation and the issue of Universal Grammar in second language acquisition. In W. Ritchie and T. Bhatia (eds) *Handbook of Second Language Acquisition* (pp. 159–94). San Diego: Academic Press.

Schachter, J. (1996b) Learning and triggering in adult L2 acquisition. In G. Brown *et al.* (eds) *Performance and Competence in SLA* (pp. 70–88). Cambridge: Cambridge University Press.

Schachter, J. and Rutherford, W. (1979) Discourse function and language transfer. *Working Papers in Bilingualism* 19, 1–12.

Schmidt, R. (1983) Interaction, acculturation, and the acquisition of communicative competence: A case study of an adult. In N. Wolfson and E. Judd (eds.) *Sociolinguistics and Language Acquisition* (pp. 137–74). Rowley, MA: Newbury House.

Schmidt, R. (1990) The role of consciousness in second language learning. *Applied Linguistics* 11, 129–58.

Schmidt, R. (1993) Awareness and second language acquisition. *Annual Review of Applied Linguistics* 13, 206–26.

Schmidt, R. (1994a) Cognitive unconscious: Of artificial grammars and SLA. In N. Ellis (ed.) *Implicit and Explicit Learning of Languages* (pp. 165–209). New York: Academic Press.

Schmidt, R. (1994b) Deconstructing consciousness in search of useful definitions for applied linguistics. *AILA Review* 11, 11–26.

Schmidt, R. (1995) Consciousness and foreign language learning: A tutorial on the role of attention and awareness in learning. In R. Schmidt (ed.) *Attention and Awareness in Foreign Language Learning, Technical Report No. 9* (pp. 1–63). Honolulu, HI: University of Hawai'i, Second Language Teaching & Curriculum Center.

Schneiderman, E. and Desmarais, C. (1988) The talented language learner: Some preliminary findings. *Second Language Research* 4, 91–109.

Schnitzer, M. L. (1993) Steady as a rock: Does the steady state represent cognitive fossilization? *Journal of Psycholinguistic Research* 22 (1), 1–20.

Schouten, E. (1996) Crosslinguistic influence and the expression of hypothetical meaning. In E. Kellerman, B. Weltens and T. Bongaerts (eds) *EUROSLA 6: A Selection of Papers. Toegepaste Taalwetenschap in Artikelen* (*Applied Linguistics in Article form*) 55 (pp. 161–74). Amsterdam: VU Uitgeverij.

Schumann, F. and Schumann, J. (1977) Diary of a language learner: An introspective study of second language learning. In H.D. Brown, C.A. Yorio and R.H. Crymes (eds) *On TESOL '77, Teaching and Learning English as a Second Language: Trends in Research and Practice* (pp. 241–9). Washington, DC: Teachers of English to Speakers of Other Languages.

Schumann, J. (1978a) *The Pidginization Process: A Model for Second Language Acquisition*. Rowley, MA: Newbury House.

Schumann, J. (1978b) Social and psychological factors in second language acquisition. In J.C. Richards (ed.) *Understanding Second and Foreign Language Learning* (pp. 163–78). Rowley, MA: Newbury House.

Schumann, J. (1978c) The relationship of pidginization, creolization and decreolization to second language acquisition. *Language Learning* 28 (2), 367–79.

Schumann, J. (1979) The acquisition of English negation by speakers of Spanish: A review of the literature. In R. Andersen (ed.) *The Acquisition and Use of Spanish and English as First and Second Languages* (pp. 3–32). Washington, DC: Teachers of English to Speakers of Other Languages.

Schumann, J. (1986) Research on the acculturation model for second language acquisition. *Journal of Multilingual and Multicultural Development* 7 (5), 379–92.

Schumann, J. (1998) The neurobiology of affect in language. *Language Learning*, 48.

Schwartz, B. (1997) The second language instinct. Plenary speech at GALA '97, Edinburgh.

Schwartz, B. and Sprouse, R. (1996) L2 cognitive states and the Full Transfer/Full Access model. *Second Language Research* 12, 40–72.

Scott, J. (1962) Critical periods in behavioral development. *Science* 138, 949–58.

Scovel, T. (1969) Foreign accents, language acquisition, and cerebral dominance. *Language Learning* 19, 245–54

Scovel, T. (1988) *A Time to Speak: A Psycholinguistic Inquiry into the Critical Period for Human Speech.* New York: Newbury House/Harper and Row.

Scovel, T. (2000) A critical review of the critical period research. *Annual Review of Applied Linguistics* 20, 213–23.

Seliger, H. (1975) Inductive and deductive method in language teaching: A re-examination. *International Review of Applied Linguistics* 13 (1), 1–18.

Seliger, H. (1977) Does practice make perfect?: A study of interaction patterns and L2 competence. *Language Learning* 27, 263–78.

Seliger, H. (1978) Implications of a multiple critical periods hypothesis for second language learning. In W. Ritchie (ed.) *Second Language Acquisition Research: Issues and Implications* (pp. 11–19). New York: Academic Press.

Seliger, H.W. (1989) Semantic transfer constraints on the production of English passive by Hebrew-English Bilinguals. In H. Dechert and M. Raupach (eds) *Transfer in Language Production* (pp. 21–34). Norwood, NJ: Ablex.

Seliger, H., Krashen, S. and Ladefoged, P. (1975) Maturational constraints in the acquisition of a native-like accent in second language learning. *Languages Sciences* 36, 20–22.

Selinker, L. (1972) Interlanguage. *IRAL* 10 (2), 209–31.

Selinker, L. (1985) Attempting comprehensive and comparative empirical research in second language acquisition: A review of 'Second Language Acquisition by Adult Immigrants: A Field Manual, Part One'. *Language Learning* 35 (4), 567–84.

Selinker, L. (1992) *Rediscovering Interlanguage.* New York: Longman.

Selinker, L. (1993) Fossilization as simplification? In M. Tickoo (ed.) *Simplification: Theory and Application, Anthology series 31* (pp. 14–28). Singapore: Southeast Asian Ministers of Education Organization.

Selinker, L. (1996a) On the notion of 'IL competence' in early SLA research: An aid to understanding some baffling current issues. In G. Brown, K. Malmkjaer and J. Williams (eds) *Performance and Competence in SLA* (pp. 92–113). Cambridge: Cambridge University Press.

Selinker, L. (1996b) Research proposal for grant application submitted to the British Library.

Selinker, L. and Douglas, D. (1985) Wrestling with 'context' in interlanguage theory. *Applied Linguistics* 6, 190–204.

Selinker, L. and Han, Z-H. (1996) Fossilization: What do we think we know? Paper presented at EUROSLA 6, Nijmegen.

Selinker, L. and Han, Z-H. (2001) Fossilization: Moving the concept into empirical longitudinal study. In C. Elder, A. Brown, E. Grove, K. Hill, N. Iwashita, T. Lumley, T. McNamara and K. O'Loughlin (eds) *Studies in Language Testing: Experimenting with Uncertainty* (pp. 276–91). Cambridge: Cambridge University Press.

Selinker, L. and Lakshmanan, U. (1992) Language transfer and fossilization: The multiple effects principle. In S. Gass and L. Selinker (eds) *Language Transfer in Language Learning* (pp. 197–216). Amsterdam: John Benjamins.
Selinker, L. and Lamendella, J. (1978) Two perspectives on fossilization in interlanguage learning. *Interlanguage Studies Bulletin* 3 (2), 143–91.
Selinker, L. and Lamendella, J. (1979) The role of extrinsic feedback in interlanguage fossilization: A discussion of 'rule fossilization: A tentative model.' *Language Learning* 29 (2), 363–75.
Selinker, L. and Mascia, R. (1999) Fossilization: trying to get the logic right. In P. Robinson (ed.) *Representation and process: Proceedings of the 3rd Pacific Second Language Research Forum, Volume 1* (pp. 257–65). Tokyo: Pacific Second Language Research Forum.
Sharwood Smith, M. (1981) Consciousness-raising and the second language learner. *Applied Linguistics* 2, 159–68.
Sharwood Smith, M. (1986) Comprehension versus acquisition: Two ways of processing input. *Applied Linguistics* 7, 239–56.
Sharwood Smith, M. (1991) Speaking to many minds: On the relevance of different types of language information for the L2 learner. *Second Language Research* 7, 118–32.
Sharwood-Smith, M. (1993) Input enhancement in instructed SLA: Theoretical bases. *Studies in Second Language Acquisition* 15 (2), 165–79.
Sharwood Smith, M. (1994a) *Second Language Learning: Theoretical Foundations*. London: Longman.
Sharwood Smith, M (1994b) The unruly world of language. In N. Ellis (ed.) *Implicit and Explicit Learning of Languages* (pp. 33–43). New York: Academic Press.
Sharwood Smith, M. (1999) Modular responses to negative evidence. Paper presented at EUROSLA 9, Lund.
Shehadeh, A. (2002) Comprehensible output, from occurrence to acquisition: An agenda for acquisitional research. *Language Learning* 52 (3), 597–647.
Singleton, D. (1995) Introduction: A critical look at the Critical Period Hypothesis in second language acquisition research. In D. Singleton and Z. Lengyel (eds) *The Age Factor in Second Language Acquisition: A Critical Look at the Critical Period Hypothesis* (pp. 1–29). Clevedon: Multilingual Matters.
Skehan, P. (1994) Interlanguage development and task-based learning. In M. Bygate, M. Tonkyn and E. Williams (eds) *Grammar and the Language Teacher* (pp. 175–99). London: Prentice-Hall.
Skehan, P. (1998) *A Cognitive Approach to Language Learning*. Oxford: Oxford University Press.
Slobin, D. (1993) Adult language acquisition: A view from child language study. In C. Perdue (ed.) *Adult Second Language Acquisition: Cross-linguistic Perspectives* (pp. 239–52). Cambridge: Cambridge University Press.
Slobin, D. (1996) From 'thought and language' to 'thinking for speaking'. In J. Gumperz and S. Levinson (eds) *Rethinking Linguistic Relativity* (pp. 70–96). Cambridge: Cambridge University Press.
Snow, C. and Hoefnagel-Hohle, M. (1978) The critical period for language acquisition: Evidence from second language learning. *Child Development* 49, 1114–28.
Sorace, A. (1993) Incomplete vs. divergent representations of unaccusativity in non-native grammars of Italian. *Second Language Research* 9 (1), 22–47.

Sorace, A. (1995) Acquiring linking rules and argument structures in a second language: The unaccuasative/unergative distinction. In L. Eubank, L. Selinker and M. Sharwood Smith (eds) *The Current State of Interlanguage: Studies in Honor of William E. Rutherford* (pp. 153–76). Amsterdam: John Benjamins.

Sorace, A. (1996) Permanent optionality as divergence in non-native grammars. Paper presented at EUROSLA 6, Nijmegen.

Sorace, A. and Shomura, Y. (2001) Lexical constraints on the acquisition of split transitivity: Evidence from L2 Japanese. *Second Language Research* 23 (2), 247–78.

Spada, N. (1997) Form-focused instruction and second language acquisition: A review of classroom and laboratory research. *Language Teaching* 30, 73–87.

Spada, N. and Lightbown, P. (1999) Instruction, L1 influence and developmental readiness in second language acquisition. *Modern Language Journal* 83, 1–22.

Stauble, A. (1978) The process of decreolization: A model for second language development. *Language Learning* 28, 29–54.

Stenson, N. (1975) Induced errors. In J. Schumann and N. Stenson (eds) *New Frontiers in Second Language Learning* (pp. 54–70). Rowley, MA: Newbury House.

Swain, M. (1985) Communicative competence: Some roles of comprehensible input and comprehensible output in its development. In S. Gass and C. Madden (eds) *Input in Second Language Acquisition* (pp. 235–53). Rowley, MA: Newbury House.

Swain, M. (1988) Manipulating and complementing current teaching to maximize second language learning. *TESL Canada Journal* 6, 68–83.

Swain, M. (1991) French immersion and its offshoots: Getting two for one. In B. Freed (ed.) *Foreign Language Acquisition Research and the Classroom* (pp. 91–103). Lexington, MA: D.C. Heath.

Swain, M. (1993) The output hypothesis: Just speaking and writing aren't enough. *Canadian Modern Language Review* 50, 158–64.

Swain, M. (1995) Three functions of output in second language learning. In G. Cook and B. Seidlhofer (eds) *Principle and Practice in Applied Linguistics* (pp. 125–44). Oxford: Oxford University Press.

Swain, M. and Lapkin, S. (1998) Interaction and second language learning: Two adolescent French immersion students working together. *Modern Language Journal* 82 (3), 320–37.

Takahashi, S. (1996). Pragmatic transferability. *Studies in Second Language Acquisition* 18, 189–223.

Tarone, E. (1994) Interlanguage. In R.E. Asher (ed.) *The Encyclopedia of Language and Linguistics 4* (pp. 1715–19). Oxford: Pergamon.

Tarone, E. (2003, March) Language play and fossilization. Panelist presentation at the 2003 AAAL Annual Conference, Arlington, Virginia.

Tarone, E., Frauenfelder, U. and Selinker, L. (1976) Systematicity/variability and stability/instability in interlanguage systems. *Language Learning* 4, 93–134.

Tarone, E. and Liu, G-Q. (1996) Situational context, interlanguage variation, and second-language acquisition theory. In G. Cook and B. Siedlhofer (eds) *Applied Linguistics Principles and Practice: Studies in Honor of H. G. Widdowson* (pp. 107–24). Oxford: Oxford University Press.

Tarone, E. and Swain, M. (1995) A sociolinguistic perspective on second language use in immersion classrooms. *Modern Language Journal* 79, 166–78.

Thep-Ackrapong, T. (1990) Fossilization: A case study of practical and theoretical parameters. Unpublished PhD dissertation, Illinois State University.

Todeva, E. (1992) On fossilization in (S)LA theory. In Staub and C. Delk (eds) *Proceedings of the Twelfth Second Language Research Forum* (pp. 216–54). East Lansing, MI: Center for International Programs, Michigan State University.

Tomasello, M. and Herron, C. (1988) Down the garden path: Inducing and correcting overgeneralization errors in the foreign language classroom. *Applied Psycholinguistics* 9, 237–46.

Towell, R. and Hawkins, R. (1994) *Approaches to Second Language Acquisition*. Clevedon: Multilingual Matters.

Trévise, A. (1986) Is it transferable, topicalization? In E. Kellerman and M. Sharwood Smith (eds) *Crosslinguistic Influence in Second Language Acquisition* (pp. 186–206). New York: Pergamon.

Trévise, A. (1996) Contrastive metalinguistic representations: The case of 'very French' learners of English. *Language Awareness* 3, 188–95.

Towell, R. and Hawkins, R. (1994) *Approaches to Second Language Acquisition*. Clevedon: Multilingual Matters.

Vainikka, A. and Young-Scholten, M. (1994) Direct access to X-theory: Evidence from Korean and Turkish adults learning German. In T. Hoekstra and B. Schwartz (eds) *Language Acquisition Studies in Generative Grammar* (pp. 265–316). Amsterdam: John Benjamins.

Valette, R. (1991) Proficiency and the prevention of fossilization – an editorial. *Modern Language Journal* 75 (3), 326–8.

VanPatten, B. (1988) How juries get hung: Problems with the evidence for a focus on form in teaching. *Language Learning* 38, 243–60.

VanPatten, B. (1996) *Input Processing and Grammar Instruction: Theory and Research*. Norwood, NJ: Ablex.

Vigil, N. and Oller, J. (1976) Rule fossilization: A tentative model. *Language Learning* 26 (2), 281–95.

Van Wuijtswinkel, K. (1994) Critical period effects on the acquisition of grammatical competence in a second language. BA thesis, Katholieke Universiteit, Nijmegen, Netherlands.

von Humboldt, W. (1836) Uber die Verschiedenheit des menschlichen Sprachbaues und ihren Einflu auf die geistige Entwickelung des Menschengeschlechts (Abhandlungen der Akademie der Wissenschaften zu Berlin). Berlin: Dummlers Verlag. Reprinted: 1960. Bonn: Dummlers Verlag. Trans. P. Heath (1988) *On Language: The Diversity of Human Language Structure and its Influence on the Mental Development of Mankind*. Cambridge: Cambridge University Press.

Washburn, G. (1991) Fossilization in second language acquisition: A Vygotskian perspective. Unpublished PhD dissertation, University of Pennsylvania.

Weber-Fox, C. and Neville, H. (1999) Functional neural subsystems are differentially affected by delays in second language immersion: ERP and behavioral evidence in bilinguals. In D. Birdsong (ed.) *Second Language Acquisition and the Critical Period Hypothesis* (pp. 23–38). Mahwah, NJ: Lawrence Erlbaum.

Weinreich, U. (1953) *Languages in Contact*. Publication of the Linguistic Circle of New York, no. 1.

Wekker, H., Kellerman, E. and Hermans, R. (1982) Trying to see the 'would' for the trees. *Interlanguage Studies Bulletin* 6, 22–55.

White, J. (1998) Getting the learners' attention. In C. Doughty and J. Williams (eds) *Focus on Form in Classroom Second Language Acquisition* (pp. 85–113). Cambridge: Cambridge University Press.

White, L. (1987) Against comprehensible input: The input hypothesis and the development of second language competence. *Applied Linguistics* 12, 121–34.

White, L. (1989) *Universal Grammar and Second Language Acquisition*. Amsterdam: John Benjamins.

White, L. (1990) Implications of learnability theories for second language learning and teaching. In M.A.K. Halliday, J. Gibbons and H. Nicholas (eds) *Learning, Keeping and Using Language, Volume 1* (pp. 271–86). Amsterdam: John Benjamins.

White, L. (1991) Adverb placement in second language acquisition: Some effects of positive and negative evidence in the classroom. *Second Language Research* 7, 133–61.

White, L. (1996) Issues of maturation and modularity in second language acquisition. In W. Ritchie and T. Bhatia (eds) *Handbook of Second Language Acquisition* (pp. 85–120). San Diego: Academic Press.

White, L. (1998) The implications of divergent outcomes in L2 acquisition. *Second Language Research* 14 (4), 321–3.

White, L. (2000) Second language acquisition: From initial to final state. In J. Archibald (ed.) *Second Language Acquisition and Linguistic Theory* (pp. 130–54). New York: Blackwell.

White, L. (2001) Revisiting fossilization: The syntax/morphology interface. Paper presented at Babble, Trieste, Italy.

White, L. and Genesee, F. (1996) How native is near-native? The issue of ultimate attainment in adult second language acquisition. *Second Language Research* 12, 233–65.

Wilkinson, S. (1998) Study abroad from the participants' perspective: A challenge to common beliefs. *Foreign Language Annals* 31 (1), 23–39.

Willems, G. M. (1987) Communication strategies and their significance in foreign language teaching. *System* 15 (3), 351–64.

Williams, J. (2001) Learner-generated attention to form. In R. Ellis (ed.) *Form-focused Instruction and Second Language Learning* (pp. 303–46). Oxford: Blackwell.

Wode, H. (1981) *Learning a Second Language*. Narr: Tübingen.

Wong Fillomore, L. (1992) Learning a language from learners. In C. Kramsch and S. McConnell-Ginet (eds) *Text and Context: Cross-disciplinary Perspectives on Language Study* (pp. 46–66). Lexington, MA: D.C. Heath.

Yip, V. (1995) *Interlanguage and Learnability: From Chinese to English*. Amsterdam: John Benjamins.

Zobl, H. (1980) Developmental and transfer errors: Their common bases and (possibly) differential effects on subsequent learning. *TESOL Quarterly* 14, 469–79.

Zobl, H. (1982) A direction for contrastive analysis: The comparative study of developmental sequences. *TESOL Quarterly* 16, 169–83.

Zobl, H. (1985) Grammars in search of input and intake. In S. Gass and C. Madden (eds) *Input in Second Language Acquisition* (pp. 32–44). Rowley, MA: Newbury House.

Zobl, H. (1989) Canonical typological structures and gravity in English L2 acquisition. In S. Gass and J. Schachter (eds) *Linguistic Perspectives on Second Language Acquisition* (pp. 203–21). Cambridge: Cambridge University Press.

Zuengler, J. (1989a) Identity and interlanguage development and use. *Applied Linguistics* 10, 80–96.

Zuengler, J. (1989b) Assessing an interaction-based paradigm: How accommodative should we be? In M.R. Eisenstein (ed.) *The Dynamic Interlanguage: Empirical Studies in Second Language Variation* (pp. 49–67). New York: Plenum.

Zuengler, J. (1989c) Performance variation in NS–NNS interactions: Ethnolinguistic difference or discourse domain? In S. Gass, C. Madden, D. Preston and L. Selinker (eds) *Variation in Second Language Acquisition: Discourse and Pragmatics* (pp. 228–44). Clevedon: Multilingual Matters.

Index